Jim Trotta
The Ice Cream Man From Hell

A Biography

Jim Trotta with Angelina Desolate

★ ☆ ★

The Ice Cream Man From Hell
A Biography

Jim Trotta with Angelina Desolate

★ ☆ ★

YOU'RE NEXT

Published October, 2006

You're Next - *(First U.S. Edition)*
The Ice Cream Man From Hell
Copyright © 2006 Jim Trotta

All rights reserved. Printed in the United States of America. No part of this book may be reproduced in any manner whatsoever without written permission except in the case of critical articles and reviews.

The information in this book is true and complete to the best of our knowledge. All recommendations are made without guarantee on the part of the authors and publisher who disclaim any liability incurred in connection with the use of this data or specific details.

This book may be purchased for educational, business, or sales promotion use. For information please contact, DTW Press, P.O. Box 277, Bunnell, FL 32110. Phone orders and information requests can be directed to (866) 731-2622. This book can also be purchased for individual sale on the world-wide-web at *http://www.icmfh.com*

Cover Art - Psycho Mike Barnard
Project Director - Elizabeth Plastina
Chief Editor - Nicole Plastina
Prepress - American Book Crafters, LLC
        William G. Carrington
        Biljana Kroll
        Donna D. Karakash

Library of Congress Catalog Number: 2006930893
Trotta, Jim, 1953 -
Desolate, Angelina, 1979 -
    You're Next

ISBN Number: 978-0-976-91400-6

The following story is true. For over fifty years, I've fought to keep my demons locked away until now…

Due to the nature of this content, all of the town names referenced in the State of New Jersey and several character names have been fictionalized to…keep the guilty—guilty, the innocent—innocent, and the dead— from walking.

This is an uncensored and shocking tale, but is also one of hope and success at this game we call life.

Foreword

YOU'RE NEXT is a snapshot of life in the fast lane. For the first time, the Ice Cream Man From Hell reveals his compelling story and is willing to share his psychedelic journey with anyone who has the notion to go along for the ride. This American Folk Hero accomplished success through violence, sexual controversy, and love and by any means necessary. He's captivated the limelight through persistence and determination and without compromise. His philosophy paints a portrait of a dying breed of man. This honest and fresh chronicle is not for the weak of heart but it guarantees to be forever imbedded in your memory bank to ensure that… **YOU'RE NEXT!!**

To God, My Loving Wife Anna, and to My Mother and Father who instilled in me the desire to succeed and assured me that I was born in the most blessed country in the world. And especially to the people that I've touched and come to know worldwide.

Acknowledgements

To the Media - "The World has Eyes and Ears!" Special thanks to each and every one of you in the media of every type. The worldwide coverage that you've given me and the wonderful job you've all done filling the public's eyes and ears has helped preserve our freedom of speech. You've all been a crucial part of immortalizing me in the minds of the people of our culture and lifestyle by helping build an "American folk hero". I know you'll understand that it's impossible for me to name you all, but my deepest gratitude will always remain with Pulsating Paula.

To Bitty - Thank God! How can I ever thank you for annoying everyone in my camp? There's no way to describe, "Bitty's Boot Camp". I'm happy to say that you've drained out of us everything that needed to be said. It's because of you that I now understand the meaning of "Passion". Without your persistence and all of your determination, this book would never have been possible. You truly are a "Chieftain" in my life.

To Angelina Desolate - You've done a magnificent job at digging up things in my life that I had buried years ago. Thanks for holding my hand on this rollercoaster ride. I pray your future will shine and the years are good to you. And sorry about the rock...thanks for not backing off! I bid you peace and keep the faith.

To Nicki P - I've watched you grow up and you've helped me to grow too. We both learned something the day we visited Duke. Nicole, this book would not be what it is without your help. I look forward to jiving with you on future projects. At such a young age, I can only imagine what the future holds for you. Embrace it and move on!

                      I Love You All!
                Sin-seriously Jimmy ICMFH

"Jimmy's personality radiates throughout these pages, I heard him talking to me like he was standing right by my side. I loved it!"
—*Pulsating Paula*

"No stones were left unthrown. What a great read! I left confused."
—*Indian Larry*

This book was written
In collaboration with
Jim Trotta,
Angelina Desolate,
Elizabeth and Nicole Plastina.

Table of Contents

Last Thoughts on Duke
1

Little Italy
8

Neighborhood Bully
44

Stenciled Angel
71

Fifth Street Tramp
93

Power of a Name Change
116

Sex Smells
131

Sidewalk Sideshow
159

Misadventures and Half Truths
181

Price of Independence
216

Full Circle
236

By Any Means Necessary
256

YOU'RE NEXT
265

Chapter 1

Last Thoughts on Duke

"Shut the fuck up and call Anna!" I reached across her to lock the passenger side door so she couldn't bail out on me. The only thing I could do to shut the psycho bitch up sitting next to me was blurt out my phone number. My left hand was gripping the steering wheel while my right was pressed against her chest until she finally got through to my wife. Mel was screaming bloody murder into the phone, while I was knocking down road dividers, climbing over curbs and speeding down one-way streets, the wrong way. "Is this mother fucker crazy?!"

We were in New York City and Mel was the kind of girl who held her own. I don't know what she's up to now, but we'd been hanging since the Psycho days, and we'd seen it all together but even this was too crazy for her. Mel felt like she was fifteen again, homeless and panicked by the fact she had nowhere else to go but my truck, but Anna reassured her that everything would be okay once we reached the Jersey side.

Those NYC tubes felt like a gateway of time travel and I was barreling through the Lincoln Tunnel with my foot to the floor, while the clunky red pick-up hemmed and groaned to keep up with me. Mel was stiff and silent. There were no more phone calls, questions, or fucking around. We were far from Queens and slipping down the coast towards Maryland on just another wake and bake morning. I stopped at a familiar gas station in Jersey, unaware that God was going to rattle my chain that day.

You're Next

In Homestead, everyone gases up and grabs their morning cup of mud at the same filling hole, so in no way did it seem strange for me to see Duke's daughter when I stepped out of my truck—but there was something unfamiliar about her approach. I had to rub my eyes to make sure it wasn't the usual buzzing in my brain. Her facial features were drawn and weary. Her frigid hug startled me even more than her appearance and it made me concerned.

"Duke is in the hospital, he's been diagnosed with cancer."

It shakes my being to even repeat it or think it. It's as if I was the one who had just been diagnosed. Numbness set into my soul and my lips turned blue, I was on fire from head to toe. Those annoying electrical shocks pulsed up and down my spine—I didn't know what to think, do, or say, and my medication definitely wasn't working. I had just crawled out of my cradle in Astoria, Queens and plunged right into the mouth of Duke's early grave. I pulled myself together for a split second, just long enough to spit out a promise that I'd be by her father's side the following day. I climbed back into my truck, and was silent the rest of the ride to Maryland. At this point, what could I possibly have to say?

This was Duke! A meat grinding, bad losing, hardcore motherfucker—he'd quit smoking cigs a year ago to pay for his new Harley—Christ! It's not justifiable or even dignified! He's supposed to catch a fast one, be thrown out of a car at a buck ten or wreck on a motorcycle—but cancer?

I kept my promise, and the next day as I stomped down the hallway towards Duke's room I could tell the doctors were serious, but he looked the same. Nothing was out of place. Duke's middle finger was held high as I walked towards his hospital bed. "What the Fuck?" That was the first thing he said to me. The only way I could respond to him was to shout back, "What the Fuck?"

After the warm welcome, Duke immediately began to express his desire to leave his grandchildren with the fondest everlasting memories stamped in the forefront of their minds. Most

Last Thoughts on Duke

importantly, he wanted to die at home. I knew I couldn't promise that, but I did have some other ideas.

A few days later, against his will, I set up an appointment for Duke with Johnny V, and because of our long endured friendship, I knew Johnny was the only photographer for the job. Duke saddled up on his Heritage and spent the afternoon in the wind roaming the fields with his grandchildren. He shopped for new real estate while Johnny followed with his camera. When I got the report of their day's events, enough of my soul was satisfied to head home. Once again, I was on that thousand mile path down East Coast America, a path I've taken a million times before—no problem. Except this road trip wasn't like the rest, it was the longest twenty hours of my life. I was lonely and needed to be in my wife's arms.

After a few speechless days, I headed back to Jersey. During those next few months, I used every bullshit excuse imaginable to fly up and down I-95. I'd drive a thousand miles north to deliver a hubcap. These weren't excuses though; I needed to see Duke as much as possible. He was dying and the pendulum of life was getting shorter and swinging faster by the second. It was turning me into a crazed lunatic—I wasn't going to let my brother go out like this. No stones would be left unturned. I was going to make sure that Duke died with dignity and respect—even if it killed me. The reality of mortality was on the front burner again, the shakes were just kicking in, and I'd be at his doorstep in minutes. What else could I do at this point but to offer my brother evil deeds on command?

By this stage of the game Duke still looked the same, just confused, or so I thought. We sat in his back yard slamming beers while I pleaded my case. You've got to understand, we've been tough guying around since vocational school. So deeds go unspoken—that's just the way it is. Revenge can be at the top of your daily list when you're a motherfucking scumbag. I was prepared to avenge anyone upon his request—no questions asked. Our "Fuck You" attitudes are eternal and there'd be no negotiation in this case—just an end result. I was prepared to do anything on bended knee to satisfy Duke's soul.

"Jimmy, right now I got to tell ya, from where I stand, that shit doesn't matter anymore. I feel no hate in my heart. Take the advice of a dead man and shake the hate. I neither want, nor need anything from you but your love and support."

"**What?**" I couldn't believe what I'd just heard! Duke was completely poker faced. "It's fucked up enough you're going to go out like this you cocksucker! Whatever ya want Duke! No worries—I'll take care of it." My fists were clenched at my sides.

With the knowledge of his demise, Duke reassured me again that violence would only make me grow old in my heart and eventually kill me. He advised me to quit hanging out with Smith and Wesson and to just keep marching forward. Did he really mean it?

"Jimmy, I'm telling you, that shit just doesn't matter anymore, now that I know I'm on my way out."

I made a promise to Duke that day to cause no more pain.

Every manic blast up the coast meant Duke was getting worse. The medications started muscling in on his brain and he was slipping out of my reach. With honor and pleasure I did it all for him during those last days, in hopes he'd crack a smile. The cocktail of chemo and meds made him vomit, but I cheered Duke on like the good ole days when he drank too much Gentleman Jack. Why would I treat him any differently in his last hours? He still had enough strength at that point to give me the finger and his notorious reply..."Blow Me."

The rattle of death was deafening by January. I was completely unleashed in my thinking, and the electrical pulses in my fingertips gnawed at me. I decided to stop taking my medication the day I found out about Duke's fate, and everything had been disoriented and irrational for months. The voices in my head were competing for attention and I wanted to stop the slow motion movie of my life from reeling—I couldn't control it. I became a puppet; I was moving unconsciously, there was no logic left in me—only action.

I picked up a friend to go along for the ride. I needed to bring someone along for confirmation of my sanity. Was Duke really dying? I wasn't strong enough to make that trip alone and there was just something inside of me that day. I knew I had to see Duke. My senses were drowned in Drambui, and I had no idea how I had made it from Florida to New Jersey.

When we pulled into Duke's driveway, I sat in the car, waiting and drifting into my alcohol induced hallucination as I stared at the Christmas lights that still trimmed the house. Duke would slink around the corner any minute in his big red suit with a brown sack full of gifts. Every other year he played Santa Claus for his grandchildren. He'd peek through the windows till each child caught a glimpse of him…yeah, he'd be coming around the corner soon. This was nothing more than a bad dream—couldn't I just wake up? She opened the car door and I rolled out, hit the ice, and busted my face. It took a lot of strength that I didn't have to get up, brush myself off and made my way inside.

I stumbled into the living room and she sat next to Duke. She began to carry on a conversation with his wife. I had no time for this small talk—I needed to know what Duke was thinking. He must've sensed that we were in the room, and in a crazed, drug induced state, he slipped back into his body for a moment and looked over at her… "Tell Jimmy I'm not working Sturgis this year and that he sucks cock."

My tears were overwhelming my speech, I tried to explain to Duke that I was standing right in front of him, breathing the same air as him, that he just couldn't see me! Duke looked different today, even from yesterday—he was a ninety-pound dead guy. The whole room was rattling and I couldn't even look at his wife, she made me shiver. I slugged what was left in the bottle of Jameson on the table

You're Next

next to Duke's stash of meds—the smell of decay was piercing my nose. Duke slipped back into himself again as I put the empty bottle down...

"Don't touch my pills you motherfucker!"

I laughed and laughed, remembering all the wonderful things we used to share. Pills, pussy, suck, cash, cars, if one had it—so did the other; that's the way we operated. I leaned over and kissed him on the forehead.

"I'll see ya tomorrow man."

He looked up at me and said, "No you won't."

I cracked a smile and did my best to swallow the lump in my throat that started to choke me as I stumbled out the door.

I was heading down south when I got the phone call I'd been dreading since his diagnosis. Duke was six feet disappeared, and all I could think was that motherfucker had gotten the last word in. Now what the fuck? Do I go back to the cold crazy north and bury the bones of my dead brother? Or, do I keeping heading south? I was so beat up. No business had been left unattended in my eyes...there was no reason for embarrassment. So I jumped in my pick-up and headed for the sun.

I was half way down the coast while big brother was in the parking lot of the funeral home with his own agenda. They were waiting to see who'd bid farewell to one of the wildest cats that had ever pounded this earth. The Feds expected a field day yet netted nothing—Duke's case was closed.

His bike, along with his leather and boots were parked inside next to his casket, and friends left behind tokens of appreciation and trinkets. An Ice Cream Man From Hell patch was left in place of me not attending, and I was happy to hear that his Crippled Old Biker Bastards patch also lay to rest with him. It was a true warrior's burial.

Seeing that I don't do funerals, I don't have much more to say about it. I heard news of the service that was held in his honor

Last Thoughts on Duke

through several phone conversations and I'm glad it was done right, but I wasn't staying in Jersey another minute. Instead, I stopped somewhere in South Carolina on I-95 and had a picnic in the bathroom with a bottle of wine and talked to the walls of a cheap motel.

Duke, I know you're with me but I just can't see you…
"I miss you terribly."
AMF

Duke shopping for new real estate

Chapter 2

Little Italy

At sunrise the concrete canyons boil over the grates and gutters into the streets in beat with the rumble of the underground. The subway purges a familiar smell like no other. It permeates your nose as you get out of bed. By afternoon, the sweet scent of grapes and tomatoes from the small plots of dirt that are tucked away in the back alleys overrides the stench of the sewer. The row houses are crammed with fat Italian women who slump over pillows in open windows, gossiping and shouting the headlines from the *El -Progresso* newspaper. Only one lady would buy the paper to save the neighborhood a few extra pennies. Their chatter and pitter-patter from the row blanketed the streets below.

Once ya hit ground level the fishing was great! I'd flip coins and baseball cards with the other kids, while the women squawked overhead...

"Lucy, where's a Luis a kid?"
"You a hear wha Lena's a boy a do?"
"Joey oudda da street!"

Grate fishing was my favorite pastime and it only required two tools, a piece of bubble gum and a stick. My Aunt Lucy had this funny little quirk; she'd wash the front stoop every single day, even when it rained. I'd occasionally swipe a piece of liverwurst from my unsuspecting aunt during her ritual. The gooey texture was prime bait compared to a re-chewed piece of Bazooka. The tacky meat made it easy to score coins and buried treasures from the sewers. Coins were rewarding and teeth paid royally, but dismembered fingers were good for scaring the neighborhood girls! I'd sell the teeth to the Catholic school kids to put under their pillows for the tooth fairy. I always had a way of knowing

Little Italy

how my fishing season would pan out—if the teeth grinding silence of the fathers dominated the mother's babble, I'd have a good month.

On Sundays, the apartment doors were left wide open so us kids could run around while our parents visited and passed the vino. The fig trees and grapes that blossomed in the alleys were enjoyed by all on

My mother, Lena

these holiest of days and my father even made his own wine from those very grapes. We couldn't afford the brands so this would have to do, and believe me, it did! It took me years to figure out why he'd make me whistle a tune while I carried the two-quart jugs in my hands. I'd start my march down to our basement distillery and he wouldn't let me stop whistling till I came back with the goods! I guess he was trying to keep me honest but there was no reason. Daddy always gave me two fingers in a coffee cup when my mission was complete. It was rare that any of us kids got punished on Sundays, unless Uncle Tony had to break up a fight in the street. Tony was so fast that I couldn't tell the front of his hand from the back when he'd lay a series of smacks right across my mouth. "Jameza! Go up a e stayz!"

You're Next

My father, (up front) and my uncle in Italy

The only downfall about being a kid back then was you couldn't get away with much because everyone had each other's back. None of us kids appreciated or valued this way of life, but we did respect it. Astoria's Italians didn't all come from Naples or Sicily. The dialects varied from row to row but that made no difference. We were all just a bunch of WOPs in the land of opportunity and that's the way it was back then. We shared everything—one hand washed the other. You were either the blood descendant of your neighbor or the sponsor that landed them in the States. It was all the same and we gladly paid homage to each other. The Irish did it, the Polish did it, and the Jews did it, so why not the Italians? This was the cradle of Astoria, Queens, New York where I was born in 1953.

People labeled us poor, deprived, impoverished, or unlucky but I just called it being short in the pockets! Whenever a family member's birthday came around, there

Little Italy

were no such things as presents or parties. We were thankful for the daily bread because most days that's all there was! I couldn't even tell ya my mother's birth date, that's how insignificant it was — no disrespect.

Our Sunday best wasn't a requirement on the row, as long as we washed behind our ears and combed our hair that was enough. I never showed up at birthday parties even if the whole neighborhood was invited, I decided it was easier on my brains and fists to stay home. I didn't understand why those whining little faggots got to have pool parties and pasta nights. I never even got to go to the zoo! Instead, every year mommy had the same encouraging words on my birthday, "You a alive today, take dadda gift and ado wadda you can wit it."

I know I'm alive today…so alive **I wanna go to the zoo!** When you're five years old, the last thing ya want for your birthday are encouraging words. I just wanted presents! I didn't start going to

Jimmy

my friend's birthday parties till the cake and ice cream was replaced with strippers and booze. Here's how I see it, I'm saving all my birthday parties for one kick ass dying day party!

The holidays in our little Queens apartment reminds me of why festivities of any kind are so physiologically uncomfortable. Our Christmas trees were straight out of the *New York Post*. Not that big beautiful tree in the middle of Rockefeller Center, I'm talking about the tree from the Peanut's comic strip! It only had three limbs, scarce pine needles, and the gifts it bore came from the same dumpster in Manhattan as *The Wall Street Journal* wrapping paper! Hey, what can I say? We knew how to get by. What really aggravated the shit out of me though was when my

Mikey, mommy, daddy and me

Little Italy

brother Mikey and I had to go back to school after the holidays and listen to all the other little bastards squawking about all the toys they got on baby Jesus' birthday. I didn't get presents on my own damn birthday let alone on baby Jesus'—no disrespect! I still hate that fat bastard Santa! What the hell did he have against me? I'll fist fight him and every one of those little elves at the same time!

    The grey skies, bitter cold, no sunlight for days, and dirty snow filled streets made for a miserable time of year in Astoria. Mikey and I'd make the best of the frost that coated the inside of our apartment windows, we'd use it as a tic-tac-toe board. I hated school more than anything growing up, but because of this holiest of bullshit—we got the week off. I still get motherfucking angry in December and as the years went by, I always found some excuse to stay away from my family during the holidays—it was too damn painful! Money is a difficult topic and poverty can cut a guy all the way down to his soul.

    My father Frank was always good to me and my brother, he provided for us in so many other ways than by playing one of Santa's little helpers. By the time I was nine and still in the second grade, he knew how much I anguished over school. He'd take me to Little Italy, for "barber supplies," at least that's what we told my mommy, Lena. Every Wednesday we'd head straight to Mott Street where my father liked to hang out. Frank would buy us sandwiches as big as my arm oozing with mozzarella and the cola bottles were always ice cold and plentiful. My father knew how to make me feel special and he wouldn't deny me anything on Wednesdays.

    I got to hang with the cool guys in the smoke filled basements while they played cards and flipped dollars across the table. Some of their mugs were stuffed with foot long fine ones, while the older WOPs choked on those De Nobili rope guinea stinkers. The good fellas knew how to make me feel like a man. Instead of dollars and vino, I was paid in coins and colas—I got to drink with the best of them! Astoria, Queens

You're Next

My father, Frank (left)

was a hard-hitting neighborhood in the '50s and '60s, but Frank got a lot of respect and no one fucked with us. That's the way it was, us grease balls governed ourselves. Even as an immigrant family, my parents knew they were in the land of opportunity and took advantage of every second on their quest for the brass ring. We stayed in Astoria for several years till my parents decided they wanted to create a better life for me and my brother Mikey—ya know, keep us out of the streets. We were slowly moving on up.

My father was making some extra cash on the side running the numbers, so he moved us into a big house on Long Island. He was hustling as a barber and making several trips to the city while mommy held her own around the house with me and Mikey. She is one tough Italian! The best way to describe her is a four foot, cotton haired, strong armed WOP and you'd agree with me if the final spoon was coming down on your ass! I think the biggest living expense my family incurred over the years were wooden spoons, one was broken over my coconut daily! My mother didn't take shit from nobody—especially me and Mikey. If ya looked the wrong way, ya got a whack across the mouth! The way it worked around our house was, my father was the director of orders and my mother was the enforcer. Even though my parents were lovebirds and would always hold hands and exchange starry-eyed glances...when mommy deemed it necessary to crack the wooden spoon, there was no time for any of that shit!

Shortly after we moved to Long Island, my mommy announced to Mikey and me that we were now to be the men of the house. My father had to leave with no explanation, I was only nine years old at the time but I did my best. It was tough getting away with any of my shit even with my father gone because we shared a roof with my mommy *and* my grandmother, Nona.

Now that I was to be the man of the house, I decided it would be a good idea to immunize myself. I ate a full bottle of baby aspirin from the medicine cabinet so I'd never get sick again! It was so easy considering they tasted like sweet orange drops. I was so proud of myself that I marched right into the living room to tell mommy what a great endeavor I had just accomplished for everyone concerned...

"Oh Yeah? Dats a nice! Now giva me dadda bottle you a **little basta!**" She grabbed me by the collar and jerked me into the kitchen to drink what seemed like an entire bottle of olive oil—I instantly and brutally vomited! She called the doctor and that prick told mommy to keep shoving olive oil down my neck. On top of it, he told her to keep me awake. That entire night I'd get a smack and a line, "Donna you a go to sleep a you little basta!" If Lena wasn't sleeping, nobody in the house was sleeping! This never discouraged me, olive oil is still a part of my daily diet. Like every good Italian boy, it oozes from my pores and leaves a ring around the tub!

From the moment I shot out of my mother's twat, I've been a tough guy. Frank was a tough guy, the gangsters on Mott Street were tough guys, but however I may've been influenced, it paved the way for my roughneck attitude. Playing with the other kids in Long Island lasted only a short while. Only a few days after we moved into the neighborhood, I called our neighbor's daughter a little piglet. I was drug home by the ear for several blocks, which in my fragile little mind felt like an eternity. Of course not before getting a smack in the mouth from her fat Italian whore mother! I should've been drug home by my prick! Have ya seen the size of my ears? It's amazing how Italian women settle everything with wooden spoons, slippers, frying pans, or anything in arms reach to whack ya with! Instead of just shutting her big pie hole, that fat little piglet had gotten me into so much trouble.

My brother was always welcome at the neighbors, but no…not me! There ya have it folks, the earliest incident of me being accused of having no respect for women. So what if at the tender age of ten I got caught pulling down that little piglet's pants? Hey, the way I see it is from the jump I've always been an honest man, and even as a child I called it as I saw it. That girl *was* a fat little piglet, and no one can deny that, not even her own whore mother!

After that incident, mommy thought it would be a good idea to enroll me in the Long Island Boy Scouts to keep me away from the girls. It only took two weeks for me to get the boot from Troop #13! Boys or girls it didn't matter, I was out to terrorize everyone! It was alone games from then on out, so I started fighting picket fences to entertain myself.

In between the bullshit of growing pains, my father finally came home. He'd been gone for six months. Whether it was a day or a year, I was missing a piece of myself when he was gone. "Daddy you're home! Daddy you're home!" Me and Mikey bolted for the door the minute we saw him walk past the living room window.

Frank's physical features and composure were exactly the same as the moment he walked out that door…he never missed a beat. From that moment on I became his shadow. I kept a close eye on him because if he was skipping out again, I was going with him. When my father left home without notice, it was the first time Frank had been institutionalized. Mikey and I never got any explanation

Little Italy

from mommy as to why our father had just up and left. I guess because at the time it was beyond our comprehension, but years later I figured it out for myself when he became a repeat offender.

Everything changed so fast and within a few months, our father decided to move us to New Jersey so he could open his own barbershop. It felt like we were shot out of a canon and dumped into the streets of Fulton. Frank picked the barbershop on the far end of Main Street, the perfect location to serve it's purpose. Our shop was located across the street from the courthouse. This made for a lot of extra business as well as some useful connections.

My father carried the word dignity around like it was tattooed across his throat. Back then, most of the Italians lived in Guinea Gulch but we couldn't afford to. It didn't matter to him that we were surrounded by the spades, it was the 1960s, and we were in the land of opportunity and did whatever was necessary to bring home the dough.

I was out of school for the summer when my father opened the shop and he made it clear to Mikey and me that it was *our* business too, so we had to pitch in and contribute whatever we could. During my summers and after school, I'd go to the barbershop and be the hand. I'd sweep floors and run for lunches, but my main gig was shining shoes. This was my first real job and my first realization of the almighty quarter! While my father would cut hair, I'd place cardboard inside his client's shoes so I wouldn't get any polish on their socks. I was so proud to have my very own shoeshine box. Back then, the going rate for a shine was twenty-five, but I only charged twenty. Most guys would flip me a quarter. There was something about that five cent tip, it gave me the incentive to work a little harder. In the '60s, Fulton was a central hub for getting in and out of the city, so that's why the barbershop was named *Travelers*.

You're Next

A barbershop is a man's world but the only reason I thought I should've been a shining curbside in the Big Apple was to cop a peek up a few skirts!

When we moved to Fulton, my parents rented a duplex across the street from the printing press of the town's local paper, the *Town Gazette*. In the summer of '64, I remember sitting on my porch with a bag full of chestnuts. I'd roll them into the street and time it just right so the nut would crush under the tires of passing cars. *My senses awoke that day to the sweet and unruly sound of a motorcycle!* A guy wearing a black leather jacket on a black motorcycle ripped up the sidewalk and parked directly under a street sign that read, NO PARKING...cool!

The bike was a 750 Triumph Bonneville. The twenty something stranger was a greaser in these tight straight-cuffed blue jeans. He was thin and his fair complexion emphasized the receding lines of his cheekbones. He started one by one taking off his glasses, then his helmet, and finally his jacket. He caught me staring at him and I was enthralled with his demeanor. I couldn't take my eyes off him, I had forgotten all about my chestnuts.

Us kids around the neighborhood used to play this game, we'd run around the hood and tag the objects of our desire..."My car! My house! My girl!" My brain started screaming..."My Bike! My Bike!! My Bike!!!" The words made their way to the tip of my tongue and right out of my mouth..."**My Bike!**"

The stranger didn't say a word, his body language was very calm, his eyes said it all..."Don't even think about touching my bike you little prick!" He didn't have to speak, I got the point. The Unknown Soldier seemed hesitant to walk away, even though I was just a little kid. I think he was debating on chaining the Triumph to the signpost just in case I decided to get cute. As he walked away and headed toward the doors of the *Town Gazette* to punch the clock, he looked over his shoulder to let me know he'd be watching. If I did anything stupid—he knew where to find me.

The next day, I casually made my way back to the front porch as my new idol was getting out of work. I wanted to feel it, the pounding in my chest, as he put the choke into position, and my eyes would widened as he primed the engine to kick start that bad ass machine! Nothing up to this point had left such a serious impression on me. Riding motorcycles, yes, yes, yes, this was something I could do and never get tired of! It took me awhile before I finally got up the balls to introduce myself and extend a handshake. Before I could say a word..."You're Frankie's kid huh? I'm Mike." He already knew who I was, and from that day on, he always paid my punk ass a little mind.

I called him Triumph Mike, and in the mornings, he'd give me a quick wave and a cocked smile. As a kid, it made me feel special to be acknowledged by such a hip creature. Everyday for the rest of the summer, I made sure I was sitting on the front porch to witness that badass machine scream into the parking lot. Triumph

You're Next

Mike's eternal coolness has left a permanent impression on my lifestyle, but there was no time for motorcycles...No! I had a shoeshine box to run.

Saturdays were one of my favorite days at *Travelers*. It was a ritual for my father to send for two New York style pies for the barbers and customers to share. After stuffing my face, Frank would let me leave early to gallivant on my own for quarters. I could hustle the corner but I was smarter than that, I went straight to the bars. I'd make my way to Lip's Lounge around the corner. Lip's was famous for their ribs...at eleven years old I was the only white guy in the joint. It was due to my father's integrity that I had the privilege to walk through the doors. Everyone knew I was Frankie's kid, so no one gave me a hard time. My father was never prejudiced and even though during the '50s and '60s most of America was still segregated. Black, white, Jew, Italian, it didn't matter, he'd cut your hair and this contributed to his success. He didn't care where the money came from—he was just in constant pursuit of it.

Lip's Lounge was always a hit and they treated me right. Men would shout across the room over the loud jukebox stomp of Muddy Waters and Armstrong, "Come over here boy, and shine my shoes!" The bar lady always had a cola straight off the tap and a bag of chips waiting for me when I arrived. I'd bop around the bar to the cool tunes that flooded the room, stuff my face, and be out the door with an extra two bucks in my pocket. I dug that place man, and I dug the black chicks behind the bar!

After hustling Lip's, I'd either go hang out with my friends in front of the courthouse or I'd head up the hill towards the Jackson Hotel to hustle a few more shines. Nine times out of ten, I'd bypass the courthouse play for a few more quarters. The Jackson Hotel has been standing since the stagecoach days and the joint was filled with transients moving from town to town chasing their dreams. I'd shine stranger's shoes as they double fisted beers. I'd listen to their stories about where they'd been and what hand life had dealt them. By nightfall, I was on my way back to the barbershop with a full belly and a pocket full of quarters.

I tried shining at Frankie and Johnny's Lounge, an upscale joint compared to most of Fulton's waterholes. I gave up stopping there because I couldn't make any money…it was too tough. Was it because those red-nosed bastards were used to seeing me at the barbershop? Who cares? Fuck Whitie! They just took me for a greasy little guinea anyway, besides it was a better hustle at Lip's Lounge and the Jackson Hotel. Making money was something my father instilled in me from a very young age— I'm proud of that.

My father, Frank (left)

You're Next

When I got back to the barbershop if I was lucky, the windows didn't need washing, the floor didn't need scrubbing, and the bottles didn't need wiping. That's when I got to sit on the curb and watch the cars go by...I loved them all! Coral colored Belairs and Hudsons as big as land yachts would roll through, "Cool cars! Yeah...someday I'm going to have that car! Man, I can't wait to drive those hotsie totsies around." It was all part of shining shoes on a Saturday and if ya ask me, it was time better spent than at school!

As I mentioned before, school was never my schtick. I stayed back two times before I finished the fourth grade. I believe that not speaking English at home may've had something to do with it. My parents could barely read or write English, but then again, my brother Mikey could speak five languages, including Latin by the time he graduated high school. When we moved to Fulton along side of opening the barbershop, my parents thought it would be a good idea to enroll me in Catholic school for a little attitude adjustment. By this time, I was constantly throwing down with other kids and my grades were failing. I had already been kicked out of public school at the ripe ole age of ten. Great! Now it was time to take on the so-called upper class Irish kids. I was enrolled at Saint Bernard's School that fall. Catholic school quickly blossomed into more fisticuffs than public school! Between the nuns and those little Irish pricks like Billy D. and their chants..."Guinea WOP! Guinea WOP! Matza Ball! Spaghetti Sticks!" How could I not clock a few here and there?

As soon as I heard their elf like chants, I'd start swinging like a windmill! It was a vicious circle—beat up a kid, get beat by a nun, beat up another kid because I just got my ass kicked by a stupid penguin, get thrown around the room by Principal Father Kelly (that revolting Irish drunk). Lump up another one of those little Irish pricks; get squashed by Mother Marie Del Fatso...and so on.

Little Italy

Between the wooden spoons, yardsticks, slippers, and fists, my days were long and hard in Catholic school leaving no time or energy for my studies. Another Catholic school punk, Mark the Fox described me like this…"Jimmy always had this air about him, like a deer frozen by the glare of approaching headlights. His eyes were always wide open and full of sheer panic; his physical being was always clenched, while his fists were balled at his sides."

Ya have to understand that even with my trash mouth, at no time in my life has race, color, or creed held any water. That's why even in Catholic school, Tommy Mc Keever (that little Irish prick), became my best friend. Tommy and I had the same attitude. It didn't matter where ya came from as long as ya were tough, so with that, we started kicking ass together.

One day in class, I raised my hand to ask the prune-faced nun behind the tall oak desk if I could go to the bathroom, "If you deem it necessary—James!" That bitch always seemed to be annoyed by my presence, "Thank you sister." After the proper respectable reply, I stood up and made my way towards the door as I flashed my middle finger behind her back!

The second I hit the door, that prune lunged towards me. Her decrepit bones lashed out and reached for the back of my head. She clamped her fist down on my skull and with all her forced anger—she ripped out a huge patch of my hair! Bloody and still having to pee, I swung around to slug her in the face. My momentum dulled the room to a crawl like in a slow motion movie, Tommy Mc Keever jumped over two rows of desks and intercepted the punch that was about to deflate that stupid nun's face! Within seconds of this heroic act by Tommy, we were both being beaten with the yardstick…again! Forget the beating, it was nothing compared to the permanent bald spot that whore bestowed upon the back of my melon!

It was inevitable; my daily routine was give a beating—get a beating. The only solitude from this during my childhood was

You're Next

shining shoes and when my father pulled me out of school to get "barber supplies." Even though we were living in Jersey, we still went to Mott Street for combs and spray bottles. Yeah...like Little Italy is the only place in the northeast that caters to a barber's needs!

Due to my lack of conformity, I was forced to attend Catechism classes after school. The classes were taught by the priests. Just what I had in mind, twelve years old and spending my evenings with a bunch of faggots—I couldn't stand it! I had to cop a buzz just to tolerate the bullshit. I knew I couldn't show up for Catechism with booze on my breath, so I chose the popular alternative. I drank an entire bottle of cough medicine for just the right glow. I was outside the church in the dark November smoking a butt and enjoying my high before opening the gates of hell. Every time I'd put that cigarette to my face, neon circles danced in front of my eyelids. As I stepped in the building the checkered floor tiles bowed into large pits of swirls, my body was crawling and my legs felt heavy. I dug that wacky syrup—man it tasted like shit but it was quick fun. I was late for my class when I entered the building, so Father O'Malley took the liberty to stop and harass me about it. I became instantly enraged, I was tired of being misunderstood and besides he was messing with my high. My long hard days overflowed into long hard nights and for that—Father O'Malley was going to pay! I pulled my serpent-handled shiv from my pocket and aimed it right at his gut..."Ya know what this little fucker's going to do to ya, don't ya O'Malley?" My eyeballs felt like ping pong balls ready to pop out of my skull—I couldn't even finish my threat. That tall, pale, lanky creature in a priest's robe bum rushed me! I was flat on my back before I knew what hit me and he was kneeling on my chest—where's my knife? I was choking! Was O'Malley going to stab me? I was so scared! I really didn't mean it...I never stabbed anyone before, I was just being a bully!

Father O'Malley, in all of his divine pale creepiness, was towering over me contemplating my doom. He revealed the blade, closed it, and then handed me back my new toy. Before he let me get up off the floor, he decided to throw me a few smacks in the trap. This entire scenario, which I'm sure only took a matter of seconds, felt like eternity in my cough syrup saturated brain..."If you ever pull this thing out again, you better use it!"

O'Malley finally got up and my chest inflated like a balloon...he had scared me sober. I felt a warm rush between my thighs and when I looked down, a stream of yellow liquid was running down my leg forming a puddle under my right shoe. I cried like a little girl and ran to class in my piss soaked drawers!

After that incident, I decided that Father O'Malley wasn't a little faggot like the rest of God's assembly that paraded around Saint Bernard's. He never told anyone about what happened between us that Thursday night and most importantly, he didn't tell Tommy Mc Keever that I pissed myself. From then on, we seemed to have a mutual understanding and I always treated him with the utmost respect. I almost felt like he knew were I was coming from. Anytime he walked into the classroom, he'd shoot me a big grin like he knew exactly what I was thinking.

When I wasn't serving my penance or saying my Hail Mary's, I was at the barbershop. Right before closing, my father would always give me the same set of instructions, "Stop a at da Acmes, an pick a up a quart a milk for you mommy, den go right a home."

Frank would stuff a brown paper bag down my pants and flip me a few coins for the milk. I was instructed to mind my own business and to never mind what was in the bag. I always knew what was coming to me but I always followed my father's orders. I'd stop at the Acme, grab the milk, then walk through the alley and cut over to my house. Most nights in the parking lot behind the Acme, there was a group of black bastards playing b-ball. They'd snatch me up by the collar and heave their callused knuckles into my guts. I never cried for help because I couldn't breathe! Eventually my little hand would loosen and the quart of milk would hit the

You're Next

pavement. Even though I rarely made it home with the milk, I never got the wooden spoon. Later on, I came to find out the milk was just a decoy for the daily bread. Those moolies never bothered to look down my pants, they just wanted something cold to drink while they played ball. It wasn't about getting the milk home. My father knew those coons were looking for an excuse to kick my spaghetti-eating ass, so he gave them one. They always got the milk but they never got the booty! My father was a smart man; unfortunately, I had to be the bullet taker for awhile. This happened early on in the neighborhood but after awhile it stopped, there was no more of that black/white shit once they got to know who Frank was.

    The Newark, New Jersey race riots of '67 had a serious impact on all of America...the times they were a changing. After three days of riots in downtown Newark, the fury spread and caught fire to all the surrounding areas. The National Guard was called in and by the time they arrived, bodies were scattered all over the streets and the city looked like a wrecking zone. Fulton started to riot, all of us kids were to stay inside and the barbershop was forced to close.

    I kept peeking out the window to watch the black clouds of smoke bellow over the courthouse and made bets with myself on the winner of the next street fight. Mommy kept shooing me away from the window and quickly grew frustrated with us kids being in the house for days on end. Her frustrations manifested into tears and Frank couldn't take it. Instead of being cooped up with two kids and a hysterical wife, he took off to the local fire station to play cards with the other volunteer fire fighters while waiting to be called on duty.

    After four days of confinement, Lena couldn't take it and had to get out of the house. My father agreed to march us down Main Street to the barbershop so that she would relax, Frank knew everything was going to be just fine. While we walked, my mother prayed in such a repetitive manner that she sounded like a broken record. I listened to the glass crunching under my shoes like hard snow to drown her out. The windows of Mary's Restaurant and the Cort Theater were shattered, the Acme was looted, it was left barren, and not a single loaf of bread was left on the shelves. The barbershop however, looked like it had been spit shined, like a beautiful shiny quarter in a pile of soot beside the railroad tracks! My father let go of my hand and lit a Winston. "See Lena, I knew a we had a friends. I told you a nothing would a happen!"

There wasn't a single scratch on our storefront window, even the barber's pole was still intact. Yet the businesses on either side stood in shambles, people's lives were ruined. My father was right— he did have a lot of friends. The air was thick in the neighborhood after the riots, so my parents sent me to Astoria to stay with Aunt Lucy for the summer. Even though we had been spared, they decided it would be in my best interest to leave town for awhile. I disagreed, I liked working Lip's Lounge, and I had no problems with anybody. Besides when your father hangs out with guys like Danny Bad Bones ya shouldn't have to leave town. Danny Bad Bones was the Jackson County Prison Sergeant who looked exactly like Dean Martin. His sharp fashion outside of his uniform was top choice. His wife had the beauty of Jane Mansfield. They were a knockout couple, and proud of each other, ya could tell by the way they carried themselves in public.

Danny and Frank were tight. On a regular basis my father would go to the jail and give the inmates a shave and a cut while he and Danny conducted business. Frank took a lot of pride in his work and did several things for the local community. Besides being a volunteer fireman, he had one day a month for senior citizen discounts, and he was a lifetime member of the Barber's Association along with Danny Bad Bones and several other people from town.

Being Frankie's kid and working at the barbershop was my identity. Everyone respected my father because he knew how to act and people treated me good because I was his son. If we didn't go to Little Italy for "barber supplies" on Wednesday, my father would

You're Next

take me to the Barber's Association meetings. Either way I felt privileged to be hanging with the cool guys.

My father hosted the meetings in a room above our barbershop and I was allowed to shine shoes. The cool cats of the Barber's Association would flip me a dollar a shine! It was unbelievable! It was like they had money growing out of their ears. Me and Mikey were shooed out of the room when the men started talking business. Our job was to wash the floors and watch the doors, we always did as we were told and never asked questions. Sometimes the room upstairs would get real quiet, and other times it was real loud. I never thought much about the occasional screams coming from the top of those stairs. Maybe they were just playing bloody knuckles.

It wasn't till I was a teenager that I realized ya didn't have to be a barber to be part of the association. Bankers, pizza joint owners, trash men, car dealers, your profession wasn't taken into account. If you were a WOP...you were in. Like I said, they could've been cutting hair, sawing wood, rolling up carpets, or counting money for all I know. I don't know what went on upstairs nor do I care...they did do a lot of cleaning up though. Come to find out back in those days at *Travelers*, Mike and I were the only ones in the place who were innocent!

By the time my brother hit junior high his physical features resembled a full grown man, he was stocky and strong like a bull, he had a brilliant mind and looked like a fresh young Allen Ginsburg. One time I'd seen him break a guy's arm in an arm wrestling contest! Mike had the ability to kick anyone's ass yet he was a man of peace. He got respect for his looks and stature, and when he walked into a room, conversations would stop and heads would turn. Mikey never took time for the ladies and there where only a few times I witnessed him throw a fist—unlike myself.

I always made sure to get home on time in fear of catching a beating. I had a lot to live up to in my mother's eyes having an older brother like Mike. One night, I was a half hour late for dinner, so mommy instructed Mike to go fetch my punk ass. As he turned onto South Street, he saw I was getting my ass kicked by these two older dudes. One jerk was holding me in a full Nelson while the other was repeatedly parking his fist into my face. Mikey, casual as a cat, slinked up behind the guy who was throwing the punches and without saying a word, thrust a fist into the back of his skull! The kid staggered several feet and dropped to the ground, his buddy let me go and started running after witnessing the massive blow to his comrade. Mike gave me a couple of smacks in the mouth after saving my ass, "See what happens when you're late, now mommy is mad and you're a pathetic mess." I don't care how old ya are, when you grow up in an Italian family, you always refer to your mother as mommy—tough guy or not.

When mommy had enough of us boys, she'd ask our Nona to take us fishing. I think it was just a ploy to get us all out of the house so Frank could throw her a bone! The spot we liked to fish at was about five miles from the house so with three fishing poles and a bucket, we'd walk through the ghettos of Fulton and over the tracks to the Guinea Gulch Bridge. All the spades I knew from the neighborhood would bust my balls as we shuffled by their porches because we were hanging with grandma. I was a little embarrassed but screw them...what they didn't know about Nona was that she'd buy us booze! We'd send her into the liquor store about half way to the fishing hole with our order scratched on a piece of paper. Every time we got to the bridge those little Guinea Gulch grease balls would tease the shit out of me..."Look here comes little nigger Jimmy from Fulton! What, ya can't go anywhere without your Nona? You're not allowed out of the house without the old lady? Ha! Ha!"

Those garlic stinking bastards always got under my skin and what killed me the most was they knew I wouldn't start swinging in front of my Nona! Hell, it was worth a few zings to get hammered by the river all afternoon. She was good to us and it was a blessing having her around while we were growing up, even though there

You're Next

was constant turmoil between the mother/daughter duo. Nona stepped up to the plate on several occasions to get us kids out from under the slipper. She went back to Italy when I was in high school, that's when things really started getting cuckoo around the nest.

Growing up in the '60s with my brother Mike gave balance to the violence that surrounded me. He was two years older than me, so naturally I considered him cool. He was intelligent beyond his years but most importantly, he possessed the gift of laughter. Mike was always introducing me to new things that would forever influence my life, like Bob Dylan. Michael was a Dylanologist, the melodious sounds and prominent lyrics recoiled off the midnight painted walls and touched the stars on the ceiling of our bedroom. We'd listen to Dylan feverishly for hours on end and everything that poured out of his music seemed to relate to Mike's life, but after spending a few more waking hours on this ball of mud, I discovered that Dylan's lyrics were relevant to the world's footsteps.

We'd entertain each other with our metaphors and play our guitars while we burned incense. My brother was also blessed with the gift of music and could capture the undivided attention of everyone in the room when he had a guitar in his hands. I started quoting Dylan and reciting quotes of my own that I felt someone else should be hearing. I managed to capture my own audience outside of Mike's arena...the chicks dug it! I guess it made me sound intelligent and it gave them the feeling that they were hanging with someone who knew a little more than them. Hey, maybe they were right. I knew I was hanging with someone who knew a little more then me and that was my brother Mikey. He'd spit on our black and white TV screen as James Brown grooved across it, and of course I'd follow his lead. I didn't appreciate how significant and powerful James Brown was at the time because it didn't matter how talented the player, if it wasn't Dylan—we didn't pay any attention.

When I was about fifteen, Mike would take me into New York City on the weekends for kicks. We'd visit my cousin Dominick

Little Italy

and a few other cats that lived in his apartment building. Mike was interested in seeing the sights of the city, while I, on the other hand, wanted to hang in Dominick's basement and get fucked up. I'm not sure which one of us was the more normal teenager. While I was kissing girls and eating pills, Mike was philosophizing and talking to God. He was seventeen years old and his desire for worldly knowledge and faith was more intense than mine, more intense than anyone will ever know. It was almost like I had to force him to be a kid because most of the time he seemed to be bored with my bullshit.

One particular New York night, me, Dominick, and another one of our friends, Slick Willie were eating acid in the basement while Mike chose to eat a handful of white crosses. Dominick and I were laughing like hyenas enthralled with the color monotones of the seconds flashing through our vision. While Mike was asleep in the corner of the purple hazed concrete basement. I shook him…

"Get up man! How the hell can ya be sleeping, you just ate a handful of speed?"

"You're boring me." He bluntly replied and went back to sleep.

As studious as Mike was, his curiosity of drugs and girls still lingered like any teenager, but it never stopped him from searching for the answers of life…

"Mig…ell…hell, hell, hell, hell don't think you're heaven."

"Mig…ell…hell, hell, hell, hell don't think you're heaven."

Dominick started this goofy rhyme to make Mikey the spoon taker for our stupidity and from that day on he was forever known as *Heller*. It was Heller's supreme thoughts that kept my head above water through the '60s. I loved the music but most of my excessive behavior was directed towards those freaky hippie chicks serving up head.

My first concert was in '69, the Singer Bowl featuring Jimi Hendrix, Janis Joplin, the Chambers Brothers, and a band called the Soft Machine. I hopped a train and met Dominick in the city. We

You're Next

walked to the show so we could leave a trail of stash for the way home. We were kicking back on Seconal and wine as we walked arm and arm laughing and talking in our loud boisterous voices.

The music pounded in our hearts and humored our souls. Even the sky was enlightened by the sound waves and the stars danced overhead. The revolution was beginning and we were right in the middle of it. Dominick and I made our way to the front of the stage. The hippies were kind enough to let us cruise through the blanketed ground of circle parties. From the front row, we were looking straight up at the angel with the golden harp. The wail of Hendrix's guitar made the air move and there was a yellow-orange glow around him while he played. It was pure voodoo...it felt so good. There was no buzzing in my brain and my high was just right. For the moment, all of my senses became one and I finally found that space occupying peace in my mind.

"Sit down or move it, motherfuckers!" A stupid ass-grabbing faggot screamed over the loud bass as he kicked me out of the way. Fuck him—I was still standing and for once, I decided to blow off my punk ass attitude. I was having too much fun. Front row, back row, it didn't matter. Dominick and I kept floating through the crowd. We had come in peace and were looking for a good time, that jock strap wearing homo wasn't going to kill my buzz.

On the way back from the show, we cut over the Brooklyn-Queens Expressway to vomit on the cars going through the lower deck. After puking ourselves straight, we remembered our stash of weed and wine. We cut through the park looking casually over our shoulders. Then Dominick and I collapsed under the tree that held our goods. We sat and drank merrily while we laughed about how we'd just witnessed a piece of history, and smoked just enough to make it to our next stash. We headed home and by 3:00 a.m., we were sneaking in the front door of the twenty-four hour bakery down the street from Dominick's pad. After stealing two loaves of bread and a gallon of milk, we slammed the door so the owners could hear us and ran to fill our bellies and call it a night.

Little Italy

The 1964 World's Fair Exhibit in Queens was hippie heaven and it was another one of our hangouts. Fuck staying home...we were free! Over a thousand people were partying at the base of the unisphere and making plans to go to the Strawberry Fields concert, it was 1969. We didn't care about going to the show. We just wanted to feast on the women and the wine for the afternoon. Dominick and I danced from circle to circle listening to the men's guitars and hitting on their women. Under the pinkish sky, we kept drinking and just kept rocking into the night. We eventually went our separate ways and made a promise to meet up later. The sweet smell of pussy was in the air and it overrode all of Dominick's senses. The party was secondary to him so I hooked up with Flavio, this slick Cuban kid from Flatbush who was a little more aggressive than me. I always dug cruising the scene with him, wherever we went trouble seemed to follow, but I dug the kicks.

Flavio and I made our way under the unisphere, we were as high as kites, and the world was looking pretty good. The girders holding up the globe were so wide ya could lean your body in the concaved eyebeams. We looked up, under the sky was a projection of the earth, it was our own planetarium. I took a couple of deep breaths in complete awe over my unfamiliar harmony..."Hey man, I bet we could climb all the way to the top of this thing. Can you imagine the view from there? Come on let's get to it man!" Flavio started climbing up the girder.

Here we go...I can't punk out now. So I started creeping up the giant beam that reached to the skyline...

"Let's keep going, were almost at the top!" Flavio had the biggest grin on his face. It was probably from the acid he took. We were half way there and I was ready to shit myself, the best thing to do was to keep looking up.

"Hey Flavio, we're almost in South Africa!"

We were just to the tip of South Africa when I was suddenly blinded by a spotlight. It was coming from the ground and was pointed straight at us..."Fuck man! It's the pigs!"

You're Next

I looked down and the crowd below was grabbing at the cops. A Mexican stand off was about to start. The gig was up and it was time to give up the goat.

"Alright Flavio, what's the game plan now? We have to come up with something quick, we're about to get busted! Think man! Think!"

"Alright man, we'll slide straight down this thing in seconds. When we hit the bottom we'll split up and lose ourselves in the crowd. Then we'll meet back up at the Roman Pavilion as soon as possible! Let's go, are ya ready? I'm not giving up my last joint, not tonight!"

We had no other choice, I turned around, lie against the grainy iron. I put my feet out, my Chucks were my only grip! I started to slide and quickly gained speed. I was body surfing down on my back on a giant steel waterslide while the magnificent view of the Brooklyn Skyline flashed before my eyes. As soon as we hit the ground, we split up to avoid the pigs. The scene set the crowd into a frenzy! The cops were grabbing random men while their women were kicking and screaming. By this time, the noise was slowly moving behind me but I could still hear the crowd chanting…"Today's pig is tomorrow's bacon! Ban the bomb! Make love not war!"

It felt like I had run for miles till I made it to the pavilion, it always feels that way when you're running from the law. I was thankful for those crazy hippies though. Their protests kept us out of harm's way. Flavio was already standing at the entrance into the pavilion when I got there. We sat down to catch our breath. We were choking on our own laughter thinking of the scene we had just created, "Let's smoke to freedom." Flavio pulled out his last joint and lit it when we sensed some rustling behind us. A couple was making out in the bushes and the chick started a shouting match. I guess we had startled her.."We just pranked the cops! Fuck that cock sucker, we're not moving till we smoke this joint!" She heard us and knew where we stood and it got silent again.

She must've put her boyfriend's dick back in her mouth. Flavio and I just kept laughing, nothing mattered that night, we were The Emperors of Rome!

When I was off from the barbershop, I'd spend my time down at the far end of South Street near the railroad station. It was one of those mythological places your parents told ya never to go to because the drifters might gut ya and sell your organs to Charles Manson for liquor money. I had a lot of confidence at a young age, or should I say balls. Being the menace to society that I was—South Street Station sparked my curiosity. As it turned out, the transients that hung around the tracks lived pretty interesting lives. They were bums that hopped freights. The locals hung around too and we'd all get smashed together. It was an easy way for me to score a bottle and some butts. I always knew the right people to help me cop a buzz.

We'd get blasted and jump over the tracks into the river. On a few occasions the ambulance had to show up, a couple of the hobos thought it would be a good idea to dive off the cliff's edge into three feet of water. Sometimes I got so caught up in the good times that I'd forget what time it was..."Oh shit, it's six o'clock! The barbershop is about to close, I've got to meet my father!" I needed to get out of there and get my ass home, but I was way too drunk. So, I'd shove my fingers down my throat and puked up the glow I had been working on all afternoon.

"Hey man, what da hell is yous doin? You be wasting all dat *good* liquor, ya crazy little whitie! What's wrong wichya? Oh, dats right, yous Frankie's kid. Yous gots to go to da babashop. Okay Jim, we'll see ya morrow."

The railroad station became a steady hangout for me in the summertime. I liked the pace, people were always coming and going. They weren't always sure exactly where they were going but they were going somewhere...we're all going somewhere.

You're Next

I spent a lot of time in the city with Dominick because Aunt Lucy's house was a lot less stressful. My Aunt Lucy was a round little Italian woman with a carefree spirit. Unlike her sister Lena, she wasn't as heavy handed and didn't give out so many smacks. Don't get me wrong, she was still a tough Italian broad who always got her way, she just went about it in a gentler manner. Lucy loved to cook and she lived to eat! It was a *sin* in her house to waste a single bite of food. Even if her guts were about to explode, she'd eat the last bite of spaghetti in the bowl. I always felt welcome at Aunt Lucy's place and I loved her dearly.

For a change of scenery, Dominick decided to hang in Fulton for the weekend and cruise for chicks. This girl Dina used to show up in town once in awhile to visit her family. She was twenty-three years old and the rumors claimed she was a super slut. Being she was much older than us, we figured she'd say no, so we never pushed the envelope. One night, Dog Shit, I mean Dina, invited me and Dominick to hang out and do some drinking. Man, we're in! She was even old enough to buy alcohol—I knew one of us was getting lucky! Dominick suggested we get her drunk and then take it from there. Judging by the smile on his face, I could tell he was happy to be in polyester.

After a few pints, Dominick and I took Dina down to the river. There was nothing lady like about Dog Shit, she didn't care about her mud soaked ankles. Oh well! She was going to be on her back in a minute anyway, she was so damn horny! My denim bell-bottoms tightened and my balls were blue for Dina. It was fuck or walk, and if you're not going to fuck—leave the bottle. I quickly chugged off the Bali Hai, which took care of my aching sack. There was confusion in the ranks between me and Dominick on how to deal with this situation, being that we've never had a girl undress in front of us before and beg for sex. We decided to forget all of that this was our chance. It was no jerk off session and may both men make it to the finish line.

Little Italy

After we both finished, we left Dina and the empty bottle in the mud. She never refused seconds, maybe because she was used to getting tag teamed at home. The rumors were right, Dina was a nice girl, but her nickname around town said it all. Yes, yes, yes, Dina looked like dog shit there's no denying that, but man could she fuck! As frequently as Dominick and I attempted to score pussy together, I would've never guessed that the first time we got laid it would've been group sex. Hey, when opportunity arises ya got to seize the moment. Even if it doesn't seem quite right and it smells a little funny! When you're fifteen and suffer from CBS, (constant boner syndrome) you'll let anyone cure it. Unfortunately for me, the only female babysitter I ever had was my grandmother.

The final straw of Catholic school was getting the trashcan. Change was in order now that Dina had made me a man. I was tapping a beat on my desk with a pencil to the rhythm in my brain. I really dug that tune by The Animals, *"Oh Lord, Please Don't Let Me Be Misunderstood."* My teacher was a sweet sticky southern whore who demanded respect. Her long southern drawl made my ears ache. I didn't care how many slaves her toothless hillbilly family may've owned, she wasn't getting any respect from me! She wasn't a nun but I despised her just the same...Tap! Tap! Tap!

"James, stop that! You're nothing but trash! Get up and go stand inside that trashcan right now before I call Mother Marie Del Fatso. Then you'll understand the kind of trash you really are!"

We bickered for a moment, and then I made my way over to the trashcan behind the door. That bitch actually made me step into that trashcan, I had no choice—this was bullshit! I was fifteen years old and still in the seventh grade. The last thing I needed was a beating from Del Fatso, I was tired of it. Mother Marie Del Fatso was the headmistress of the school and the leader of the penguin clan. Her fury burned a flame big enough to set the building on fire. Meanwhile, unknown to me, the few words that were exchanged were being heard in the main office over the intercom. That sneaky little southern witch had flipped the switch! That fat mother had heard it all, and I could hear that penguin panting as she stormed down the hall.

    The enormous oak door flew open so fast that I thought it was going to fall from its hinges. I was safe for a moment, the door was blocking her view, and she couldn't see me standing in the trashcan behind it. The whole class stood up to greet her, "Good morning and God bless you Mother Marie Del Fatso." She didn't answer the class in her usual proper reply...**"Where is he?"**

    Despite her great divine fatness, she managed to spit out the words between long-winded breaths. The whole room was frozen in sheer terror and most of those scared little pricks pointed in my general direction. Del Fatso slammed the door shut and exposed me. "Get out! Get out you piece of trash!" Her deep voice bellowed off the walls and her eyes were full of rage...I knew this was *it* for me! She ordered Christian Chris to get the yardstick and he gladly obliged. That little faggot had the biggest snide grin on his face. (Yes, I remember who ya are Christian Chris, and if I *ever* see ya again, ya two bit little punk I'm going to kick your teeth down your throat!). Mother Marie Del Fatso dragged me out of the garbage and started viciously beating me!

    "You're nothing but trash! Don't you understand this by now James?" Del Fatso managed to scream at me with every thrash of the yardstick...

    I wasn't going to take it anymore! No more rulers across the knuckles, no more slaps in the face, no more hair pulling, and definitely no more brutal insults from these stupid whores! I bolted for the door and ran towards the boy's room. No way would she follow me in there, she's a nun and has never laid eyes on a guy's meat before. Well, except maybe Father...aw forget it. I was wrong! Del Fatso barged right in, copped a look at all the little dicks as they pissed themselves and continued attacking me even more furiously! Bobbing and weaving I managed to escape, I ran out the door, flew down the hallway, and headed straight for the exit—I didn't stop running till I reached the barbershop. I wasn't turning back, the wooden spoon was child's play compared to the lashing I had just endured.

I was completely out of breath by the time I hit *Travelers*. I stood in front of my father and re-enacted the scene as tears streamed down my face. Then I went where I've never gone before with my father. I raised my voice and made it very clear to him I was done. "I don't care what ya do to me. I'm never going back there again, I quit!" I squinted for a moment in anticipation of the backside of his hand across my face, but I opened my eyes to my father kissing me on the cheek. He gave me a hug then sent me home to tell mommy. My father must've called home before I arrived because mommy's reaction was quite humane and civil. No smacks, no slippers, no frying pans, I guess she knew how serious the situation was. "Nobody whacks a my Jameza but a me!" It was time to go cut a deal with the public school system—again.

To this day, I still hate nuns. It was so bad at one point that when I'd see those fucking Brides of Christ—I didn't think twice about spitting on them. I'd experience "nun rage" when I was on my motorcycle. If those bitches pull up next to me, I christen their windshield with spit and ear splitting blows of, "Fuck you stupid cock sucking, motherfucking, dickless whores!" Hey, you would too if ya had a permanent bald spot on the back of your head! My method of dealing with my anger may repulse you, but it's cheaper than paying Fran the "psycho" therapist two bills to "talk" about it. Thanks Fran but, fuck that! Talk is expensive and spit is effective.

Shortly after I left Catholic school and was making the transition into the public high school, Heller was graduating. Even though we were two years apart in age, I was four grades behind him in school. I turned sixteen before I hit the ninth grade. Heller appreciated Catholic school much more than I did, so much that

You're Next

My brother, Michael

after graduation he enrolled in the Seminary to become a priest. Maybe he'd find what he was searching for and be around people who were more in tune with his infinite wisdom.

After a few months of my brother being in the Seminary, my mother put in a request for all of us to go visit. She wanted to cook a meal for the family. The priest granted her permission to use the kitchen to simmer her sauces and work her magic and the dining hall would be just fine for the four of us to enjoy each other's company. While mommy was cooking, Father Fitzjames came into the kitchen for a formal introduction. He asked if I'd accompany him downstairs, he needed assistance checking a light bulb. I looked to my father for the nod of approval and he waved his hand. The basement was very dark, but Father Fitzjames managed to prop a ladder in the middle of the room. He shooed me up the ladder to investigate if the bulb was blown. I didn't notice he was up to a little investigating of his own. He stopped me half way up the ladder. In his left hand was a brand new bulb and in his right was a handful of my cock! What was Fitzjames thinking? Hum, let's see…F-I-T-Z-J-A-M-E-S. Fitzjames! Wait, this can't be right! Even if his name is Fitzjames he's not supposed to fit his cock anywhere near James and James's cock shouldn't be in his hand! I was sixteen years old, I knew this wasn't right. I was already screwing chicks! Wait, maybe he has a pussy? No! I jerked his hand away and scurried down the ladder. He grabbed me by the arm as I made a move towards the door.

"Where are you going? You're not going to tell anyone about this…right?"

"Of course I am you stupid queer!" As I hustled up the stairs, Fitzjames tried to make light of it but the only thing that was light was his loafers. My adrenaline was pumping hard by the time I reached my father. As I was explaining in Italian what just happened to me, I reached over and grabbed a piece of Italian bread for comfort. I lifted the lid off the pot of red sauce and dipped the bread. Aah…it was so good—**Whack!** Another spoon over the head and a couple of smacks across the mouth. I had broken the cardinal rule, "You basta! You a know a you donna eat afore I'm a done a cookin!" I was right in the middle of explaining that the priest had just tried to molest me! Mommy didn't care, she was waiting for an explanation and an apology because I had just fucked with her sauce! My father went down stairs to have a little chat with Fitzjames. I was so worked up over the spoon that had just been bestowed upon my melon that I had already forgotten about that faggot priest. After my father had his little talk with Fitzjames, we didn't see him for the rest of our stay.

Now that I'm looking back on the situation, I should've let that cocksucking queer blow me! At least I wouldn't have caught another beating from mommy! I guess it's my black humor that keeps me sane. The situation with Father Fitzjames hasn't traumatized me in the least. If ya wanna experience real trauma — try living with my ma!

    A few months after being touched by a priest, we got a phone call from my brother in the seminary. Heller confessed to my parents that he was psychologically uncomfortable and pleaded that he was desperate and wanted to come home. The urgency in his voice was serious, so we jumped in the car and headed north to give him our immediate attention. We didn't know what popped, there was no comforting my brother. He was still distraught by the time we got home. His body language made it clear that his mind was frantic. This made my parents extremely nervous so they decided to consult with the family doctor. They were at the doctor's mercy because they didn't speak much English. The doctor reached a prompt and harsh decision. Within days of Heller returning home, he was admitted into a mental institution. The only thing Heller said to me on that long ride home from the Seminary were these words…"I learned *too* much *too* fast."

    Heller spent the rest of his natural life in and out of mental institutions. When the insurance money ran out, he became state raised. No one ever attempted to console Heller in his times of tribulation. It's still a mystery to me why Heller pained so deeply after leaving the Seminary. Instead of solving that mystery, the state deemed it necessary for Heller to receive electric shock therapy in order to subdue his behavior. Electric shock therapy has been proven to cause irreversible brain damage, so naturally it would alter ones train of thought. He eventually became mesmerized as the treatments continued, not by his own intellect, but by the electric shocks to his brain.

    Did Heller learn too much at such a young age from the elders in the Seminary? Is that what made him question this life so deeply? Did this knowledge frighten him? Were there too many Fitzjames? Or, was he just mesmerized by the State of New Jersey?

Little Italy

There was a time in my life when I started to think about Heller only in my dreams and less and less during conscious daylight hours. At that point, Heller slowly drifted out of my life, our bond was broken for reasons of self-preservation. Heller will forever remain in the background of my mind and in the forefront of my heart.

Heller, my brother, you are, older than me, do you still feel the pain?

Chapter 3

Neighborhood Bully

The noose around my neck was tightening and the gun at my back was suffocating. It was causing my brain to swell and my teeth to grind. I had the ability to stop it all, this relentless headache, if only my parents would let me drop out of school! There'd be peace in the valley and I wouldn't be so pissed off all of the time. The odds were against me and my chances were slim because I refused to live by the rules set by the world. I was "Frankie's kid" and that's the only reason why I had passing grades. Every single teacher shuffled me through the system so they wouldn't have to deal with my miserable existence another day…or they'd just kick me out of school. I believe despite my wickedness, I was in the prayers of every authoritarian in Fulton, "Please Lord, I beg of you, let James get hit by a bus…I can't take his torturing another day!"

After leaving Saint Bernard's School, I finished the semester at Fulton High School. Saint my ass! There were more whores there than matches in a matchbox! I have to say, as much as I wanted to just be done with the whole thing it was liberating to at least be out of that stupid Catholic uniform! Being that I had a few extra quarters from the barbershop, I decked myself to the nines in a coral, wide lapel, polyester suit and tan suede platforms. Yeah, I was the man, and I was known around the slums as "Crazy Whitie."

By the time I hit high school, I was known only for my bad reputation and not for my stunning personality. Throwing fists was the core of my identity. I was the oldest kid in my class, a dirt-poor flunky. Teachers hated me because of my badass attitude, fathers

Neighborhood Bully

hated me because I was fucking their daughters, and the pigs hated me because I jammed up their coffee breaks. I had to throw a beating to some of the spades that were bussed in every morning. They thought I was on enemy turf because I was white! This was *my* hood, black or white and I couldn't tarnish my reputation by backing down. I was constantly criticized and condemned for being alive — the world was against me. The school system wanted me to stand around thick-skinned and not fight back. Fuck that! I counted down the days for that chapter of my life to end. Needless to say, I got the boot from Fulton High School after the first semester because of all the fighting.

Pride, prejudice and superstition has always surrounded my existence, which has forever crowned me the neighborhood bully. The alternative to public school was vocational school which was a holding tank for all the born to be losers. This place was serious. I'm telling ya it was full of hitters. I had to change my coolness stature immediately! My look needed to be toned down, I stuck out too much around the whities in Vo-Tech, and they could tell by my duds that I lived on the other side of the tracks, besides high tops and jeans were easier to throw down in. The vocational school building was an old warehouse. The outside looked like a prison because of the mesh wiring that covered all the windows. Inside the building, the walls that divided the classrooms were cut off about four feet

from the ceiling. Why? I don't know, but it sure provided us with a great deal of entertainment. Shoes, books, panties, everything came over those walls! Aah...there's nothing like coping a sniff off some girl's panties before lunch.

As a vocation, I decided to try my hand at being an electrician. I figured I could slack off there. Come to find out, after I already signed up, the instructor was an ex-State Trooper and didn't take shit from nobody. Mr. Manhandler took his stance immediately by rounding up the class of flunkies in the locker room. We formed a circle and he stood in the middle, "Which one of you fuckers wants it first?" His breathing was heavy, like he was getting ready for a bullfight. His eyes were bulging out of his head and his pale blue veins pulsed vigorously throughout his forehead and neck. This ex-pig, crew cut wearing, motherfucker wasn't screwing around. Someone was about to get squashed—nobody moved! Was this guy serious? He reached his long muscular arm out and slam-dunked this little pipsqueak's skull into a locker! The kid stumbled around as if he was punch drunk after taking a hit like that!

"Come on! One of you little faggots hit me! We're going to end this right now! You all need to know who the toughest guy in this room is, and let me give you a little hint—it's not any one of you!"

We all went nuts, everyone started swinging, it was a free for all! Mr. Manhandler grabbed the pipsqueak again and started using him as a body blocker! It was literally over in seconds...he had taken on the entire class! Mr. Manhandler used us to block our own punches; we were punching each other...genius! We got the point, and after a show like that, I always treated Mr. Manhandler with respect. He was okay in my book and he knew what scrapping was all about. He had proven it twenty-five to one.

Speaking of tough guys, Tommy Mc Keever was doomed for eternal damnation in Catholic school while I was busy sticking my fingers in light sockets! I had fun busting his balls about midget wrestling with those little leprechaun faggots. Mc Keever and I still got into trouble together even after being separated in school. The word on the street was that ya didn't go to Cobbstown unless ya wanted some action, so we met up and headed straight over there. We stumbled upon a construction site to split a quart of beer. The dirt lot was the site of the new vocational school, and among the dust, all that stood was a steel frame. Just to be jerks, Mc Keever and me crawled around the steel beams and loosened every nut and bolt that was holding it together. A group of local kids spotted us on the lot and approached us because we were whities and weren't supposed to be in their town. Mc Keever and I got squashed by at least a half a dozen spades. It was one of the worst beatings I'd ever taken. You'd think I would've been a little thicker skinned by then! They had no idea who "Crazy Whitie" was and they didn't care.

    We finally got up the strength to dust ourselves off and drag our asses back to Fulton. We were on a mission and tried to round up some troops, we were determined to seek revenge but no one would follow our lead. The blacks were busting our balls and jiving about the Cobbstown incident because the Fulton kids knew to stay away from there. We did too, but part of being a tough guy is having no fear. Mc Keever and I'd be back another day to claim our victory!

    Looking to escape the daily grind of school, I decided to drop a hit of acid with these two cats, Kevin and Joey. School had never opened the doors of perception in my mind, so maybe dropping acid would liberate my thoughts, at least for a day. If nothing else, it would keep me occupied for the afternoon and hopefully calm. By midday, I was at my desk preparing for take off. I could feel that big grin creeping its way across my face—I was feeling fine. While the empty space in my brain sat quietly, Kevin was wigging out and decided to go to the school nurse for help. Kevin's panic-stricken brain caused him to rat out on Joey and me! He was so fucking freaked he didn't even realize what he had just done. Kevin's only focus was anxiously awaiting a big shot of

You're Next

Thorazine to quiet the voices in his head. I heard my name loud and clear over the intercom, I was instructed to go to the principal's office. Or at least that's what I thought I heard. How could they possibly know? Maybe they don't know? What else would I be in trouble for? For once, I was keeping to myself. I hadn't thrown a fist all day. Maybe it was in my head? It wasn't in my head! The teacher repeated the message and pointed her long ghoulish finger towards the door.

By the time I reached the principal's office, the school nurse, the principal, my father, and a cop were all there waiting for me. It was an interrogation and I was put in the hot seat. The nurse was shining a pen light into my eyes, dumb bitch, as if I wasn't seeing enough colors already. I had to stay calm! The principal was speaking Italian to my father. He was trying to explain the effects of tripping on acid. Although I'm almost positive he had never taken the trip himself.

Two languages were being spoken at once, which created a weird vibration in the room that caused the walls to breath. Nothing made sense everyone was talking in tongues. The cop was hound dogging me—he wanted the connection, the source, and he wouldn't stop asking questions. The whole time I couldn't stop staring at the big chrome buttons on his uniform, they gave off a strange glare that made me squint. I looked up at him. His mad grin and towering height led me to believe he was really an evil clown under that uniform—it's a clown conspiracy! I knew no one would ever believe me, but I denied everything and I stuck with my story till the bitter end…there was no way I was folding. I wasn't going to let that clown drag me off to his evil clown lair! My mouth was so dry— did I lick a toad? It took every ounce of my squirming guts and whatever brains I had left to pass the test that was being giving in tongues, but I did it—I beat the system! Everyone started to leave the room. The principal instructed my father to take me home. They had had enough of me for one day.

Neighborhood Bully

    The twenty questions made my trip take a turn for the worse and I was trying not to freak out! As I reached for the door handle of my father's Chevy Wagon, my hand went right through the door panel—strange. All I wanted to do was go home, lock myself in my room and search for my sanity. Maybe it was behind the door, or on the floor, or maybe it was in the mailbox. It wouldn't surprise me—I had my suspicions about the mailman being a communist. Communist! Sheer terror set in! I wanted to tell my father that my blood was pumping so hard it made my veins raise and weave through my skin like a pile of worms and I couldn't shake them! I needed someone to tell me that everything was going to be okay—I needed some comfort. There was no way in hell I could handle a beating from mommy right now! My father's curiosity was getting the best of him. I couldn't jump out the window, so I had no choice but to let the interrogation carry on...
    "Jameza, tattoo gradite il vostro galleggiante?"
    "No! I don't feel like I'm floating!"
    "Sentite dei rumori bizzarri?"
    "No! I don't hear weird noises!"
    "Vedete dei colori?"
    "No! I don't see any colors!"
    "Jameza, Avete preso l'acido?"
    "No! I didn't take any acid!"
    "NO! NO!! NOOOOOOO!!!"
    That was all I could say, Frank had me cornered, and I felt like he could read my mind. Cars were zooming by us at mach speed in the opposite direction. They'd come crashing through the windshield if I didn't pay close enough attention. When we finally reached the house, I immediately bolted for the stairs to find a quiet place. My father stopped me dead in my tracks and with his hands pointed towards the sky he said "Where a ya think you a goin? Ya not a in a school? No drugs? Ya come a to a barbershop and a work!" Fuck me! All I needed was some solitude! I needed to remember what planet I was living on. My trip had gone too far,

You're Next

but I couldn't turn back now. I had no choice but to ride this rollercoaster out at the barbershop.

My brain was bouncing around like a pinball machine by the time we got there. My paranoia made me question whether I was ever going to be in my right mind again. It just happened to be senior citizen discount day at the barbershop. Lucky for me because seniors are already out of their minds, so maybe I'd be in good company. Ya know, I drool, you drool, we all drool! The barbershop was real busy and it took everything I had to keep it together to shine shoes. The waiting area was filled with old people and it looked like a giant puppet theatre. I was shining this old man's shoes that was sitting in my father's chair when his long wrinkly face came alive. I could see every molecule of his skin begin to multiply. Every time he talked, his face would melt. It started to drip down his leg and settle into a pool on the floor. The butterflies in my stomach were searching for an exit! I couldn't look up! The man was making me nauseous. His breath seemed to reek of embalming fluid. I needed to get a grip before I blew chunks all over his pants and shoes. Where were the merry pranksters when ya need them? I was ready to run out of the barbershop screaming like a guy too high.

Suddenly I had a moment of genius! I remembered talking to this guy who was more experienced than me with taking hallucinogens. He told me how to shake a bad trip through repetitive thought. So I kept repeating to myself...Everything's going to be okay...it's just a bad trip! Everything's going to be okay...it's just a bad trip! Everything's going to be okay...it's just a bad trip!

It was like a tape recorder playing in my head. I decided to take it a step further and turn it into a prayer. I pleaded with God that if he got me out of this one, I'd never do hard drugs again! I quickly learned that the power of repetition is the only known way to the subconscious mind. Before I even understood the power of this formula, I was putting it to work. "Everything's going to be okay...it's just a bad trip!" It saved my ass! I had made it through the day and was somewhat sane by the time I crawled into my bed. I had weird dreams though—too many shoes and not enough feet!

Needless to say, the acid incident determined my fate in vocational school…I got the boot. I guess it just wasn't my calling to be an electrician. So it was time to go back and cut a deal, yet again, with the public school system. Through all the insanity, the one thing I did do was keep my promise to you know who. Being a man of my word, I ditched the narcotics and started hitting the bottle pretty hard. Spooliolli or Jack if I was lucky. Or Mad Dog, cough medicine, mouthwash, gasoline, whatever was cheap and readily available.

These two guys in their 60s, Mr. Bojangles and Joe Gee were cruisers who always offered to drive my drunken ass around on their dime, while we juiced. The rumors around school were that they were two pickle smoking pervs that would do anything to lure in a fresh young piece of meat. The word was, if ya got smashed and passed out in their car, you'd wake up with your pants around your ankles and a sore asshole.

Fuck it! I decided to go cruising with Joe Gee one night despite everything I had heard, I wasn't scared. Besides when it comes down to it, I'm not opposed to kicking any queer's ass! I had no gas money and I wanted something to do, so why not cruise around, get drunk and sniff glue! I was leery at first but as time passed I realized they were saviors, not psychos. We cruised around for years together, jiving about life and listening to tunes. Bojangles and Gee were my guardian angels that always made sure my ass had a safe place to crash. If I didn't, they'd drag my dead weight onto ma's porch and wait in the car till she came out and whacked me one. Not once did they attempt to give me the Jersey reach around! Back then I couldn't understand why two old guys would want to spend their time jerking around with a bunch of unruly teenagers. Now I know they just needed human contact, someone to talk to, and a sympathetic ear once in awhile. Just like the rest of us…no one should ever feel alone.

You're Next

Staying on the straight and narrow and getting passing grades was virtually impossible for me. I needed to find something to do. I wasn't into sports or any after school shit. I already had a job at the barbershop, maybe I just needed a hobby, something I was truly passionate about that would occupy my time and keep me out of trouble. It didn't take me long to find that certain something...SEX! Black, white, fat, skinny, ugly, pretty, toothless, or ya motha, I fucked anything that walked. No, I take that back, even if ya couldn't walk I'd still consider ya! If it smelled like pussy— I'd fuck it. Hey, ya can't get arrested or kicked out of school for fucking...right? While the guys were out blowing their minds on the drug of the day, acid, speed, mescaline, I'd occupy my free time screwing their girlfriends.

Dog Shit was still a regular on the weekends. The older I got, the more I appreciated Dog Shit because she'd let me screw the shit out of her and then leave. This cat I used to hang with, Dixie Darrell, would always bust my balls about Dina, claiming that someday I'd care about the face. On one of those afternoons down by the river, I convinced Dixie to join me and Dog Shit. I told him that if he stuck around long enough, he'd no doubt catch dirty seconds. The girl was going to fuck him and that's all that mattered. As I was getting ready to mount Dina, Darrell pulled down his pants, but I told him to slow down because I was first. I started fucking Dina but I was losing my concentration. I just wanted to cum, but I kept hearing all of this rustling coming from Darrell's direction. I looked over and that stupid hillbilly had his pants down around his ankles and was beating his own dick with a switch from the tree..."Hell Jimmy, you have at her. I'm just going to stand here and beat myself off!"

After the party was over, Darrell kept busting my balls about Dina, "Hell, Jimmy! They don't call her DAWG SHIT for nothing ya know. What the hell ya doin stickin yer dick in that? She's so ugly I couldn't even get a hard on! Man, I tell ya what Jimmy, some day yer gonna care about the face. Maybe ya should start havin sex with yer eyes open!" I was fueling his fire and it was funny! I kept telling him it wasn't my fault, that I slipped and my dick fell into her. Darrell and I truly had a lot of fun and ya know what, he was so right. Dog Shit Dina was *so* ugly, but that still didn't change my mind.

    Dominick and I started hitting clubs for pussy in New York City in hopes that it would be an easy play. We made our way to the Tamble Inn because we heard they were lenient about checking IDs. We got a pretty good glow on before we hit the bar because we couldn't afford to buy all of our drinks there. The action was so fast inside the club that within minutes a chick approached Dominick. With no introduction she clamped down on his ball sack, "Are you straight or gay?" What a strange question, of course he was straight! Fuck this stupid broad—we both started aggressively groping her. After the first few minutes of submission she panicked, "I gotta go! My girlfriend is looking for me!" She slipped right through our hands like boy butter. Oh well, blue balls were only temporary and we didn't have to buy her a drink, so we treated ourselves to one.
    The club was a little strange, but there were a lot of cool chicks in the joint and we were hot! Before Dominick and I could even finish our drinks, two more chicks approached us at the bar. One for each of us, this would be a change of pace! The groping started immediately. I was making out with this tall confident blonde who seemed to be very aroused so I decided to go for it. She was so horny and seemed to like the rough stuff. She didn't care that we were in a bar. I slipped my hand up her skirt to feel her hot blonde...rock hard cock?? "What the fuck!" I wanted to look up her skirt to make sure it wasn't the booze. No need to second-guess myself. I have one of my own! I pushed her, uh, him, away from me and onto the dance floor—I was ready to puke! I rinsed my mouth out with the rest of my drink like it was mouthwash and spit it on the floor—my rage was boiling! Everyone in the club was

about to pay for my humiliation. Before I started cracking skulls, I turned around to grab Dominick. He had the horns going and was so into this chick (uh, dude), that he didn't even notice what just happened. I tried to explain the situation but he couldn't hear me, he was obsessing over his boner! All he could do was mumble about what a good kisser she was and how we were invited to her apartment. I grabbed Dominick's hand and shoved it into her crotch…he got the point. "Aah, who cares?" Completely drunk and belligerent he turned his back to me and started kissing it *again!* All I could think about was choking everyone in the joint, but instead I grabbed Dominick by the collar and dragged him out of there. He might've thought it was a good idea at the time, but I knew if he woke up hung over with a cock in hand that wasn't his—he wouldn't be able to handle it! Isn't alcohol great? So I guess I take it back, I won't fuck just anything that walks!

  By my *second* sophomore year in high school, I hated my existence and my misery kept spiraling. Our house had literally turned into a nut house. Heller was constantly in and out of the mental institution, and when he was home, his actions became dangerously violent. My mother was going out of her mind and was under a lot of stress as his caretaker. She lived in the middle of all this dysfunction, yet she was the only one to remain sane. The tension was high and it was a miserable place to be! My mother sent Nona back to Italy to live with her sister. Lena had enough on her hands with Heller and couldn't take any conflict between her and her mother. Everything was piling up on her shoulders and it seemed like she was ready to go off like a shotgun at any moment.
  Growing up, I didn't realize how strong of a woman my mommy really was, and I'm not talking about her spoon arm. Looking back on it all now, I realize that she was the one who held us all together. Being the son-of-a-bitch that I was, I only added to her aggravation. So between school and the barbershop, and let's

Neighborhood Bully

not forget about drinking and fucking, I managed to keep my time occupied and stay out of her hair.

I wasn't keen about having a steady girl, so I joined a motorcycle club called the Night Raiders. I was patched pretty quickly being that it was run by a bunch of screwed up teenagers. Besides I knew most of the guys before they patched me. We didn't take ourselves too seriously. We just liked to get drunk, fight, and pick up girls. Our patch was a three piece. The centerpiece was a large Maltese cross with a skull wearing an old style German War Helmet. The skull's eyes were mean with purple and red threaded

Heller wearing my vest

fury. The top rocker read Night Raiders and the bottom rocker carried Central Jersey. They were both threaded in red. The side rocker of course read Fulton-wide—just kidding. It was tough I tell ya, so tough it was taken from a kid's model car box from the late '60s. Even back then I was a fan of Ratfink. Big Daddy Ed Roth

You're Next

designed most of the model car boxes and I was proud to wear his art.

Not all of our members had motorcycles, so a few of us pitched in on some house bikes. Yeah that's right we had Honda 350's, we decided not to go too crazy considering most of us didn't even have our license yet. We pitched in on a used limo so we could cruise together and get liquored up. The limo was the core of our scene, the trademark for our badass motorcycle club. I guess we should've started the first limo club! We would hang riverside slugging gin because the pigs would fuck with us if we drank near the road. Back then, all the cops would do was confiscate the bottle. No big deal right? Bullshit! When you're not old enough to buy it, this could be a real pain in the ass!

I can't stress enough that the Night Raiders was no ordinary club. There were only a few guys in the club that were not deaf mutes. I wasn't the president, I was the spokesman. I spoke a little of their language and they understood mine. No matter how great the communication gap was, one thing we all had in common was our attitudes. Anywhere the Night Raiders went together, they came back together. No one was ever left behind. Ever since, I've kept that same attitude with everyone I hang with, no matter what the circumstances...no one gets left behind!

One night, we were cruising around in the limo jerking off and Deaf Charlie was at the wheel. We were on our way to score some pot, get drunk, and kiss girls. Our typical Friday night. Hey, maybe we'd attempt to beat the record of how many times we could continuously drive around the Fulton Circle. At some point we needed to take that title away from those Millville punks! We pulled into Johnny's Diner, it was always a good hang out. The fuzz followed our limo into the parking lot. We had nothing on us because we hadn't made our way to the taste shop yet, so this should be fairly quick. The pig was bored and determined to find something, he hauled our ass's out of the vehicle and made us hang curbside. That jerky cop spent at least fifteen minutes crawling around on the floor of our limo. He looked like a crack head scratching the shag to find a rock! In the end, the stupid pig only managed to scrounge up two pot seeds.

Being that I was the only dude in the bunch that was shooting off my pie hole, the cops pulled me aside, "You better make it clear to the rest of these punks how serious this is." I stepped away from the pig to translate to the rest of my crew. All the guys were good at reading lips, so communicating his message wasn't a problem. Someone had to fess up or they were going to impound the limo and haul us off to jail. The cop stuck out his hand and shined his light on the pot seeds. The pig was yelling at Charlie, but of course, he *couldn't* hear a fucking thing! Charlie's facial expression looked perplexed, he didn't understand what was happening—at least he acted that way.

It was time to confuse and bamboozle the bacon breath motherfucker—he needed to be distracted. When Charlie started talking, small screeching noises were coming from his mouth. His boisterous hand signing and body language made it apparent that he was confused. The cops started to get nervous. In the midst of Charlie flaring his arms, he ever so slickly smacked the backside of the cop's hand in an upward motion and the pot seeds went flying! Man, that cop started jumping up and down while frantically shining his light looking for the lost evidence. He went totally ballistic! That doughnut-eating faggot had to push his nose through our dirty carpet to come up with that evidence and now it was gone! We laughed in his face till he finally gave up and they had to let us walk with no charges. Our badass motorcycle club had claimed victory. Fuck Whitie!

The Night Raiders were very short lived, it was really just something for us misfits to feel apart of. It worked for all of us. We shared some really cool times together and had a lot of fun. It's exactly because of those memories that our friendships are still alive today!

You're Next

In 1971, my father's mug was front and center in all of the New York City newspapers. He was accused of laundering money for the Mafia and our barbershop was supposedly the headquarters. The rumors spread around town like wildfire and the news articles became the talk of Fulton. My family was crucified for it. I stayed out of it the best I could, no one ever told me anything and I never asked. What I do know is there were never any convictions or indictments. The air about the barbershop drastically changed and so did the clientele. My father's so-called friends and prominent clients decided that gossiping about Frank and shunning my family was the best way to handle the situation. A lot of people turned their backs on us. I felt my family was disrespected and I've always been offended by that!

My father had decided to take a sabbatical in the mental institution, so we were forced to close the barbershop for what we thought would only be the summer of '71. It was the first time he had been in the nut house since we lived in Long Island and it scared the shit out of me. Did my father go into the mental institution to avoid jail time on federal charges? Did he plead insanity? Or did he just crack under the mental strain? Did Heller know more than I did? These questions have never been answered.

Immediately after the newspaper incident, my mother slapped me in the face by telling me I had to go. Like I didn't have enough problems in my life already, but fuck her, I didn't need my family anyway. She told me I could eat, shower, do laundry or whatever chores I needed to do, but she made it very clear that I was no longer allowed to sleep at the house. "What the fuck did I do?" I knew I was a troublemaker and probably did cause a lot of the burden on her, but I had put in my time at the barbershop since day one. I did as much as I possibly could for my family. I would've done more if they would've just let me drop out of school! So why was I getting kicked out?

At the time I had a VW Van. I didn't need anyone and I didn't need to sleep at home, I'd be just fine—Fuck it! So I'd park my VW in the city or out by the Jersey Shore to sleep. I could do whatever the fuck I wanted and that's exactly what I did. I'd occasionally sleep in the hippie patches. No matter what, there was always a place to crash. Self-preservation was in order, I didn't need to be wrapped up in my family's garbage. I was sick and tired of trying to gain the same level of acceptance in my mother's eyes as that crazy motha fucker Michael!

My father spent close to eight months in the mental institution right along side my brother. Even though I wasn't living at home, I was pardoned from the final draft for Vietnam in 1971 because I was labeled as head of the household. Due to my father's condition, my mother had to finally step up and make the decision to permanently close the barbershop. This was a very sad day in all of our lives. We had all put so much time, effort, blood, sweat, and beards into that barbershop. It was my childhood, my identity, my upbringing. No one ever gave me any direct answers as to why we closed the barbershop, but it was pretty obvious due to everything that had happened.

I've always lived in constant fear of my family's mental illness. I knew that I was capable of slipping into the genetic cesspool of this disease at any moment. Thorazine and shock treatments were being passed around my house like candy and no one seemed to have their shit together.

I found a lot of ways to make money and to keep my time occupied now that the barbershop was closed. I got several job offers from the Barber's Association. I'd drive into the city, pick up a car, drive it through the Lincoln Tunnel and drop it off. I'd pick up another car and an envelope, and then head back to Jersey. I got $100 per car and I never knew what I was driving, where I was dropping, and I sure as hell didn't know what was in the trunk. I never looked or even dared to ask! Besides what did I care, all I wanted was the hundred—the rest was none of my business.

You're Next

I started this hustle when I was seventeen because it was better than working a real job. I moved four to nine cars a week. I was fat city...you do the math! What was I going to do for that kind of cash, flip burgers? Someone could've held a gun to my motherfucking head and I would've had nothing to say.

My father and Heller were in and out of the looney bin and I had four people to take care of. I landed this gig along with several others because I was still "Frankie's kid." I'll tell ya what though, my heart would be fucking pounding every time I'd make a run into the city. Traffic jams would throw me into a panic! I could never get out of there quick enough. I remember this one time, I had gotten hung up in a roadblock coming out of the tunnel. It was over for me for sure.

I was sure they were looking for me—I was trapped! My mind was telling me to get out of the car and run like hell through the sea of traffic back into the tunnel and look for a good hiding spot, but that would be too obvious...I would surely draw attention. By now, I was six cars deep from the law. Fuck, I could of swore I heard noises coming from the trunk, or was it just in my head? I slammed my foot on the brake, but I was already at a complete stop. It felt like the car was rolling backwards. The heat curled off the hood. It was a cool car, one like my daddy used to drive us around town in, but this is no time for reminiscing. My vision was blurred and I shook my head—my breathing was quick and short. I was drenched in sweat so I turned up the radio to try to drown out the thumping and the voices in my head. Three cars deep—fucking New York traffic! Damn it, I'm screwed! Fuck Me!

The car along side of me rolled up their window after seeing me talking to myself and swaying back and forth like a mad man. I was going to puke, just one more car to go. I put my head down on the steering wheel. Everyone was honking their horns. Did they know it was me? When I lifted my head, I could see the cops moving the barricades! The blue lights of the five NYPD cars started up and

Neighborhood Bully

they pushed through the traffic as they continued on their way. My knees gave out—I couldn't step on the gas. Fuck Me! I needed to get a real job. I was losing sleep, but I was back in the city the following day to make a run for another hundred.

After finishing my junior year at Fulton High, I got kicked out. Not bad for me actually, I was pretty proud of myself, I made it through two more years. Now it was time to take the situation into my own hands and just drop out. I was sick of the everyday torture and there was so much turmoil in the family. It would be easier to just focus on making money. My father and my brother had become state raised and even though the bills were overwhelming, there was no way my mother could leave the house to go to work. So when my father was released from the mental ward, I made the grand announcement that I was dropping out of school. Despite the fact that he was still trying to recover, my father

You're Next

refused to accept this. So he took matters into *his own hands* and set up a meeting with Mr. Cheese, the principal of Fulton Vocational School. I don't know what the hell he was thinking—I had already gotten kicked out of there my freshman year for the acid incident.

Frank managed to cut a deal with Mr. Cheese to get me back into Vo-Tech. Ya see, us WOPs had to stick together, because that's the way it had to be. What the Fuck? Why were my parents so hell bent on me graduating? The deal my father cut with the WOP master was this, he agreed to work at the vocational school as a janitor for the entire year. This way, my father could watch over me and keep me out of trouble. Frank promised Mr. Cheese he'd keep an eye on me at all times and if I did get into trouble, he'd deal with me personally. Cheese agreed and once again I was back in school. How wonderful this was, my father, a once respected businessman in Fulton was the fucking vocational school janitor. Dignity was lost for all when this deal was sealed. I don't know what the fuck my father was thinking, I just hoped like hell he'd spend a lot of time in the broom closet.

For my *second* crack at vocational school, I tried my hand at auto mechanics and auto body repair. Fuck being an electrician, mechanics get more pussy anyway. I started off in auto mechanics thinking I could be a wise guy. As usual, my humor and sarcasm were not appreciated—no one cut me any slack. I did however, have the privilege of sending the freshmen who didn't know shit about cars to fetch me parts from the shop teacher, Mr. Thor. "Hey kid, tell Mr. Thor ya need a sky hook and a radiator cap for this VW!" It didn't take long for Thor to crack and when he finally did, I was cutting sheet metal and minding my own business when I heard him scream my name from across the room—"Jimmy!" I stood up and looked towards the front of the classroom just as a fucking lump hammer was flying through the air and headed straight for my skull. I had just enough time to duck! Okay...Okay...I got the point! It was time to relocate to the body shop for the rest of the year.

Neighborhood Bully

From the first moment I stepped foot into Mr. Rusty's classroom, he made it perfectly clear he wasn't taking any of my shit, "I've spent enough years dealing with punks like you—let's just get through the year!" The way Mr. Rusty worked was if ya bummed a smoke off of him at break, ya owed him two the next day. He reminded me of Johnny Carson and he had the same sarcastic attitude. When Mr. Rusty wanted to make a point, he'd bust your balls in front of the entire classroom. He was good at the ridicule game, so out of fear of embarrassment he made ya stop and think before ya opened your mouth. He busted my chops a lot about beating up my classmates and huffing lacquer thinner. He made me the poster child on why not to kill your brain cells. He'd yank me out from under a car knowing there was a shop rag across my face saturated with lacquer thinner or gasoline. I'd be totally fished out and everyone would be laughing by the time I came to. I got tired of hearing from Mr. Rusty about how stupid I was to kill my one and only brain cell, so my huffing days were short lived. That was Mr. Rusty, he had his own way of dealing with my stupidity—and it wasn't running like a rat to the principal!

By my senior year, I was surrounded by some heavy hitters. I had to get serious about my attitude and take care of my own ass. With tough guys like Big Dick Duke and Slick Nicky walking around, I had to crawl the halls with a constant chip on my shoulder. On the right day, there'd be nothing less than a food fight in the cafeteria! Man, of all the things I've done wrong, if my mother ever found out I had wasted food—she'd put her foot up my ass. I was the oldest cat on the boulevard at Vo-Tech but this other roughneck Harley Charley (not to be confused with that deaf fuck Charlie), ran a close second. So together, we ruled the school our senior year.

Harley Charley and I were notorious for pulling pranks around the school. One of my favorite stunts involved a motorcycle, of course. Hey, they didn't call him Harley Charley for nothing! He was a badass motorcycle mechanic and rider...it's his life even now.

You're Next

The corridor was a straight shot with double doors on each end. Classes were going on so no one was in sight and all the classroom doors were closed. Harley Charley started his 900 Sporty and cracked it up the stairs and straight through the doors. He shot clear down the hallway at nuts speed—straight out the other set of doors and Evil Knieveled it over the stairs and into the teacher's parking lot! The pipes echoed so loud through the enclosed space and Charley was going so damned fast, that by the time any of the teachers came out of their classrooms to see what the hell was going on, both sets of doors were already closed and Harley Charley had already left the building—with Elvis in tow!

Besides motorcycles, I can truly say that Denise was the first love of my life. She was the first person to ever make me feel that special feeling. I didn't know then but it was called love! Denise was a few years older than me, and was fucking hot. She carried herself well for a girl in her twenties and she always spoke her mind. There was nothing timid or shy about her. Denise was very independent and would make heads turn when she opened her mouth. Everyone paid attention to her, no one brushed her off. She was a tall brunette with fiery blue eyes who was ready to go out and see the world by the time she was out of high school. She was just itching to get the hell out of Fulton. She wanted me to cut out with her because things were so fucked up on the home scene for both of us. My mother needed so much help…there was no way I could leave her. I'd have to pick up ma and take her to run errands and try to get her out of the house as much as possible. Sometimes this annoyed Denise because we never got much time alone. We always wanted to fool around but I always seemed to have that little four foot, garlic stinking, cotton hair in the back seat.

One day when I picked Denise up at her house, she was babysitting her nine-year-old little brother Chris, so he had to come along. We cruised into Pennsylvania to check out some used rides, little Chris was glowing with excitement. He was the first one out of the car. As soon as that little shit head stepped foot on the gravel,

Neighborhood Bully

I slammed the door and gunned it down the street so I could get a few pokes at his sister. Chris was hysterical! He was out in the middle of Pennsylvania and didn't even know his own phone number! What a scumbag, right? Well I know ya would've done it too...Denise was hot and if it wasn't for her, I would've left him there.

After graduation, Denise begged me to move to Tucson, Arizona. She wanted to cut out and Tucson sounded as good a place as any. She decided to split, probably because she was knocked up by some other guy. Needless to say, we broke up and she went on her own leaving me more alone than ever. We all have different paths in life, we just weren't supposed to walk ours together, but it's cool because we're still friends today. I'm also still great friends with that punk Chris, although now I don't leave him all alone in car lots, he leaves me. Chris and Denise also had another sister Debbie, who was a dear friend of mine. She was taken off this earth too quickly, but I'll always cherish the good times we had and she'll never be forgotten in my heart.

Denise wasn't the only broad I was hanging out with my senior year but she was my only girlfriend. One of my teachers, Miss Hot Twat, well...she's another story. Hot Twat was twenty-four and fresh out of college. In Vo-Tech we were segregated into all male classes. I guess they figured we shouldn't hang with the ladies if we were just going to beat each other up. But for some fucking reason...they threw us a pretty pink pussy for a teacher! Hot Twat announced that she had just moved into her new apartment down the street and needed a volunteer. In her girlish giggle, she explained that ya could see right through her windows. She didn't know how to hang a curtain rod and needed a man to come over and help her. I looked around, raised my hand and told her I'd be happy to hang a rod for her. I wasn't stupid, I knew what she wanted.

I called her that Saturday to ask if she wanted me to pick up anything, she requested a bottle of Blue Nun. Blue Nun? What the

You're Next

fuck? That was more expensive than the Bali Hai that I drank! Fuck it man, I knew I wasn't going over there to hang curtains. I was going over to give her my rod, so I guess I could spend the extra buck. It was well worth it, I ended up staying at her place all weekend and let me tell you, everything got hung—except the curtains!

Miss Hot Twat was never my girl, so I gladly shared her with my brother Harley Charley. Occasionally, when the three of us were too drunk to make it back to her place, we'd end up at ma's house. Miss Hot Twat would wake up hung over, dripping in whip cream, and sandwiched between me and Charley. Our alarm clock was my mother pounding on the ceiling with the end of a broomstick, "Get a up you bastas! You a gonna be a late for a school!" Hot Twat would come down stairs, say good morning to my father the janitor and drive us to school.

My father always knew I was running around with handfuls of women at the same time. I used to screw around with Black Betty and a few other chocolate honeys in those days. He knew me and Hot Twat were fuck buddies because of the broom stick banging on the ceiling in the morning! He never asked me any questions about the chicks I was hanging out with but on occasion he'd throw me a line, "Wha, ya can't a do bedda den dat Jameza?" I think it was just to bust my chops, because my father liked pretty women too. One day Frank was whistling away, minding his own business and mopping the school floors. He went into the broom closet to get some supplies and found Black Betty giving some other whitie a blowjob. That night after dinner he pulled me aside to tell me about Betty hunkering down on some other dude's cock…"Jameza, dis a Betty a Black a, she a suck a da cock a dis a boy today!" I couldn't stop laughing—it was cool he was looking out for me! He wanted to make sure that Betty wasn't my girl, because if she was, it should've been my cock in her mouth, that's all!

I used to wise off to Hot Twat in front of her class because I knew she wouldn't do shit about it. I'd tell her to stop being a bitch and to shut the fuck up in front of everyone..."James, can I speak to you in the hall please?" Hot Twat pulled me out into the hallway and pinned me to the wall. With all of her sex appeal she pleaded with me, "Jim, I can't have you treating me like that in front of the other students. Please baby, they'll know something is going on between us if I don't send you to the principal's office. Please, just stop it, okay?"

I agreed and walked back into the classroom and sat next to Harley Charley. I leaned over and told him to stay after the bell rang and as soon as it did, everyone shuffled out of the room, but Charley and I didn't move. We knew there'd be only a few minutes before the next class started, so I went for the door and locked it while Charley pulled all the shades. I grabbed Hot Twat and told her to never fucking talk to me like that again! As Charley moved towards her, I could see the fear in her eyes. He pulled off her blonde wig and smeared the onion mask of makeup on her face as I leaned in close and told her how pretty she looked. I could feel her heart beating out of her chest—she was terrified and didn't know what to think. Charley forced his hand up her skirt and started finger fucking her through her nylons while I was kissing her and ripping her shirt open..."Oh stop! No—don't stop! OH! OH!! OH!!!" Right before she reached pure ecstasy, Charley and I pulled away leaving her a hot and disheveled mess with only seconds to put herself back together before her next class came in. She never spoke to either one of us like that again and she still came around that night begging for cock!

Fucking my teacher or not, my grades were still below average and I had a bad habit of skipping class. I needed to pass more than just one subject and there was no way I was fucking Mr. Rusty! So, the school decided I had to make up for my absences by assigning me as the tool crib attendant. I'd like to thank Fulton Vocational School for giving me the opportunity to get some much needed equipment to start pounding out dents and painting cars— but we'll get to that later!

You're Next

Jock Strap the gym teacher, unlike Hot Twat, had a serious problem with me and Harley Charley. He had a chip on his shoulder because he knew…that I knew…that he knew…that Charley knew…that we were ALL fucking Hot Twat! So Jock Strap abused his authority and was a complete asshole to us all the time. He was jealous and humiliated. Here's the thing Jock Strap, something ya may not know to this day—I never cared that you were screwing Miss Hot Twat. I'm not the jealous type. Shit, that's why I shared her with Harley Charley. Live and let live—right? So we made it as tough as we could on Jock Strap for trying to push us around and would retaliate by not showing up for gym class and reeking havoc when we did. I think Jock Strap came to the realization that the count down to graduation was on, so he didn't dare fail us in fear we'd just torture him again next year.

One day in gym class, Harley Charley and I made it clear to the rest of our classmates that if anyone of them moved on Jock Strap's command, they'd get their brains kicked in. "Okay everyone, get changed! Let's go! Get outside! It's time to do some laps." We were lined up military style and no one moved an inch. No matter how many times he blew that fucking whistle, no one moved. He repeated himself, "Let's go! Get outside, it's time to do some laps—what the hell is wrong with you kids?!" The whispers went down the line from ear to ear that no one was to move unless they wanted to get stomped. Finally, Mr. Strap realized that the class was paralyzed by our threat. He pulled us out of the gym and dragged us to the principal's office. My father wasn't there for that particular incident. He must've been in the broom closet with Betty—just kidding. Mr. Cheese was pleading with us…"Guys, let up on them. This is ridiculous! Just listen to Jock Strap."

Harley Charley and I both agreed to give Jock Strap a break, just so we could get the hell out of Mr. Cheese's office. When we went back into the gym, the whispers started again and we reassured every student that if they moved they could expect to take a beating before the day was out! Strap announced, "We still have a half a period to go. Let's not waste any more time. Everyone needs to change and get their asses outside!" No one moved an inch! Jock Strap was beside himself and was pleading with the whole class. "Don't listen to these punks! You're going to grow up to be losers if you listen to guys like these! They're not leaders! Stand up for yourselves. You don't have to take this abuse from them, they're losers! You're supposed to be listening to me! You have your own minds! Stop this! I'll take care of those bullies later—now come on people!"

Strap blew that whistle till he was blue in the face and he didn't stop begging till the period was over. The air in the gym was so tense that as soon as the bell rang, it was like a gun went off and the finish line was beyond the gym doors. Not a single one of those miserable pukes could take the pressure that was causing their brows to sweat. They all ran for their lives! That was one of the heaviest power struggles of my senior year. Harley Charley and I never did stop screwing Miss Hot Twat. What was Mr. Jock Strap going to do, explain to the principal what was really going on? Fuck no! The only person who truly won that senior year at Vo-Tech was Hot Twat. That dumb slut was getting more cock than she could handle! Jock Strap should've been happy that we didn't march the whole damn class over to her apartment for some real gymnastics.

Finally, on the day of my birthday, June 16, 1973, I got the best present I could even ask for! I graduated high school at the tender age of twenty. My father's job as my babysitter was over and my parents had finally gotten their wish. Unfortunately, they didn't make it to my graduation ceremony. It was just one of those nights around the house when everyone needed a double dose of meds. As Mr. Cheese handed me my diploma, he looked me in the face one last time—I just turned and walked away. Of course, not before grabbing his ass right in front of everyone there, I had to break his balls one last time. My friends wouldn't have expected any less of me! That night, us roughnecks went out to celebrate and reminisce about our years in hell school. I have to admit, I felt an overwhelming sense of accomplishment considering all of the bullshit I had endured—I finally made it! Graduating was a bittersweet ending to some of my friendships while others became eternal...like Duke. I was happy to close that chapter of my life, now maybe the insanity would mellow out. My anxiety over school was no bullshit. Even now as an adult when I'm having a bad day, I reassure myself that whatever the problem...it's better than being in school!

Chapter 4

Stenciled Angel

It took me over thirty years to reconcile my feelings about ma giving me the boot. Only now do I understand why she did what she did because one of her oldest friends, Bernie Pure Buns, told me—it was for my own protection. Why hadn't I thought of that? Sometimes we get so caught up in our emotions that we don't take the time to see what's right in front of our face. Lena was just making sure the "madness" didn't rub off on me. She was trying to ensure some kind of normality in my life. I'm sure my mother knew there was a bag of pot in my underwear draw and a stolen motorcycle in the shed—she wasn't stupid. After Frank got accused of laundering the dough, we never knew when or if Johnny Law would come a knocking. Because of her love for me, Lena kept me from going down the drain with Frank's dirty water. Maybe *institution* was just the family code for *jail* and nobody clued me in.

I said that I wrote my brother off after the first time he was institutionalized. Well…I lied! I tried to write him off, but I couldn't. Mental illness was going around my house like a virus and I thought for sure I was going to catch it. I was afraid it would manifest in my brain like a tumor if I stayed around and let it! Obviously, I understood the dynamics of mental illness and that you can't catch it like a cold. But certain thoughts creep into my head while I sleep and I'd try hard never to let them gain ground.

When Heller was on leave from the institution, my mother took care of him. I was only called when he roamed. He started hitting the road to experience the world. He was in search of his purpose, and he'd take road trips around the country with no means of getting home. Nine times out of ten, he'd end up in the slammer and I'd have to go bail his ass out. Heller strayed far away from the path he worked so hard to beat down. I believe he was traveling backwards in time to experience the spontaneous behavior of a normal teenager. Then again...I'm no shrink, just truly shrunk— ninety percent of shrinks are nuts anyway! Maybe if Heller had studied psychology instead of theology, he could've been fucking with other people's brains instead of his own! He'd set up his life to follow the Good Book and he was always told he'd receive great rewards for his gallant efforts and intellect. My parents put Mike on a pedestal, which can put a kid under a lot of pressure.

When you go probing for the answers of life and the true spirit of the Holy Ghost and come up with abuse and corruption, well this would obviously send anyone over the edge. Man, sometimes we all need something so bad, something to fill that void in our existence, but that doesn't mean it can be found in a pharmacy or in an alley. There's no substitute for faith, and when the worlds got you beat, you just need something to give you hope.

In the '60s, when people started to experiment with LSD, they discovered that Thorazine would reverse a bad acid trip. If that were the case, the theory would be that Heller was naturally on a bad trip and the Thorazine was supposed to straighten his ass out. There is no question that the medication along with the electric shock treatments made Heller's brain take a turn for the worse, it was ultimately his demise. He kept up the good fight by pushing his creativity to the outer limits, but the fucking drugs kept him down. My buddy Jeff and I were curious and wanted to know what was going on inside of Heller's head. So we each took half a dose of Heller's daily diet of Thorazine and went for the worst ride of our lives. The only thing we could do to calm ourselves was to flush the shit—it was a long three days. Was Heller having a bad trip? Or did the Thorazine put him on a bad trip like Jeff and me?

Stenciled Angel

I'll never forget the singsong voice of that fucking nurse. It still rings in my head today, "Michael…take your medication Michael…come on Michael…you must take your medication to get better…Michael." What did that stupid whore know? I repeated myself to Heller over and over again in fury, "Just tell everyone fuck you! Fuck you! Fuck you! Fuck everything! You have to stand up for yourself, or you're never going to get out of here alive! Who cares what the fuck these people think? Fuck you! Fuck me! Fuck them!" But that wasn't Heller's style.

Several people who've harnessed greatness because of their supreme drive and desires have also fallen victim to these cruel treatments and a life of *One Flew over the Cuckoo's Nest*. They've thrived on their creative imagination in the quest for infinite intelligence—Ernest Hemingway, Frances Farmer, Vincent van Gogh, Robert Pirsig, Heller, and my own damn self.

With all this insanity and trying to recover from the hell of high school, I began to search for people I could relate to. I started hanging with this cat Skeets. We were a couple of tramps, like two stray dogs. We bummed around the country riding motorcycles and digging the hell out of life. We eventually became best friends. There was something forever young about Skeets and our parties never stopped. Our backgrounds were similar and we had the same opinions about life. Skeets was one of the guys I'd drink the holiday blues away with. We felt no reason to start a so-called real life, that was a drag, and besides, we refused to conform.

Skeets and I terrorized our way through the Carolinas and ended up on the beaches of Florida. By the time we had gotten home I could tell how uncomfortable Heller was, the anxiety on his face was obvious. He was desperate to get the hell out of dodge, so I gave him a '68 Ford Country Squire Wagon. I figured if he had some wheels he might feel a little better. After I delivered the car, Skeets and I split to have a few beers. Hours later, I came home and found Heller under the dash cutting up the electrical wires with a

You're Next

Bowie knife. When he saw me standing in the driveway, he grabbed a hammer and started smashing in the gauges and the windows. Then he popped the hood—not the engine! He had totaled the fucking car! I was furious. What the fuck was he doing? This is the kind of thanks I get for my good gesture. Fuck him! He wasn't going to treat me like that. Heller really was crazy if he thought I wasn't going to say something to him, "Dude! A Wagon isn't a bad ride, especially for someone who has no wheels!" We started arguing and it was getting heated…we'd be toe to toe any second. Wrong! I was running for my life—Heller chased me down Warren Street with that huge Bowie knife in his hand! Fucking crazy bastard, I knew he wasn't right but I couldn't figure out why he was trying to kill me over a car! Mommy saw the whole thing from the living room window and put an end to it. If there's anyone who Heller listened to it was mommy. She got me in the house safely and I called the junkyard. Now the wagon wasn't even worth its weight in scrap metal. This was virtually the beginning of no communication with Heller—he was shut out. I still had to be there for him though. He was after all my brother, and I couldn't leave him behind no matter what the circumstances.

As I mentioned, Heller started taking spontaneous road trips to get the lead out and break away from being locked up. After the car incident, he and his buddy Rudy took off to North Carolina in a '68 VW bus I scored for them. While cruising south they got caught in one of those freak snowstorms. Heller lost control of the bus and it ended up on its side in a snow bank. Heller, being the physical powerhouse that he was, along with the help of a couple of dudes, managed to get the bus back on all fours and back on the road. Somehow, the mangled VW got them home safely. The damage to the van didn't matter much to Heller because he never did care about material possessions.

A few months later, Heller was off again, this time to Florida. He got locked up for stealing shrimp off a fishing boat and was charged with a misdemeanor. He only stole a handful of shrimp.

Stenciled Angel

Can ya blame the guy? He was hungry! I had to cruise down the coast to bail his sorry ass out, and do his bidding over a few shrimp.

The adventures of Heller became a regular thing, every couple of months I ended up somewhere in the USA with a pocket full of bail money and instructions from mommy to get him home safely. Heller ended up down in the Carolinas and back in the slammer shortly after going shrimping! Being that I was the man of the house and couldn't even sleep there, every time I started a new gig, mommy would call me in a complete panic and I'd have to drop everything to bail her precious Michael out. I was fed up with the bullshit. That's why I never could hold down a real job! My mother and I decided that the next time we got a phone call, I shouldn't immediately run to Heller's aid. Maybe if he sat in jail and stewed for awhile he'd learn his lesson. Heller…that poor lost soul, as if he didn't spend enough time being locked up. The next time he was in jail for trespassing because that's what happens when you're a stranger in a strange town. He never even had a license and his only form of ID was his fucking library card. As massive in size as Heller was, he was a timid man. When it came to being locked up, he didn't enjoy breaking skulls. The people working at the jail quickly came to realize how harmless he was, so they gave him kitchen duty.

When I showed up in court with the public defender and saw Heller, I was completely stunned. He entered the courtroom in his jailhouse rags shackled around the waist and hands. This is normal, but what caught me off guard was that he had shaved his head! He was as bald as a buzzard and had lost the Roy Orbison glasses. I didn't recognize my own brother! Heller was acting completely insubordinate in the courtroom. I had no time for this bullshit—we had to get home! I asked the Judge if I could approach the bench. I informed him that Heller wasn't playing with a full deck and was all out of his crazy pills. Honestly, Heller was smarter than everyone in that room but in this case, the crazy ace would work in his defense. Luckily, in the end, this got us the fuck out of there and on a plane back to Jersey.

During the flight home, Heller wouldn't calm the fuck down, so I put up with it by busting his chops about his new look. He told me that he was locked up with a bunch of cats from a motorcycle club, so he decided to adapt a harder image. That was Heller's style all right. He'd rather shave his head than throw a punch. Mommy was going to be pissed off because Heller didn't have his glasses. Oh well, at least he still had his teeth!

I had to move on with my life. What I really had to do was to get my own life, so I decided to rent a garage with my friend Dumblay. Remember my tool crib attendant gig at Fulton Vo-Tech? Yeah well, that's how I was able to start a body shop straight out of high school. Tools aren't cheap you know, and you can never have too many!

By 1974, the body shop was doing well enough to put a few extra clams in my pocket, so I decided to take a road trip with Skeets. I was hanging with this chick Carrie and she told me if I was going to leave town, I'd better take her out on a date before I go. So we cruised down to a club called Rum Runners. You know, one of those dark shit holes that should be passing out oxygen tanks at the door—only the best for my dates! We were at the bar when I caught a glimpse of Anna. She was a beautiful Puerto Rican Goddess. My buddy Oscar had introduced us a few months back, and I had almost forgotten about her. Carrie caught me looking at Anna one too many times and started copping an attitude, "As much as you're staring at her, you might as well go talk to her!" Yes! This was my chance to make my move. Besides, Carrie was being such a bitch. It was like she dared me...I'll take it! I quickly made my way to the other side of the room to ask that black haired beauty if she wanted to sit in my ride for a few. It was too loud in the club to talk, so she agreed to follow me outside.

We climbed into my pick-up and reintroduced ourselves while I smoked a joint and jived with her. Anna and I started making out, she was such a good kisser that I had forgotten all about Carrie waiting for me in the bar. I explained to Anna that I was skipping town for awhile to take care of some business but that I wanted to see her when I got back. What a great summer night I thought to myself, what the hell am I leaving town for? But the road always calls. The olive skinned enchantress gave me her phone number and we went our separate ways.

    Carrie was still at the bar and nine eyed drunk by now. She was so pissed off by the time I slipped back into the club, she instantly started swinging! She was hysterically screaming and crying. I physically had to drag her out of the bar as she wailed her fists at me. I wasn't going to put up with her shit. She was the one who fucking dared me! What the fuck was wrong with this broad? Needless to say, that was the end of Carrie, and I hit the road.

    When I drifted back into town, I went straight for Anna's phone number. I'm so glad I called her. Anna is truly one of a kind, she's a completely down to earth hippie chick. We made plans to get together. Anna told me she couldn't believe that I actually called, and how pleasantly surprised she was when her mother gave her the message. She never needed me to wine and dine her. She just wanted to get to know me. Anna wasn't full of herself even though her Puerto Rican beauty was stunning. She had her own confidence and didn't need a thing from me. She was able to stand on her own just fine.

    When we first started hanging out, Anna was working as a teller at the local bank in Homestead. I was still running the body shop in my spare time, when I wasn't running around the countryside. I called her as much as I could. I had a constant desire to be around her. She wasn't the only chick I was hanging with, but I slowly started to get rid of the hang arounds so I could spend more time with Anna. The more we got to know each other, we realized that as children we had passed through the same apartments and dark hallways. Turns out, they were the ones above Lip's Lounge. We were so young back then that all that boy-girl stuff didn't matter. We played different games, but I quickly remembered exchanging several innocent glances with her so many years ago. Sometimes fate toys with you before it gives you the big break! Anna was a solid straight-line connection.

I kept hanging around with her through the summer, and it was finally time to meet her family if I wanted this to continue. Juanita, Anna's mother was an easy person to get along with. She was a free spirit and we had a lot in common. Juanita had a great sense of humor and loved to call me a stupid guinea. As carefree as she was, everyone in town knew not to fuck with her. Her hot-blooded Puerto Rican temper was not to be taken lightly. She wouldn't think twice about giving you a fresh one—she was quite the Spanish spitfire! Everyone who knew her loved her. God Bless you Juanita. We miss you!

Anna's father, Mr. Alcaide, was a military man. He was very set in his ways and had a stern attitude that demanded respect. Although we were very different, I never once busted his chops. Anna has twin brothers, John and Raymond. They had a hard time with me at first because I was hot on their sister. I was envious of Anna's family life, they seemed so normal. Mr. Alcaide told me right from the jump that I'd better pay respect to his daughter if I wanted to be welcome in his home. So I gave him my immediate attention—it was worth it! I really dug Anna, I was impressed that she had so much damn self-respect and wasn't another stupid whore like most of the girls I dated. Mr. Alcaide was one of the few people I never stepped off the curb with. My big stupid trap was definitely off color for him, but hey, that's just my lingo. I said something to him like, "yous PR's are a lot like us Italians."

"Yous PR's? What do you mean, yous PR's?"

"You know Mr. Alcaide, yous Puerto Ricans."

Let's put it this way…he wasn't impressed! He told me never to use that term in his presence again. He was a Puerto Rican not a PR and that I'd better get it right! I guess he felt I was insulting him. I

Stenciled Angel

should've called myself a WOP instead! From that day forward, I made sure I paid mind to his wishes. I had better if I wanted to keep kissing his sweet little Puerto Rican daughter.

With all the family how-do-ya-do's out of the way, it was time for me and Skeets to hit the road again. I told Anna I'd see her soon. We only had one bike for the trip but there was no shame in that, so few people were riding motorcycles then. That bitch with a stick shit didn't exist! We tromped through Central Jersey and Pennsylvania drinking beers and sleeping roadside. By day two I was done and I asked Skeets to drop me off at Anna's house in Homestead—I wanted to see her.

You're Next

Skeets busted my balls, "What, that little Puerto Rican chick that works at the bank—why man? She's cute and all, but come crash at my place. We'll get loaded and take off again in the morning! Ya think we could make it to California on the Yamaha?" As much as I enjoyed the trenches and a trip to California did sound sweet, I told him to drop me off. All I could think about was kissing Anna.

Skeets got the hint and headed towards her house. We stopped at Farley's Tavern to get a couple of beers before Anna got home from work. Farley's was the one and only tavern in town. The locals ruled the joint and didn't take kindly to newcomers, especially the likes of us. The minute we stepped foot in that shit hole, the drunks started in on us..."What do you two creeps think you're doing riding motorcycles around here? You got no business being here—get out!"

Of course it only took one comment like that to get Skeets and I riled up, we weren't scared of nobody. Before it got bloody, the bartender decided to call the coppers. They immediately showed up and hauled our asses out of there. The pig threw us in the back of his squad car and questioned our intentions. I explained to the fat fuck that I was in town to see the Alcaide girl. He was straight with us, "The next time you boys roll through town on that faggot motorbike, you best not stop at Farley's. And if there are any disturbances while you're here, it's going be your fault!"

He was trying to bully us into leaving, the ignorant fuck. I wasn't going anywhere—I was there to see Anna! After the lecture we were released from the car, Skeets grabbed the cop's briefcase fucking around. The cop didn't think it was funny. Then Skeets started coming loose and was acting like he didn't know what the problem was. The officer announced to Skeets it was his one and only warning!

Anna's house was right around the corner so we split. I hopped on the bike, I was driving this time, and Skeets took the back seat as he waved goodbye to the disgruntled pig. As we turned onto Anna's street, Skeets jumped on my shoulders with his arms spread eagle. We did this kind of shit all the time and luckily, just as we were pulling up, Anna was in the front yard and snapped a picture of us coming down the road.

He dropped me off at Anna's and hooked up with our friend Bobby, then set off to pack for California.

I spent most of the evening with Anna and I eventually made my way back to ma's place. The following morning mommy barged into my room with the phone. What the fuck? I was still in bed, I had gotten in late and was running on E…I didn't need to face the slipper right now! It was Anna, she was at the bank, and it was about Skeets. He never made it home. Skeets was dead. When he split from Anna's, he was going a little too fast on a hairpin turn and hit a tree. Bobby was following him in his Galaxy 500 and when his headlight disappeared from the road, Bobby turned the corner and found him in a tree. By the time the meat wagon showed up, Skeets was already gone. I told Anna I'd catch up with her later. All I wanted to do was hang up the phone. Out of shock and confusion, I sat at the edge of my bed and cried my eyes out. I had dealt with death before but nothing this close. Skeets was too young to be done with this life and we had so many plans! My mother asked me what was wrong. When I explained in Italian she left me alone.

Later that day, the town started an investigation. Skeets' parents wanted some closure. The police blamed the accident on faulty brakes. The day before the accident we had done an adjustment on the rear brakes, so there's no way in hell that had anything to do with his untimely death. Skeets and I knew what we were doing when it came to wrenching bikes. I told the police that the Yamaha had just gotten an adjustment and that they better take a closer look. The closing investigation stated that he was going too fast and said nothing about faulty brakes.

I had to visit Anna, I didn't know where else to go, I was totally flipped. She held me and told me that everything was going to be okay. The only reassuring thought I had for years after Skeets' death was that somehow Anna was my guardian angel. To this very day I have to take comfort in the thought that this was some kind of divine intervention between me and Anna. I had lost my closest friend but Anna was right there. I was supposed to be tramping with Skeets that night, but instead I felt a strong urge to hang out with that little Puerto Rican girl.

Eventually, Anna and I moved in together, and in 1977 I decided to ask her to marry me. I couldn't live fast anymore, not if I wanted to stick around. This was my one shot at true love and possible sanity. Prior to our engagement, I decided that I should get a real job. The body shop had been short lived. My partner was a flake who was just waiting around for his father's inheritance. I was still lying, stealing, and cheating but I knew I needed to do something legit if I wanted to marry Anna. I started working for an engineering company as a service tech. They asked me to relocate to Ohio and offered me benefits, an apartment, a car, and better pay. This would be a perfect opportunity for me and Anna to start a new life together and leave my mess behind! It was the only way I could see us having a long enduring relationship. I needed to start over if I was going to be any kind of a husband. I had too many skeletons in New Jersey.

That spring we were cruising around Warren in my '69 Ford pickup with our dog Levon. He was a real cool dachshund, our first of many over the years. I was casually explaining the offer I

Stenciled Angel

had just gotten from the company to Anna, and how I felt I should take it. I told her she should come with me and that I wanted to marry her. Anna looked over at me and her face lit up. She immediately said yes! We both felt a wonderful unity that day, and I knew I had just been gifted with the most precious angel on earth!

Anna started planning the wedding but only a few weeks before our big day, the owner of the company died, change was coming on quick. The new chief decided that it would be too costly to relocate me to Ohio. They wanted me to stay in New Jersey. Our plans were already under way and I wasn't backing out. I was stressing, my plans were squashed, and I really wanted to split—I had to get out of that fucking snake pit. Even though I couldn't go to Ohio, I wasn't going to let that stop me from marrying Anna.

The night before we got married I didn't do any of that bachelor shit. Instead I spent the night in the chicken coop next to the barn at Dumblay's place, where I lived prior to moving in with Anna. I wanted to be completely thankful for everything I was about to receive, even with the bad news from the company. I wanted to be straight with myself and start our new life together. After twenty-five years on this planet, finally something was making me look up.

Anna and I were married on July 1st 1978. She did a great job planning the wedding and looked absolutely stunning. The only roughhousing that day was over a fur coat. Mark the Fox's girl at the time decided to smack around some broad over stolen merchandise. No big! I can't complain. Usually there's a hell of a lot more damage at an event when I'm in attendance! By this time my brother and father were so overmedicated that they were walking around the reception like a bunch of zombies, but I tried to keep my emotions under wrap. Today was for me and Anna.

We headed to Nova Scotia for our honeymoon. I had a bunch of vacation time and decided to use it up. I was so pissed off about the company stiffing me that I decided I'd quit when we got back. We cruised up to Canada in our '66 Malibu, and on our way back

we got stopped by the border patrol. The chick with a dick wanted to search the vehicle, she was hell bent about finding something. When she started talking about the dogs, I decided to turn over the little bit of weed we had on us to keep Anna out of trouble. I wanted her to have some peace, this was the first road trip since we got hitched, but trouble seems to follow me wherever I go. I was trying to keep it as far away from Anna as possible. The border patrol sent for a State Trooper to book me and take me downtown. Believe it or not, he was actually a really nice guy and was giving me the ins and outs about the area. I explained to him that Anna and I had just gotten married. The cop congratulated me on my new life and on the fact that the possession law had just changed a few days prior. A fifty dollar fine, my name on a list, and I'd be free to go. After everything was said and done, I paid the fifty and we got the hell out of there.

When we got back to Jersey, my mother wanted to see us. To my surprise she had a hefty wedding present in hand. Ma managed to save a few G's over the years from my contribution of quarters from that blessed shoeshine box. Not bad considering I was only charging twenty cents a shine! I never had any idea where those quarters were going...I thought they'd turned into red sauce. I followed through with my plans once we got home and I told the company to go screw. I decided to get back in the car biz while keeping a few dirty deeds in my back pocket.

Ever since Skeet's' death, it became tradition for me to visit him on Christmas. For years, I'd get juiced in the bone yard and jive with him. I'd take all the Christmas blankets off the other graves and drag them through the snow to the point of complete exhaustion. Then I'd pile them sky high on top of Skeets' plot. He was the fattest cat in the graveyard, I made sure he was tops. I had to keep changing the days I'd show up to visit him, in order to keep any onlookers confused. Someone was going to catch me sooner or later, but that wasn't stopping me from making Skeets' holidays special!

Speaking of holidays, another way I'd shake the woes of the so-called Christmas cheer was jumping in my car, driving through the Lincoln Tunnel leaving my troubles miles away. My Christmas hate was so deep rooted, that I'd justify parking my car and grabbing nameless bums off the street and kicking the shit out of them. I was miserable, so I decided to make other people miserable too. This went on for way too long. I was doing it for my own selfish reasons; you couldn't possibly begin to understand how serious my pain lingered to justify engaging in such vulgar acts. Violence has seriously fucked up my life. I spent several years all by my damn self at Christmas so that I wouldn't hurt others—that was even scarier. Every December the same feelings start to grind in my guts, I don't know if they'll ever go away, but I do my best to keep them under control.

Anna made the attempt to spread some holiday cheer around the house, but a couple of the dudes living with us felt the same way as I did. We were shooting hand held crossbows, throwing knives, and acting like a bunch of animals, which was somehow comforting to us. We bastardized Anna's Christmas tree just to be

You're Next

funny. We took down her angel and replaced it with a giant Swastika and we decapitated her Santa Claus.

One year before she got a chance to decorate the tree, I dragged it outside and coated it with flat black spray paint. That was the last year she put up a tree. Anna is the most patient and understanding soul I've ever met, but that particular evening her Puerto Rican temper reared its ugly head. She finally let us know that enough was enough...and we all listened. The guys knew what a cool chick Anna was and that she never says shit. So when she speaks her mind, it stops everyone dead in their tracks.

The easiest way for me to relieve anxiety has always been to escape on two wheels. This was virtually impossible in the middle of December being a wild man fighting the northern blizzards. I'd haul ass up and down Fifth Street where we lived, sliding through the snow with my back tire all over the road and the bike's pipes roaring. You can imagine how much the neighbors loved this. They finally smartened up and started leaving town for the holidays. I guess I'm like my mother, if I'm not sleeping, nobody's sleeping!

My life was set in the path of born to lose, but I've always known in my heart that I was meant for bigger and better things.

Stenciled Angel

Since I was a child I've always been motivated by the hustle, but it seemed that I was always stepping on my own dick and could never get out from under my mental anguish.

When I entered the used car racket, Chrysler sent me to a motivational seminar. I didn't think much of it at the time, but luckily for me I paid attention. The seminar introduced me to the power of positive thinking and the book, *Think and Grow Rich*. After the seminar, I immediately ran out and got the book. From that day forward, and for the first time in my life, I had a charted course for success. I had finished reading my first fucking book ever and it's been a daily part of my life ever since. It's shown me how to turn my burning desires into reality. The book itself isn't magic, it just introduced me to a new way of thinking, a change I was ready for, and this book was just the beginning.

Music has also had a positive impact on my life and has helped me to stay sane. I've been strumming guitars since the days when Heller and I shared a room, but I'm not a guitar player, harmonica player, or a singer. I've never claimed to be good at any of those things, I just happened to be a good Dylan impersonator. I've been told by a few dudes I used to jam with, that I could barely play guitar and that I shouldn't attempt to sing because I was tone deaf. All I know is that I can play along with Dylan, song for song, start to finish through every album. In spite of the criticism, I started fooling around with a group of guys in a Dylan cover band back in 1979.

Like all of my accomplishments and eternal friendships, the band was originally formed out of frustration. It's just a matter of turning a negative into a positive. Johnny Pizza was on guitar; he had an unbelievable spirit behind him and went with the flow. He was capable of falling into any song. Crip Mane Jackson was the bass player. He was confined to a wheelchair and paralyzed from the waist down, but man could he wail! His physical condition didn't matter. He was an exceptionally talented musician. When

You're Next

he was playing in front of an audience, you'd swear that motherfucker was going to stand up! My brother-in-law John was on the drums and I was the lead man. The chemistry was right on...we were poetry in motion. I called the band, *Shot of Love*.

We'd jam several days a week and work some local gigs. I was able to devote a lot of my time to the band. I was flipping used cars at a pretty fast pace and it was paying the bills. We decided to get into a recording studio and lay down some tracks. That's when I met Stick. He had a state of the art facility with all the bells and whistles, and he took his job seriously. The first time we were in his studio I noticed that everyone in the recording room was looking at me sideways. Maybe those dudes were right, maybe I shouldn't sing. Stick flipped the switch halfway through the song, turned on the intercom, and asked me to come into the recording room. Everyone was standing around with great big grins on their faces..."Do you know you sound just like Bob Dylan?" Stick couldn't wipe the sly grin off of his face.

"Yes, yes, yes, well I hope so seeing that I'm in a Dylan cover band! Now stop jerking me off, why the fuck did you just cut me in the middle of that song?" I couldn't understand where this conversation was going or what the fuck these guys wanted from me. Stick insisted that I listen to myself coming through the sound track. To tell you the truth I was pretty embarrassed, I really didn't want to hear myself. I figured it would discourage my creativity, but he flipped the switch. The song was *Precious Angel*. I needed to hear it twice to make sure it was me and not Dylan, I couldn't believe it. I looked up and shot that sly smile right back, we had something and I knew it. Stick had everyone lay their tracks and told us he'd be in touch with a finished product. After that day, we always had an open invitation to his recording studio and we rocked the joint till we were all satisfied.

The studio was the perfect setting for the spirit of the '80s to give birth to the new radicals. Everyone was waiting their turn to be heard, to be seen, to be something. There was an endless supply of women and wine around the studio. The drugs were served up like coffee from a waitress that would never let your cup go dry. The Quaaludes made me feel like a rock star as I swayed back and forth on the stool with my hands over the earphones. The talent poured out of every lung and fingertip. The enchanting power of music has its way of captivating the ladies.

As fashionably lame as these women were, they flocked to the cool moments in hopes they'd be able to come along for the ride. They didn't talk elementary or flaunt their philosophies. They were just a bunch of groupie bitches. Lord knows I was having my fill of them. Their flattery was amusing, besides I thought I was a rock star. The musicians were aplenty, and I was being introduced to all of them. The guys running the studio were show boating me around in hopes of creating a better band. I wanted nothing to do with it, I wasn't interested in changing any of the players. The band wasn't broke and it didn't need fixing.

We started getting booked for more gigs around Central Jersey and I was feeling large in my '71 Cadillac Convertible. It was white with blood red interior, a definite rock star ride. All of my life I'd been wheeling and dealing with words, I can get anything I want with my cunning yet diplomatic way. Basically—I'm a hustler. I was starting to realize for the first time that I had the ability to capture the attention of entire audiences and it felt great.

One night in the club, this woman in the first row was carrying on and crying hysterically. I looked down at her, all I could think was that maybe her old man caught her fucking around and smacked the bitch up. When we broke the set, she came running to me and claimed it felt like I was singing directly to her. I had no idea where this chick was coming from…had I ever seen her before? Maybe she had been hanging around the recording studio. Who knows with all the Quaaludes going around? It was so strange, she was quivering as she explained the feeling of being entranced by the vibe of the room as we played. I thanked her but moved on, we

You're Next

needed to book more shows. The band was working, the shows got larger, and for a bunch of locals we were sold out.

Shot of Love booked a gig at Island Park, it was an outdoor venue, and there were a dozen bands scheduled to play. I was so fucked up on pills and wine that I couldn't get my ass to the stage. Someone threw me in the Caddy and barged through the crowd as people stepped to the side so I could get on stage. The band was already set up waiting and I came in like a fucking train. The audience must've thought I was a real star because my entrance was so lavish that it distracted the crowd from my drug-induced stupor.

I really started to think I was something special, there always seemed to be a chick on my lap and some pills in my pocket. The studio and stage became one big party and I was enthralled in the moment. I kept slipping off the curb and was losing complete sight of my marriage. I had several opportunities to be with other chicks, and I took advantage of them all. It was more than a touch and go situation. It became convenient and went on for way too long. I was over two years into my marriage and I still didn't have a grasp on things. Even though I was always fucking around and not giving Anna the attention she deserved, I still got love and understanding from her. God bless her for that, I wouldn't be where I am today if it were any different.

Stenciled Angel

I split from the band and gave them no explanation. Being that my brother-in-law John was the drummer, you can imagine why.

I was still hustling cars and dodging the law after the band broke up. Shortly after my farewell, I was faced with some pretty serious news. Someone was gunning for me and this time, it was serious—I had crossed the wrong motherfucker and he wanted me in a body bag! I didn't know if I'd be on this planet another hour, another day, another week, or another month...so I made a decision. If this was going down, I had to come clean. I couldn't leave this earth a liar, and the only person I owed any motherfucking explanation to was Anna. I figured it was best that she hear it from me instead of someone else after I was landfill. The guilt was overwhelming. What the fuck did I do to her? I just couldn't take it anymore—I had to tell Anna the truth about my infidelities. I told her everything, I didn't sugar coat it or leave anything out. I had no reason to ever hurt her. I knew how much she loved me.

At first it felt like a tremendous relief to tell her everything, but that only lasted a second. I had to go back to square one with Anna in an attempt to completely regain her trust. The general consensus was that I was crazy for leaving the band because we really had something going. I decided that it wasn't a good idea for me to be around the bar and club scene anymore. That scene fed my addictions that made me unfaithful to my wife.

Nothing ever did become of that hit. The guy dropped off the face of the earth. I guess he had bigger problems than me, so I had opened a big can of worms for nothing. Actually not for nothing, it put me in my place. I spent a lot of time being bummed out about myself. I tried to get a real job and change my way of thinking...again. I opened a sandblasting business in hopes that it would keep me out of trouble. What the band didn't understand, was if anything was going to keep me alive...it was Anna!

You're Next

Anna, the Stenciled Angel

Purple light beams heading out beyond the end.
Smiles of sly, Latin wisdom…floating out of time.
The tramp waiting in the alley by his pearl blue Harley.
San Francisco nights on a Homestead afternoon.
Anna dancing with Levon in the upper room.
You think of yourself as a little girl and laugh beyond control.
And yet when the time comes for blending back situations and remembering Oz,
You whisper,
"Jimmy, come here."

Poem by Heller: 1987

Chapter 5

Fifth Street Tramp

The bitter cold causes a chain reaction in me, which eventually leads to brain freeze, which ultimately means I lose my mind! The only cure for my winter blues seemed to be my garage. My life long obsession with classic cars and motorcycles has always made me a few extra beans and the garage is where all my demons go to get the lead out. It's taken some convincing over the years, to get Anna to agree that it's a good thing every time I get a harebrained idea to do another restoration. Anna's so laid back it's never been a struggle. I know the money is better spent somewhere else, but when you're a jerky punk like me you'd rather make up a story (plea to the wife) about why building another radical machine *is* a good idea. Anna has always let me pursue my madness in that ole sacred garage. She's been putting up with me dragging my mud flaps through the living room since day one. She even lets me sit on the furniture with my motor oil stained duds. She's always known that my most creative thoughts have been daydreamed under a hood and besides, it keeps me out of trouble.

On another one of those cold ass winter mornings, I was sitting on the throne having my morning constitutional and reading the bible, the *Want Ad Press* classifieds. I saw an ad that read, *good cash business*. It was for two original 1954 Chevy Ice Cream Trucks and the phone number was local! Even though it was snowing like a bastard, I called my buddy Zap and asked him to take a ride. When Zap and I got to the dude's house, I did the wheeling and dealing. The guy wanted to sell me a package deal with all the ins

You're Next

and outs of the ice cream biz. Man, I wasn't about that, I was drooling over the rides and day tripping about my next restoration project. I sure as hell wasn't thinking about slinging ice cream! The cat told me that he had made enough money every summer to put himself through law school.

I nixed it off and told him to skip down over all that. I just wanted to see the trucks. The only reason my eyes bulged out of my melon when I read, *good cash business* was because it would be an easy play when making excuses. I mean explaining to Anna why I had the burning desire to restore not one, but two ice cream trucks! "No Anna, you see, these are rare specimens. Good Humor Ice Cream wagons were all Fords but these are Chevys—ya dig Anna? Yes, yes, yes...now you see why it's of the utmost importance that I purchase these vehicles! Right Anna?" I spent the trip home practicing my rap, meanwhile the trucks were already loaded on the flatbed, and the bill was paid. When a man works for the love of it, he knows that coming up with a logical plea to the wife is how you seal the deal! After I scammed the twin '54 Chevys, I was off to my garage. I spent the winter restoring one of them, stripping it down, and pounding out the dents.

During the '80s, my sandblasting business gave me the extra bread to feed my car and motorcycle addiction. This was good because I wanted to back out of the car biz for awhile and focus on my company. I recruited Big Dick Duke, Junior, and Woodman on my crew and we were master blasting everything from skyscrapers to sewers. The Reaganomics was a glorious time to be alive. I was making more money than a dead guy with a hefty life insurance policy! The four of us were absolute madmen. We'd work twenty-four/seven and took advantage of every second to make a buck. It's amazing what you can accomplish with the right chemistry of people.

The three of us would sleep under the sandblasting rigs and bathe in the river to beat our own time on the job! I got so good at estimating pools that before I even pulled into someone's driveway,

'71 Moto Guzzi Ambassador

judging by the neighborhood and the price tags on the cars they were driving, I knew what to charge. Man, things were going great and the business was doing well. I was patching up things with Anna and my life was getting back on track. I was on a regular schedule, and I had a sense of normalcy—wait a minute! What the fuck am I doing? I started feeling tied down, schlepping, stealing, lying, cheating, wheeling, dealing and cutting my own throat to make a buck is how I was used to getting by. Besides, flipping rides has always been my favorite addiction. So much that I still lock slide across four lanes of traffic—pull a U-ee and jump a curb or two when I see a "For Sale" sign! That's what I should be doing, after all, that's what I do best—so I sold my sandblasting rigs.

Right around the time I bought the two '54 Chevy Ice Cream Trucks, Anna was thinking about leaving her teller position at the bank. She started slaving there fresh out of high school and for all the years she had given, she wasn't receiving. When you're working for the man, the ladder is short, because the man's always on the top. Between the law student's comments and a buddy of mine who owned a deli, I realized the profit margin on ice cream started to taste sweet. So why not give it a go! It would be rewarding for Anna to do something on her own that she could be proud of, and I knew her winning personality would make it happen. Oh, she could make it happen all right...but not in *my* two Chevys! These vehicles were way too cool to serve their purpose. I wasn't going to let my vintage sleighs rack up the miles so some little puke could get a popsicle! It was time to lay the *good cash business* rap on Anna again, and convince her that we needed yet a third Ice Cream Wagon.

I'm a complete lunatic when it comes to two, three, or four wheels. I'll even take it with one wheel, that's why they call me Jew Bag Jimmy! I bought a 1968 Chevy Ice Cream Step Van with a three speed on the column, and it didn't take much to get it on the road. So now, I owned three ice cream trucks and I wasn't even in the ice cream biz! Duke and I blasted the hell out of the '68 in my garage. We painted it white and dolled it up with some colorful balloons. On the display panel, we painted *Anna's Ice Cream.* That was the day Woodman dubbed Anna the Ice Cream Queen.

I decided it would be a good idea to replace that annoying carnival like music that blasted from the speakers with a cool bell. Not the typical ice cream bell that you can barely hear, but a battery operated school bell. I knew that bell would get the kid's attention because they were so damn used to hearing it. I also thought it would be positive on their psyche to give the sound a new meaning, rather than just feeling like a lab rat. At least I know that's how I felt in school. We called the bell, *The Salivator.* When those little rat bastards would hear *The Salivator* — they'd run down the street with their teeth showing and stand in a crowded puddle of their own drool outside the truck in anticipation for one of Anna's tasty treats!

The first day that Anna went out to sell ice cream, she came home with a Franklin. We were in business! Man, I knew if this thing was guided in the right direction, Anna would be a hit! I started paying a little closer attention to the All American Treat to help ensure her success. Fortunately, I was able to go back to the man I stole...I mean purchased the two original ice cream trucks from. He hepped us to his wholesalers and tipped Anna off about the baseball games, the local swimming pools, and the right time to be at the parks. After a few weeks of her part timing it, we knew we were in business to stay. At the end of the summer, we closed up the truck and headed to Florida for a few months with the extra cha-ching!

When we got back from our vacation, I decided to go visit ma. I hadn't seen her in awhile and I wanted to share the good news about *Anna's Ice Cream*. My buddy Junior came by to give me a lift, we were both traveling in the same direction so why not share a few laughs. I hopped in the driver's seat of Junior's '64 VW Bug. We headed out of Homestead down a country road and crept up to a four way stop. The car behind us rear ended the bug and pushed us into the middle of the intersection. Then we got rammed on both sides causing a pile up. There was instant confusion and at first reaction, I was enraged! After I came to from bouncing my melon off the steering wheel, my instincts told me they were all unmarked cars. I reached for the door to see what the hell was going on. As I opened the driver's side door, someone threw me a punch to the side of my face! Alright now, it was time to kill someone. I jumped out of the car and started swinging, within seconds another guy had me pinned against the side of the Bug. What the fuck?

"Police! Police! Get down on the ground and don't move motherfucker!" I was still in a haze from the accident. I had no idea what the fuck was going on, the cops were acting like they'd just caught the head of a cocaine cartel. Oh yeah, it's just that regular clowny cop garbage—what was I thinking? These small town punks always have an authority complex! Before I knew it, I was on the ground handcuffed from the back and they were wailing the shit out of me. One was punching me in the face…while the others were kicking me in the ribs. There was a fucking gun to the side of my head! Nice intro, huh? Those faggots didn't even know my name as far as I could tell. There were three cops manning Junior on the passenger's side. Luckily for him, no one was breaking his face. The feds decided to get cute. They stood me up and grabbed me by my beard so they could use my face as a punching bag.

"What do you think about that tough guy?"

"Why don't you take these handcuffs off me and I'll show ya how bad this bastard is." At that point, I should've just kept my mouth shut, but I fucking hate getting pushed around!

"Threat! Threat!" The fed was screaming at the top of his lungs. Man I got to tell ya, as many fights as I've gotten in over the years, win, or lose, this was one of the hardest beatings I had taken since the Cobbstown incident.

"Stop! Stop!" The officer on the passenger's side manning Junior pointed at me. "That's not Junior!" It took well over ten minutes and my gruesome face for them to realize they had the wrong guy. They were gunning for Junior, for what, I had no clue! Junior had been one of my closest friends for years. I knew he wasn't involved in any heavy shit. So there I was…in the wrong place at the wrong time…rare but true.

The cops dug out my ID and left me standing bloody while they interrogated Junior for awhile. We were rushed down to the local zoo and handcuffed to the animal bar. Junior ended up with possession of a controlled dangerous substance because he had a chunk of hash in his pocket. As the day's events unfolded, the coppers knew they had done wrong by kicking the shit out of me. There was no warrant out for my arrest, yet somehow they managed to scrounge one up along with a warrant to search my house (like I didn't see that coming). Right then and there, I knew my long endured, successful carrier of hustling weed was over.

Meanwhile, back at the ranch, Anna had no clue what the hell was going down. Even though a swarm of cops showed up at our house early that morning, the search warrant didn't show up till late that afternoon. That didn't stop them; they were already hours into their search. There was nothing Anna could do, and as far as she was concerned, let them search the place—there was nothing they'd find that would do us in. She immediately showed the pigs a small stash of weed on the dresser. Then she was guarded downstairs while they ransacked the rooms, played our records, and ate our food. The feds found a roll of roofing tar and put it in as evidence—the dumb fucks thought it was hash! They also found a pretty good lump of cash in the house. It was the portion I had left when I sold the sandblasting rigs. When the money was reported as evidence, it came up over a grand short. Somebody had a heavy coffee break that day!

To Anna's complete surprise, three pounds of pot were found buried in the walls. While I was downtown, I couldn't help but think that she was going to kill me. I hoped she'd understand why I never told her...it was because of this very moment! Between the cash and the pot, the feds thought they had a pretty big bust and had found their man. They searched every single vehicle on the property. It was quite a chore, Anna and I had several rides at the time. The car they targeted was a BMW. "Package! Package!" The feds ran over to the Beamer like a bunch of monkeys. The screaming apes supposedly pulled out two balls of hash from under the driver's side mat. I'm not denying that there was three pounds of pot in the house, but let me tell you something—they planted that hash! Anna had been driving it at the time and there was no way in hell that car was dirty. Someone must've put a call into Weasel, the head prosecutor, to see what kind of car he wanted that day. He must've picked the Beamer because that's where they found the hash! Needless to say, that was the end of Anna's car.

Within a few hours, I had over seven charges against me ranging from possession with intent to distribute, to atrocious assault on a police officer. Junior and I were hauled off to the local jail. When we got to the slammer, there was a shit load of guys there. Some we recognized from a few towns over, but I didn't hang with those faggots so I was unsure of the connection. Turns out, there was a sting operation and they rounded up thirty-six people including Junior and me. With eight guys to one cell, it was hard to talk. I tried to see where Junior's head was at and if he knew he

You're Next

had been under surveillance... "If I did, do you think we'd be sitting in here?"

I told him I just couldn't understand why they'd be watching him in the first place, and as for me, what the fuck did I know? I'd been out of town for months, so they wouldn't have been watching me!

I decided to shave my face, I wasn't going to let those cock suckers grab me by the beard and use my face as a punching bag again. I borrowed a couple of razors from one of the cellmates. As the hair came off, the damage to my face became more apparent. I didn't even recognize my own ugly mug. When the turnkey came to check on the cell and didn't see the guy with the beard, he started screaming. The station broke into complete chaos, they thought I'd escaped and several guards were bum rushing the door! "Hey! Hey! I'm right here, calm down!" Among all the madness, this older cat Eddie, who was as bald as a baby's ass started busting my chops, "Auhh! You'd think the guy would've given some of that hair to me. I could've used it on top ya know." The whole cellblock burst into laughter.

"Eddie, what the fuck is wrong with you? Cool it man, like my face isn't fucked up enough!"

"Hey, I could've used that shit ya know, and ya threw it in the garbage! I'm not a garbage picker Jimmy!"

The guard walked over to the garbage can, as soon as he spotted all that hair, they calmed down, and everything was cool again. Junior and I made bail by Monday; we couldn't wait to get the fuck out of that urine soaked hellhole. The turnkey came to tell us that no one was getting out today because it was Veteran's Day. The judges were off and the banks were closed. Shit, we had to wait it out for another wake up. The entire time I was in the zoo, I couldn't help but think that these fucking suits weren't done with me yet. I hadn't slept for days and my mind was racing like a madman. I couldn't stop thinking about what Anna must've gone through during the search.

I stayed on my cot and gazed out the window hoping to feel the sun on my face by tomorrow. Outside, I saw myself as a child playing on the curb and creeping my way over to the jailhouse. I forced my little feet up the building's concrete ledge so that I could hang on the window bars and look inside. Out of nowhere, a man rushed the window and howled, "You'll be in here some day little boy, just you wait and see!"

I felt a rush of fear come over my body, the man scared me so much that I let go of the bars! I fell flat on my back, I wanted to get up and run away, but I couldn't. I had the wind knocked out of me and was paralyzed for a moment. "You'll be in here someday, just you wait and see!" His eerie hackle scared the shit out of me and I started running like hell even though I couldn't breathe! Whoever thought that stranger so many years ago was going to be right? Now I was the man sitting in the Jackson County Jail.

When Anna came to my arraignment, as soon as I saw her, I knew she was devastated. She had been through so much over the past couple of years. We were still patching up our marriage, her mother had recently died, and now this. I could tell that my shaven, lumped up face frightened her. Even though we didn't exchange words, I could read her eyes…"I can't believe you had three pounds of pot in the house!"

Like I mentioned before, Anna was completely shocked when the cops found the pot in the house. She was clueless to the whole thing, just like I had planned it. The purpose of this was not to deceive my wife, but to keep her safe. The less she knew, the better off she was, and as far as I was concerned…I knew what I needed to do. I learned that from my barbershop days, you never talk business around the house.

Anna's girlfriends used to say that God was saving a special little place in heaven for her because she was married to me. It pissed me off because it was a cheap stab at me, but for the first

You're Next

time...I believed it. As serious as this whole situation was, all I could do was smile that goofy smile of mine because I knew I was about to get out of that soup can stinking, over crowded jail! When we finally got to split, I told Anna there was no way we were going back to the house. My guts told me the cops were on their way and I still had that feeling they weren't done with me yet. Anna thought it was paranoia. She wanted me to see the damage that still remained from them ransacking our home. I refused to go there under any circumstances. Besides our two roommates Jesse and Dickey were at the house, and they would let me know if something came up. There were no warrants out on them, which kept them out of this whole fucked up mess!

We spent the night at Anna's brother's house. At five in the motherfucking a.m., the cops were at my house looking for me. They had another warrant for my arrest. They were interrogating Jesse and Dickey to no end and wanted to know where the hell I was. The boys couldn't give them the answers they wanted, so the cops made themselves at home...again. With flash lights in hand, one of the monkeys moved through the upstairs hallway. Jesse tapped him on his shoulder..."We already told you he wasn't here, what are ya going to do, beam him up Scotty?"

The cop instructed one of his apes to get Jesse downstairs. They were convinced I was there. When they finally realized that my roommates were telling the truth, they split, but not before they left three unmarked cars on Fifth Street. I got a phone call at Anna's brother's house that they were looking for me. I called my lawyer and he wanted me to meet him at the prosecutor's office to turn myself in. I told him to go fuck himself! There was no way I was going down there. I'd already gotten the shit kicked out of me once. I wasn't going to set myself up for another beating!

We arranged to meet so my lawyer could escort me into the administration building. The first cop that recognized me drew his gun. My lawyer stepped in and asked the cop what the hell was the matter with him! "Jimmy's here to turn himself in! Do you really think he would have anything on him or attack you? What the hell is going on here?" The officer wasn't letting down, he called for backup and a few more clowns showed up. All the while my lawyer was trying to break up the commotion. Finally, one of the guards slammed me up against the wall and handcuffed me.

I was being charged with conspiracy! The drug ring was all news to me! I wasn't associated with any of those people I shared the cell with. The prosecutors were way off base. All I was doing was smoking weed like a Mercedes uses diesel! Sure, I was selling to a few people here and there if they needed it. The only reason I had such a large amount in my house was because I scored a really good deal. So I tried to explain myself to the judge and said, "Your Honor, if you find a bottle of fine wine at a good price, do you buy the bottle, or do you buy the whole damn case?" Besides, it was easier than fishing for a bag every week, which is typically more dangerous!

The stupid cops actually made the interrogation easy on me. I just gave them what they wanted. They named off all the people that had been arrested in the sting and wanted to know my involvement with them. It wasn't even about the weed. They were cracking down on a meth lab a few towns over. "Yeah, yeah, I know that one. Yep, I'm involved with that one too." I yes'd them to death, meanwhile I didn't know who the fuck any of these people were! Man I'd never associate with a bunch of speed freaks, that's never been my style! I kept telling the prosecutor what he wanted to hear through the information *he* was feeding me. Talk about instant specialized knowledge. I knew this would keep my people safe—it was the right thing to do. It's called street courtesy. Keep your mouth shut at all costs.

Junior's lawyer told him that for his own safety, not to have any contact with me. My lawyer told me I was on the list with Junior, due to association. I was in Florida, so they had no action from tapping my phone and had no sightings of me being involved in anything illegal. I was just in the wrong place at the wrong time

You're Next

when they crashed the VW, or I would've been clear of this whole mess. The bust was broadcasted all over the east coast, which put pressure on the feds to throw darts, even though I wasn't their target.

I made a deal with Junior. He had a new baby on the way and couldn't afford to do any jail time. Because I didn't have any kids, I decided to take the rap for both of us. I told him to tell the cops that he had gotten the hash from me. As bad as he felt about my suggestion, he came to realize that it was the best way out. After his confession, they went light on him and then turned to me to determine my fate.

The whole gang was rounded up and marched across the street to the courthouse like a heard of cattle at auction. Being there were over thirty people, the station ran out of handcuffs and I was wire tied to Vinny the Guinea. I couldn't stand the tension or the fucking stink anymore so I decided to lighten things up a bit. I broke into song, "I love a parade! I love a parade!" After the first chorus, Vinny the Guinea and Junior joined in. I was hoping our stupidity would bring the men some relief. Eventually, most joined in but the band was broken up immediately by the guards.

I was the last one in the bust to be indicted. The state held back over a year before handing out a five-year sentence. During that unusually long wait they literally tortured me, hoping that I'd hang myself. I hadn't given them any new information, only what they already knew. So they figured by making me wait it out…I'd eventually crack. They kept grabbing me off the streets and at work to see if my story would change. In the end, the joke was on them because the dirty motherfucker was one of their own.

The agony of waiting for my future to be decided by someone else was nothing more than spiteful torment. I started drinking heavily in hopes to make the clock move faster. Waiting to be sentenced was a good reason to drop off the face of the earth. I couldn't think clearly during that year and a half of my life. For the first time I wasn't living…I was learning to die.

Fifth Street Tramp

There were other people involved in the sting that got away because they were tipped off early in the game. That Fat Baker Man was one of them—he wasn't innocent. He was just supplying the cops with their heart's desire. The fat man owned a bakery that all of the pigs flocked to for free coffee, doughnuts, and even some of those magical brownies. Due to the baker's, oh so very brown nose, he was tipped off by the local authorities about the chain of events long before they happened. So that fat bastard sold his bakery, packed up the wife and immediately moved out of state. I don't blame him for splitting town, it was a matter of self-preservation, but a scared little pussy shouldn't be running around with the big boys. He could of at least hepped us to what was going down. That fat fuck and me were supposed to be tight. He could've saved me years of aggravation if he had acted like a man, but who can ya trust?

When I finally got to see the judge, I was let off the assault charges and I pleaded out the rest. I had to leave my money on the table that they confiscated even though I was able to prove that it had nothing to do with drugs. I had all my paper work in order when I went in front of the judge three different times. He refused to give it back. I was facing twenty-five years on the conspiracy charge and pleaded out to five. When the hammer came down, the five were to be served on weekends because of presumption of non-incarceration for first time offenders.

My lawyer wanted me to re-negotiate and do the five straight, he figured I'd fuck up and dig myself a deeper hole. He made me sign a release stating that the plea to five on weekends was against his better judgment and counsel. I signed it to shut him up! What my lawyer never realized through all of this was that I could accomplish anything I desired. Positive thinking can be applied to any scenario in life, not just making money.

Remember the layout of Fulton? Go back to the barbershop, which was across the street from the courthouse. As soon as I walked out the door, I headed up the hill. Where do you think I ended up?

You're Next

The Jackson Hotel! This is America, land of the free, and when a man wants a drink, he can have one. Which was exactly what I needed after waiting a year and a half for this day to come.

After my sentencing, I knew I had to tell ma because I knew that somehow she'd find out. Anna and I decided not to tell her father, by this time he had moved back to Puerto Rico. We decided it would be better left unsaid; it was going to be hard enough dealing with ma. So, Anna, Junior, and I made our way over to her house. When I explained the situation to my mother, she was completely heart broken and became unglued. Lena told me in Italian that there was no way in hell she'd ever come to visit me in jail. It was hard enough for her going to see Frank and Heller in the institution. She then proceeded to take off her slipper and told Junior and me to kneel down in front of her. The Italian strong arm started whacking the shit out of us! Like two little kids, we were on our knees as she strategically smacked every inch of our melons! We were both crying our eyes out. Not because it hurt, because it was so damn humiliating! Anna just stood back. She knew not to get in Lena's way, and the best thing to do was to let her have at us. Junior and I had been under the gun for so long and the last thing we needed was the slipper! There I was, a thirty-six year old man, being assaulted in front of my wife and friend. I thought to myself, I was once the Emperor of Rome!

Lena let out a big sigh…"Okay—now we a eat!" My mother had her fill of stomping us and now she was hungry…typical Italian. Junior and I sniffled all the way to the dinner table, the last thing we wanted to do was eat. But the smart thing to do was to sit down and shut the fuck up before she gets the wooden spoon!

"Aah, you a see, you dona learn a you lesson in a school! I dona come an see you Jameza. Now, boat a you stop a da acting like a baby, no more a cryin!"

"Yes, Mommy."

Fifth Street Tramp

So we sat quietly while we shuffled our food around. I don't think ma completely understood that I'd only be in jail on the weekends. Either way, it didn't matter right now, I was happy with her response. I wouldn't want her to come see me anyway, because the last thing I needed was to get a beating by my mommy in jail. I'm sure that would've gone over real well with the other inmates!

My first weekend in jail, the guard dropped me off in the day room where everybody was playing spades. The turn screw pushed me into the room and closed the door. It was by no means a social situation. It was every man for himself. For the first time I knew how it felt to be a woman. The catcalls and hissing started immediately and everyone was calling me baby and shit. This big black bastard got up to check me out. He was the biggest, blackest, motherfucker there. He looked me dead in the face and then at everyone else in the room and put his arm around me. "Nobody fuck with this bitch. This one is mine." I was ready to shit myself! I knew I had to do something! I wasn't getting raped my first time

in—or any time for that matter! So I smiled and casually put my arm around the giant spade and said, "Yeah, that's right—I'm with him!" The room erupted into laughter as the big bastard immediately pushed me away...

"Mothafucka, get da fuck away from me ya little queer! Y'knows I was just playin'!"

"How was I supposed to know you were fucking with me? I thought that's what you wanted. You're the biggest guy in here, and if I'm going to get raped let's just get it over with!"

"Get the fuck away from me, ya crazy little whitie!"

The guards heard the commotion and entered the room to see what was going on..."You starting trouble already Jimmy?"

"Yeah, it's me against all these guys! What do you think?"

The attendant wasn't happy with my smart ass remarks, so to fuck with me he told me to take off all my clothes, "What, in front of all these guys?" He wasn't budging and insisted that I get out of my street clothes and into their orange jumpsuit. I turned my back to everyone in the room and started to undress. As the clothes came off, the whistles got louder. I couldn't help but to stand there with a stupid grin on my face. I couldn't understand how I ended up in here with all these low lifes. The guard took his sweet ole time walking me into the showers. He told me to stop laughing, "What are you smiling for boy? You're in jail. Do you think this is funny?" I didn't think it was funny—it was degrading! I just kept my mouth shut. I wasn't going to let them know it was a nervous laugh and that I was seriously concerned.

That evening the big black bastard came over to my bunk and re-introduced himself. He told me he ran the shit hole and if I needed anything to come to him because the rest of the cocksuckers in there were scammers. He explained that the bullshit earlier was nothing more than the welcoming committee.

"Damn mothafucka! You're fruitier than a Knee High! What the hell were you saying that shit for?"

"Look man, I ain't no queer or nothing. I just thought to myself, if I'm going to side with anyone in here, it's going to be you. Why you ask? Because you're the biggest, blackest, bastard in here! That's why…ya dig?!"

Thank God, the gift of laughter had prevailed again! This guy didn't want to kill me for calling him a big, black, bastard and I was happy about that. At least now I didn't have to worry about sewing my asshole shut! I was on good terms with everyone in the jail but I decided to keep to myself. I wasn't there to make friends.

One of the stipulations of my parole was that I had to have a legit job. Junior set me up with Bomba, the owner of the company he worked for hanging sprinkler systems. He knew what was up with me and was real easy going about the whole situation. As long as I showed up for work, he stayed out of my business. The parole officer kept showing up on the job site to interrogate me and to collect my piss. I was so concerned that it would get mixed up with someone else's. It's a huge inconvenience when someone shows up during all hours while you're working or at home. This was something I knew I had to keep my big trap shut about. I wanted to move on with my life eventually.

Bomba knew I'd have to get out early on Fridays to make my way to the jail. A few hours before I signed myself in every weekend, I'd slug a bottle of booze and pop some sleeping pills. That way I was out of my mind and could sleep through the whole experience. One of the guards, Sal, told me no one had ever successfully completed a five-year term on weekends and asked me why I thought I was so special.

"Sal, I know what I got to do and I know how to do it." That was all I said. I knew in my heart that I could accomplish anything I desired. The positive thinking formula can be used in any of life's battles, and this was a battle I refused to lose. Sal always made sure I was on the straight and narrow and helped me keep my nose clean.

You're Next

He tipped me off to the dudes whose job it was to fuck with me in anticipation that I'd crack.

I leaned back on my cot and gazed out the window of my cage at the sunny street below. I saw Heller shuffle by talking to himself. I tried to figure out what was on his mind. He was probably working out some metaphysic formula in his head or maybe he was reciting Dylan. For the first time in my life, I had to wonder which one of us was better off. The guy I was sharing the cage with spoke up and jerked me out of my haze...

"So I hears yous doin five on weekends?"

"Yeah...so?"

"Man, let me tell ya somepin, I'm in here for eighteen months straight as a first time offender. Ain'ts nobodys goin to fuck up my weekends bro. I gots bitches to see and bottles ta drink, if ya knows what I'm sayin?"

"Hold on a minute, you're doing straight time and you're breaking my balls for coming in on the weekends? Let me get this right, what you're saying is, you wouldn't let them fuck up your weekends. Don't ya get it man? You're fucking up eighteen months of your life—forget about your weekends!"

"Like I said ain'ts nobody goin to fuck wit my weekends bro."

It was truly one of the most idiotic conversations I had ever had in my life! I'm no scholar, but what the fuck was rattling around in that jackasses brain? I kept to myself the rest of the weekend, the conversation had pushed me into deep concentrated thought. That stupid cocksucker pushed me over the edge! I took the negative ignorance from that numbskull below me, and decided to concentrate on reinforcing positive thoughts into my mind. I made a promise to myself to successfully get through this five-year sentence—it became the focus of my determination. I didn't want to spend my life around these ignorant fucks—I knew this wasn't my destiny!

I worked hard during the week and had ditched all my recreational activities. When I was at home, I stayed in the garage and focused on my restorations. I was still drinking heavy to tame the stress. I had minimal social interaction outside of work and the house. My boss approached me one afternoon and expressed how he felt about my situation. He felt it was a shame that I was under so much pressure and that it was stunting my creative train of thought. He had seen some of the vehicles I had built, and he knew all about the wacky ideas I had. He told me how much he admired my talents. Here we go, this guy is being too nice…he must be getting ready to serve me walking papers!

To my complete surprise, he shot me a truly generous offer. Bomba felt that I was wasting my time and talent hanging sprinklers for him. He knew I only needed that job because of my parole. He told me I didn't have to show up for work anymore and that he'd still keep me on the payroll. If the law showed up, he'd tell them I was on another job site and to come back the following day. Then he'd tip me off with a phone call. I couldn't believe that he'd just laid this whole scenario on the table and was cool with it! Bomba's concern for my creative well-being was one of the greatest blessings I'd ever received! His kindness and open mindedness is one of the reasons I'm successful today.

With Bomba's help, every weekend in jail got a little easier. I was feeling more and more confident that I'd make it through my sentence. I did everything that I possibly could to stay out of that cage and away from the negative vibes that surrounded that jail. I had gained the respect of the jail attendants so they let me work outside in the yard washing cars. Those spade playing, motherfuckers would break my balls calling me a cop kisser, but the truth was I just wanted a breath of fresh air. The less time I spent cooped up in that building with those can soup stinking losers—the better off I was, so fuck them.

Sal, the prison guard, was pretty tight with someone from my past. Remember Danny Bad Bones from the Barber's Association? Yeah, well…around a year into my sentence, the jail became so overcrowded that select people were released early. When the connection was made that I was "Frankie's kid," I was sent home right after roll call!

When I went in front of the parole board, I was feeling pretty confident about my situation because I had a lot of ammo. I had gotten a letter of recommendation from Danny Bad Bones. All of my piss tests had come back clean and as far as they knew, I had a steady job working for Bomba. The officer that was getting ready to walk me into the parole hearing turned out to be Big Dick Duke's Uncle Joe. He recognized me as Duke's friend and pulled me aside before we entered the room…"Listen kid, these guys are going to mess with your head in hopes that you crack. They're purposely going to try to antagonize and belittle you. All you have to do is keep your mouth shut and don't speak unless you're spoken to and you'll be just fine! These people are trained to break you down, just stay strong or you'll end up right back where you started. Good luck kid!" Joe patted me on the shoulder and walked me in.

He was right. The parole board was in my face the whole time. The board was complaining that I was getting off too easy. One guy was roaring so loud that his face was beet red and the spit was flying! He was in my face the whole time and was absolutely certain that I'd fuck up and be right back in here, "Six months of parole and a year's probation? There is no way you will sustain that without getting yourself into trouble! You think like a criminal because you are a criminal!"

I did nothing but sit there, I didn't even blink. Every time I wanted to say something, I'd look over at Joe. I noticed that the guy who seemed to be in charge was the youngest cat there, and it dawned on me that he was probably in training. When I realized what was going on, I told myself there was no way in hell I was going to cave into this little parole faggot's trap. I kept my mouth shut. When I was finally asked if I wanted to make a statement, I stood up and explained that I'd found a formula to change my way of thinking. I no longer wanted to hurt my wife or family. After having my freedom taken away, I now understood the severity of my crimes. The parole officer wasn't letting up, but eventually he got tired of shouting and realized he couldn't crack me.

Once again, I walked out the door of the prosecutor's office and headed straight to the Jackson Hotel for a drink. It was the first calm moment in over three years. I stayed resilient to everything that was going on around me. I kept on the straight and narrow with a legit job building condos at the Jersey Shore. My garage got me through the six months of parole and a year's probation without any trouble. It's amazing the way a chain of events will unfold when you're in control of your own destiny. If I hadn't been so determined to make it through serving my sentence, all of the helping hands along the way wouldn't have been accepted.

People like Anna, Bomba, Sal the turnkey, Danny Bad Bones and Duke's Uncle Joe gave me the specialized knowledge and compassion that I needed to make it through my hardship. I guess you could say they were my guardian angels. Because like Sal said, "No one ever completes a five year sentence on weekends!" Hadn't they gotten the point by now—I'm not like the rest of them!

A few years down the road, the head prosecutor of Jackson County, the big man who calls all the shots downtown, and the same fucking scumbag who okayed the planted hash and ended up with Anna's Beamer, was indicted on numerous criminal charges. The head prosecutor, Mickey Weasel and his wife were accused of white-collar crimes of money laundering, misappropriation of funds and conspiracy! He'd been cleaning out his own gas stations and evidence rooms for years to pay for his big dollar house in his big dollar neighborhood. They were put on house arrest because he was the local prosecutor. The state couldn't put him in the slammer for obvious reasons—someone would've shanked him for sure! Weasel was known on the streets for being dirty, if you didn't give him what he wanted, he took it! It's pretty scary if you think about it because he had a tremendous amount of power.

You're Next

This is a story we like to call *The Self Dismissal
of Mickey Weasel!*
One day while the kids were playing inside the gate.
Little Mickey was planning an escape for fear
of being raped!
Off came the bracelet and started the race.
So Mickey could land in some far away place!
Leaving the wife and kids behind.
He decided that gambling in Nevada would be just fine!
He knew the judge's hammer was going to send him
to the slammer.
With only five days to go before his sentence!
Little Mickey's face was all over the papers with mention.
In Las Vegas, the feds tracked him down on his phone!
Mickey knew they'd never leave him alone.
The feds kicked in the door and Mickey decided he
was no more!
He put the gun in his mouth that he clutched.
Not thinking about the wife and kids he supposedly
loved so much!
Ten years in jail was too much for Little Mickey to endure.
So bang went the gun! He hit the floor!
Now Mickey Weasel was no more!
Because of his actions and the men, he condemned.
That is why he had to blow off his head!
Remember kiddies, watch out for the white devil
and don't ever doubt.
If you grow up to be a crooked faggot, your ending
might be just as tragic!
May it be written by me or someone named Seuss.
Little Mickey Weasel really had no use!

Fifth Street Tramp

When the news got out about *The Self Dismissal of Mickey Weasel,* my phone didn't stop ringing for days. It rang with apologies due to the disbelief of my association with the drug ring. It rang with congratulations that I was finally free from worrying what this prick might have in store for me next! The party went on for days and I ain't lying! I felt that my life was a little more clear sailing after Weasel's departure. My paranoia of being set up again had subsided. I knew that I was going to be freed of him for the rest of my life!

Chapter 6

The Power of a Name Change

My wife took a year off from *Anna's Ice Cream,* but she was back slinging twin pops and strawberry short cakes by the time I was sentenced in 1987. We worked grand openings, pool parties, and company picnics on the weekends with *my* '54 Chevy that I restored while on probation. It was time to upgrade Anna's '68 Chevy Ice Cream Step Van because we needed a new neighborhood cruiser. So, with the extra weekend coin, we purchased a '72 Ford Good Humor Ice Cream Truck for her to run the roads with. I was sticking to my guns, there'd be no greasy little paw prints on my '54 Chevys!

Anna was still a hit with the kiddies even though she had taken a year off. It was like she was a local celebrity! The first year Anna started the whole ice cream thing, I actually went out and did a few neighborhood runs with my buddy Johnny Pizza. I quickly realized that it wasn't for me. Sometimes I'd lose my patience with the little people, but the true problem believe it or not, was that I had too big a heart. I gave away so much ice cream that I wasn't making a profit. I felt bad for those little pukes that didn't have enough coin to buy a pop, so I'd give them one on the house. Hey, I've been in those shoes and I know how much it sucks. I couldn't be a hard ass about it. When the kids caught onto my weakness, I think they started conning me—suddenly everyone was short in the drawers!

We decided that Anna would be better at selling the ice cream, besides she was a perfect role model! Being that Anna and I never had any kids of our own, I admired her for the way she

The Power of a Name Change

handled all those little brats. Anna used her common sense when dealing with those miniature meatballs and she was stern when necessary. She'd bust their chops if they didn't look both ways before launching across the street for a rocket pop. She'd point out all the things they needed to hear. As we all know, little kids can be mean but Anna never let anyone get away with picking on the retards that hung around her truck and I don't mean me...I mean the other retards. The kids never crossed her because they knew she had the goods!

Anna's kind ways made the kids pay attention and they respected her to the point that the truck became the, "Ask Anna" stand of the neighborhood. She also found a good way to take care of those not so fortunate rat bastards. She started a jar for the kids who weren't able to float the entire bill, that way everyone could enjoy her All American Treat. All the coins in the jar came from the silver-spooned kids who had no respect for the almighty quarter. When Anna would give these brats their change, they'd throw it on the ground. After the little monsters would run away with popsicles in hand, Anna would get out of the truck and collect all the loose change for the jar.

Even the dogs knew when it was time for Anna to come around. Before she hit the streets, the dogs would start howling. It was like clockwork. They too, were mesmerized by *The Salivator*. Anna, being the animal lover that she is started carrying frozen doggy treats in her truck. It wasn't for profit, it was for her love of dogs. They deserved a cold little something too!

All of the parents really liked Anna, even though they were tortured by their young when awoken by, *The Salivator*. Anna was always considerate and came by early in the afternoon or late enough not to spoil anyone's dinner. It was like she got to see a whole town full of kids grow up. I think that's what made her emotionally sound over the years about not having any kids of our own. She has a lot of good memories of the *Anna's Ice Cream* days, and there's always a big smile on her face when she talks about it. Even today, when we stop in Jersey, those once sticky fingered little brats now turned adults, come up to Anna and praise her as, *The Ice Cream Queen!*

While Anna was running the roads in Homestead, I was spending most of my free time in the garage restoring random stuff,

The Power of a Name Change

pushcarts, pedal bikes, and anything antique. I refurbished an original PT Barnum and Bailey horse drawn popcorn wagon to bring along with my '54 Chevy Ice Cream Truck on our weekend gigs.

These projects kept me out of harms way. Ironically, I always seem to get into less trouble when there's a torch in my hand. I decided between the popcorn wagon and a few other marketable items that I'd go to Homestead Township to get a vendor's license. I had to start something, the sandblasting business was gone, dealing weed was out of my life—I needed a drastic change. I had to stay off the streets. There was no way I was going to waste my life rotting in jail.

When I went downtown to ask for the application, the lady told me not to even bother filling out the paperwork. There was no way in hell they were going to give me a license—I was a felon! They warned me that I better not get caught working *Anna's Ice Cream* truck either. Fuck this! We had come so far and I was still working to put this bullshit behind me. Out of anger and frustration I kept pounding away in my garage…there was no way New Jersey was slowing me down!

Suddenly, I had a stroke of genius! Even though these thoughts can be few and far in between, you got to be keen on your

My '54 Chevy

hunches and when you get them—act on them immediately! That's right. I did buy my '54 Chevys to feed the grease monkey that lived in my garage. Then I thought to myself...how cool would it be to do more private events with my little gems. If I kept working private functions, then the whole permit thing wouldn't come into play. I could sweep Homestead Township under the carpet. That's it—it would work and I knew it! So I placed an ad in the newspaper and the phone started ringing immediately...

"America's Favorite Treat"
Service with a Smile
The Old Fashioned Way!
Book Us For Your Next Event!

Anna and I started dressing the part. We wore red and white striped shirts and a white skirt. Well Anna wore the skirt. I wore the pants...because she beat me to it every time. I found an old Good Humor Ice Cream hat and don't let me forget my red Chucks! The whole get up was straight out of the era...Service with a Smile! The more we got booked, the more elaborate I got with our ads. I started this rap...

"From The Cradle To The Grave!"
Book Us For Your Next Anniversary,
Divorce, Wedding, Barf-mitzvah, Birthday, Funerals,
Polo Party, Car Show, Grand Opening, KKK Rally
Or Just For Fun!

The Power of a Name Change

The phone was ringing off the hook! All I could do was grin, my demons advised me that it was time to build yet another ice cream machine (plea to the wife), "Anna can't ya see we *need* this one?!"

I had this idea that I wanted an ice cream motorcycle. I had no idea what the hell I was going to do about it. I just knew I had to have one and somehow, I'd make it work! Then I decided that a servi-car would do the trick because I knew I could convert it.

Around the time that Anna and I started this whole ice cream thing, I purchased a '56 Harley trike. It had three wheels—I needed it! I bought it just so I could sell ice cream with my '54 Chevy Ice Cream Truck at Harmony. Harmony is an antique motorcycle rally in Jersey. It's the real McCoy, if you don't have an antique motorcycle you can't get in. I purchased the classic trike to park next to my '54 Ice Cream Truck so they wouldn't bust my chops. Harley Charley's dad was there and made the comment that I should turn the trike into an ice cream slinging machine. Since the day he planted that thought in my mind, I just had to have one—I couldn't shake it.

Servi-cars, if you don't already know, are three wheelers that were originally used to tow vehicles back and forth by auto mechanics. They'd drive to the customer's house on the servi to pick up their vehicle. Back in the days before these wicky tricky computers, bumpers were universal so the servi-car could be towed back to the shop by any vehicle, or vise versa. This way, the customer wouldn't have to stop what they were doing in the middle of their workday to drop off their cars. That's when the word "service" was still part of this country and you got something for your buck. In the '60s and '70s, they were used by meter maids because it had a storage unit on the back that was used to hold ticket booklets, doughnuts, hairspray, or whatever else those little meter Nazis carried around with them.

I found a '71 Harley Flathead servi-car in Paterson, New Jersey. It would be less heart wrenching than cutting up the old '56 Harley Davidson trike. A Shriner had owned it and he used it to drive in parades. It had low mileage and was in good shape — sold! I took it home and measured it up for the freezer. I brought the box to this cat Mr. Mott, and told him what I had in mind. Mott specialized in building ice cream vehicles during the '30s and '40s. He'd converted all kinds of vehicles into ice cream wagons, and luckily for me, he was right in Jersey. Mott thought I was crazy, he told me to go buy something nice for my wife rather than be caught up in these kinds of ideas.

Even though he protested, he ended up doing the stainless work and installed the freezers with two latch doors. He said it was going to take months because he didn't have time to fool around with something so stupid, but I got it back within a few weeks. In the end, he was just as excited as I was and had spent the last couple of weeks working on it non-stop. I loaded up the servi-car and stopped by the local bike shop for some parts. Frito, a friend of mine who had been riding motorcycles since the beginning of time, was hanging around the shop. He asked me what I was going to do with the servi-car, so I told him my plans. Frito started laughing hysterically — I hit the roof! I was so pissed off that everyone was dogging my dreams. It drove me over the edge to the point that the ridicule lit the spark under my ass to see the project through to completion.

Pulsating Paula, a photographer for Biker magazine, who documented the biker's life style of the '80s, wrote an article about the trike shortly after I completed it. She called it *The Ice Cream Dream Machine* and commented on how cool it was to get ice cream straight from a biker's hand. Paula did a photo shoot of me and

The Power of a Name Change

Anna on our rides handing out ice cream to my nieces and nephews. I was so excited to be in a biker rag, it was my first piece of serious publicity! It almost felt like I was getting back at Homestead Township for denying me my permit, and all the guys who told me what a stupid idea the trike was. That's why, no matter what anyone says, when you have a hunch—you got to go with it—because you're probably right! I had an idea and I followed my dream! Fuck Jersey!

In 1990, Pulsating Paula and her husband Jeff the Axe, a.k.a. Flat Black Jeff suggested that we bring my puttsicle to a biker party in Cobleskill, New York called Am Jam. Aah, Pulsating Paula…the name says it all, she can melt anyone's popsicle. More importantly, she's one hell of a photographer and a pioneer for tattooed women. Paula and Jeff always had it going on and have been great friends to Anna and me over the years. When she suggested we hit the party,

You're Next

Jeff and Paula

I thought she was crazy! I'd done a few car shows and antique swap meets with my '54 Chevy, but the idea of the trike was still so new to me. I decided to go anyway because in my mind, it was another way for me to shove it up Homestead Township's ass. Besides, Paula was definitely a hot tip when it came to the motorcycle world.

When we got to New York, I was uncomfortable with the idea of running around in my ice cream get up. I mean it worked for the kiddies and the corporates, but at a biker event? I felt like a jackass, I looked like a complete faggot amongst my peers! I was hiding in my box truck with the bottle and refused to come out. I had to get drunk before I could show my face in public. Suddenly, my brilliant idea of wearing this uniform seemed so stupid. I pleaded

The Power of a Name Change

with Anna and Paula in between sips off my bottle that I wasn't going out there. Paula was giggling her little girl giggle while trying to lend encouraging words. Anna however, wasn't taking my bullshit anymore—she pushed me out the door! I had no choice but to jump on my trike and start my rap...

"Ice Cream! Ice Cream! Take your tongue for a sleigh ride! Ice Cream! Ice Cream! Ya can't holla for a dolla! Ice Cream! Ice Cream!"

The people started paying attention to this goof ball ice cream man and I was actually making a few bucks! Slowly, I grew more comfortable in my get up around the tough guys. Hey, at least they were buying my product, and it turned out to be a late night and a quick profit!

We got up the next morning in preparation for another great day of sales. After shaking off the dust, Anna and I went cruising by the Porta John in search of a cup of mud. A hung over, drunken, scooter-riding zombie thrust open the shit hole door and almost knocked me over. I stepped back waiting for him to blow chunks... he was looking at me cross-eyed. In between belches, the poor bastard managed to muscle up enough strength to speak, "Hey look...it's...the Ice Cream Man From Hell!"

The birth of the *Ice Cream Man From Hell* had just boiled out of the deep dark bowels of a Porta Shitter! My gears started turning into overdrive as the drunken buffoon stumbled back to his campsite. Genius...but now what do I do with it? Maybe a name change **was** in order? I was turning a new leaf. My probation was finally over so why not call myself, the Ice Cream Man From Hell!

So, now what about this Ice Cream Man From Hell guy? Wait a minute, who the fuck is this guy? I had no time to figure it out, I just had to play along. Besides, it seemed to fit me quite well, and it instantly stuck. From that foggy morning forward that name became a part of me...it was my Excalibur.

As silly as the whole concept was from the beginning, I got up the nut sack to run with it. Pulsating Paula saw my potential

You're Next

way before it ever smacked me in the face and if a visionary like that could see it, maybe I really did have something! I came to the realization that the power of a name change could be my foot in the door to be accepted in this wild world of motorcycle shows.

The day my first Ice Cream Man From Hell tee shirts arrived hot off the press, my friends didn't understand what it was all about. Nor did I, because I had no idea where it was going—I was still confused myself. That didn't matter because we shared some good laughs while brain storming about some crazy ways I could work it. Then they gladly reached into their pockets to purchase a shirt. I

The Power of a Name Change

had already made some sales, and the new me hadn't even left my front porch.

One of the first people to expose the antics of the Ice Cream Man From Hell was a local Jersey boy, Dickey Craig. We shared several hilarious interviews on his cable show called *Not Just Rock 'N Roll*. I only hoped the rest of the world would see my vision the same way. You know you're on the right track when you can make people laugh!

From years of hustling cars, bikes, pottery, snot and ya motha...I've always known that—Flash is Cash! It was time to start working on some more creative concepts and logos to make this Ice Cream Man From Hell guy come to life. I already had the ice cream parlor uniform but it was time to spice it up. I pasted together a skull with some flames, a true biker tradition and added my own twist, or should I say a fudgesicle—I shoved one in its mouth! It was the first Ice Cream Man From Hell design ever known to man— *The Rugged Original!*

I was already in the know that the almighty biker's patch had been a tradition dating back to the ole #1 logo because I had been riding for years. With that in mind, I took my *Rugged Original* design and concocted it into a two-piece back patch. From that day forward, the name ICE CREAM MAN FROM HELL would be on my back at all times while slinging ice cream. My patched vest made me feel a little more at ease with my image. It was a rougher look that I was more comfortable with and felt like myself. I've taken and given a lot of beatings over the years for my patch and it's caused several unreal images and distorted facts, and if you give me a fucking minute...I'll explain it all!

By 1994, I decided it was time to take my image to the next level. Knowing that the Ice Cream Man From Hell had been surrounded by controversy since day one and my *Rugged Original* patch was the source of my troubles with the motorcycle clubs—I still wanted to continue forward. When I had reached this decision,

You're Next

I knew I had to talk to Heller about it. Even though he had hopped off the fast moving train called life a long time ago, Heller was someone who understood my feelings of needing a purpose in life. Neither one of us had ever been satisfied with the notion of walking through life unconsciously or having a meaningless existence.

Heller told me he was sick and tired of feeling like a mouse waiting for the piece of cheese. I understood everything he was saying, and I knew I was faced with the same reality right now. I couldn't go back to a regular humdrum job, what was the fucking point? Even with the controversy of the clubs, I knew I had to push forward and that Anna would understand... she always did. Just like my brother, I've always had visions of grandeur in my heart as to why I was on this ball of mud and I wasn't going to spend it running the maze. So, marching forward with the Ice Cream Man From Hell was the right decision—my conversation with Heller confirmed it. Those were the last words I ever exchange with Heller, a few months later he died in a mental institution.

Years before Heller died, he made me promise him that he'd never be buried in Fulton, New Jersey. He always hated Fulton and was never there by choice. Mommy would never understand why it was so important for Heller to be anywhere but next to her. So when it came to the particulars, I told mommy that I would take care of it. We decided to cremate him, and bury his ashes. We held a ceremony at the Fulton cemetery where he would lay to rest. It was the dead of winter, but I decided to ride to the service on a chopper in Heller's honor. As cold as the day was, the bike started first kick. There was no procession or onlookers. Mommy, Anna, the priest and me were the only ones present for the service. Ma was wailing and carrying on in a fit of tears as she clutched the urn containing Heller's remains before they lowered it into the ground. What mommy didn't know was he wasn't in there. I filled his urn with cement, a rubber skeleton, John Lennon glasses and his opal and gold confirmation ring engraved with his initials...MT. It wasn't to disrespect my family or my mother's wishes. I knew I was doing

The Power of a Name Change

the right thing by keeping my promise to Heller. I reduced some of his ashes on the stove that created a mixture of black ink and was tattooed with it—I even smoked him with some of my friends, and for years, I'd leave a little piece of Heller everywhere I traveled...as a reminder to keep on keeping on.

I wasn't giving in and I sure as hell wasn't giving up. That same year I decided to make my way to Daytona Bike Week in Florida for the first time. When I got there, I had the opportunity to meet Kram. One of the hottest airbrush artists to ever walk the boulevards of any bike week. For years, he had been blessing the pages of *Super Cycles* and official bike week memorabilia with his outrageous artwork. He created several of the designs that some of you wear on your backs today. That's if you rock an ICMFH tee shirt.

Hold on, let me back up a little bit. The flash on my back that I'm famous for actually started with Flat Black Jeff, who was flat blacking rides before any of you motherfuckers thought it was cool! Jeff was a dark soldier, a bat out of hell. At least that's the feeling you'd get when you saw him on his bike. Everything Jeff owned was christened by a can of flat black paint. His signature was always a long black leather cape that hung to his ankles. He was a leather craftsman on the side and used to make his own garb. When I started banging around ideas about this Ice Cream Man From Hell concept, Jeff presented me with my first full-length custom-made leather cape.

I took it to Kram and he turned it into one of the most explosive works of art I've ever laid eyes on. The black and white capes that I parade around in at every motorcycle event are the best advertisement I've ever had. The outrageous leathers and my trike are what drew the attention of all the photographers and their pictures of me that were popping up worldwide in all the motorcycle magazines. Beating the streets with my name on

You're Next

I've gotten to meet so many people and to enjoy so many good memories that I'm about to share. Like I said—Flash is Cash! I proudly wear the words Ice Cream Man From Hell across my back even though it's made me a moving target.

Chapter 7

Sex Smells

My extreme personality has always allowed me to take everything over the edge and that's why I started selling pussy back in the 1970s. Before I realized that—Flash is Cash, and long before I was the Ice Cream Man From Hell, I knew that—Ass equaled Cash!

They say its women that keep the American economy in the bank. I'd beg to differ; the cock is a pretty big spender too! There's only one thing more powerful than the almighty dollar and that's the almighty pussy. Being a savvy hustler, I immediately realized my potential clients and what their needs were.

My next move was to find some employees. Back then, I knew several married women, so at first this appeared to be a problem. Turns out, they were the perfect candidates. They constantly bitched about their old men never being home and that they were too busy pissing away the daily bread on booze and dope. "Well don't ya worry little ladies, I've got a solution." With that, I had my staff and I didn't need to hit the streets for backup, we were in business. It was a no nonsense deal and like everything else, I never asked for anybody else's opinion. I guess you could say I became the Man-dame of the neighborhood housewives!

We all got ours, that's the way the deal worked because I wasn't out to scam the girls or get anybody hurt. The housewives would supply the pussy and I'd supply the protection. Remember it was the '70s…I'm not talking about condoms! It was a sweet set up. I'd screen the clients, book the rooms, and guard the doors. I never had to put my girls on the street, everyone was safe, and we all got paid—royally!

You're Next

The only potential job hazard we faced were their husbands. Of course, they didn't know what their wives were up to...are ya kidding? I would've been out of business! One evening when I brought one of my girls home, her husband was waiting outside their apartment. A neighbor informed the guy that his wife was hanging out with a scumbag like me, so he was waiting for her to come home. When we pulled into the driveway, she was still disheveled from her hot and heavy session. She was fixing her face in the rear view mirror, unaware he was waiting for her. I managed to smooth things over with him as soon as I got out of the car. As she ran up to him with hugs and kisses, she casually invited me upstairs so nothing seemed suspicious. I didn't notice till she was smooching on her husband that her skirt was hiked up and stuffed down her panty hose. I followed them upstairs and quickly tugged at her skirt. She was smart enough not to look back—talk about a close call!

After a hard day of pimping, I decided to go prowling for some of my own action. Luckily, it was easy pickings that night and I didn't have to waste too much time. When a man works this hard, he needs to stop the clock for a few hours and rub one out, if ya know what I'm saying! I hooked up with this chick Lola, and she took me to her brownstone in New Brunswick. We were digging each other and things were moving fast. Before the first cork was popped, I had her fully undressed and I was down to my underwear. There was a knock on the door and I could see the panic in Lola's eyes.

"Is it your husband?"
"No."
"Boyfriend?"
"No."
"Pizza man?"
"No."

"Then what the fuck are ya freaking out for? I'll open that motherfucking door and stomp him right now!" Her lips were quivering and I could tell she was on the brink of tears.

"It's my pimp! He's going to kill me because you're here!"

"What? Why the fuck didn't ya tell me ya were a motherfucking whore? Are ya trying to get me killed?"

There was no question that Superfly was about to kick in the door. I knew no words or fists would be exchanged and even though I was packing heat...I had no time for this shit. I wasn't a paying customer, nor was I about to be. I had to get the fuck out of there and fast!

Fortunately for me, Lola lived on the second floor, because my only option was the window. I didn't have time to get dressed. I threw my duds out the window and heaved myself over the sill. I was hanging by my digits! I cocked my head backwards to see what the commotion across the street was all about. There were two black guys sitting in a Riviera sharing a bottle and enjoying the view. So there was my pimp ass, hanging out of some prostitute's window in a pair of tightie whities and my powder pink platforms listening to two black guys bust my balls. Does this shit only happen to me or what?

"Hey mothafucka! Whacha doin hangin out dat winda in yer drawers? Ya best be hurrin up and hit the street fore I come over and shank dose pleated duds!"

I heard the apartment door kick open—I closed my eyes and let go! As soon as I hit the pavement I grabbed my shit. The two guys in the Riviera were still laughing at my expense but I ignored them, my ass was on the line. I hobbled towards the alley in back of the brownstone, my legs were throbbing. I needed to get to my car that was parked behind the apartment building. Stupid move...the one-way alley was going to restrict my get away.

I tried to flag a cab because I needed to go around the block and have someone wait till I got in my car. No one was stopping

You're Next

and I realized I better put my clothes on if I wanted any help. The cackling coming from the two guys in the Riviera was making me lose my focus. I finally got dressed and hailed a cab. I quickly explained my situation, the driver agreed to go around the block and wait for—twenty bucks! For a hundred foot ride? I couldn't argue I needed to get my ass out safely.

The cab driver started to back out of the alley before I could get my car door open. What the Fuck? He wasn't holding up his end of the bargain! I hopped in my Pontiac and rammed the front fender of the cab—I was heated. He was blocking the exit and I started seeing red. I rammed him a second time! By now, Superfly had made his way to the alley—I slammed the car in reverse. I knew that motherfucker was going to start shooting! I ducked my head below the steering wheel. The alley was tight but I had no choice, bullets started flying! My ride got all fucked up. I was backing over all kinds of shit and swerving into buildings! At the end of the alley, I slammed the car into drive and headed for the hills as the two black guys in the Riviera were cheering me on. It wasn't till I hit my driveway that I realized I had left my brand new suede coat in that ho daddy's apartment. Fuck! It had my clip in it! I started slamming my hands against the steering wheel. Fuck me! Fuck me! I couldn't go back, at least not tonight.

The next day I grabbed one of my girls, jumped into my Caddy and headed back to Brunswick. I had already taken the Pontiac to the crusher. I sent my girl up to Lola's apartment and told her to make sure that whore was the only one in the joint and to check the pockets of my jacket before she split. I parked down the block and waited. When she returned with the coat, she informed me that our business arrangement was over. She said she was done and threw the jacket at me, then hailed a cab. I couldn't understand why she was so hell bent, but I wasn't going to force her to do anything she didn't want to. I was her pimp. What did she care if I had fucked another prostitute? I tried to get the info out of her, but she wasn't talking. The only thing she told me was that Lola was home alone. I parked my car under the window of her apartment (just in case I'd have to use it again), and marched upstairs packing. I had to find out what this was all about.

When Lola opened the door I didn't even recognize her, her face was bruised and swollen. The red and purple finger marks around her neck were gruesome, and she was walking with a limp... "Haven't you already gotten me into enough trouble? Unless you have intentions on getting me out of this mess, get the fuck out of here!" She slammed the door. I couldn't get the image of Lola's busted up face out of my mind. By the time I hit Fulton, I decided that my pimping days were over. Smacking chicks around had never been my thing. The money was great, but I truly didn't want to be involved in the reality of the scene. I guess I never really was a true motherfucking P-I-M-P.

Here's one I never saw coming. Twenty years after hanging up my pimp hat, I was crowned the "Hardest Working Man In Ice Cream!" Please understand that it wasn't due to record sales in the rocket pop division. Actually, Anna sold most of the ice cream over the years. The crazy sex-capades I became notorious for was how I earned my title. There's no question that the, "WHAT tee shirt?" contests I've hosted and the exhibitionists who've used my booth as their stage, with a little coaching of course, is what truly put me on the map in the motorcycle culture.

Unfortunately, over the years as the laws became stricter, several townships decided my fate. What I mean is, my bail started to eventually equal my pay. Because of this, I've had to give up a lot of gigs over the years. Not that I'm a pussy or that I knuckle under to Johnny Law, but because people were scared to hire me in fear of being fined. Bike weeks across the country have had a, "No Tolerance" law pertaining to nudity since the mid '90s. A lot of states feel that bike weeks should be more of a family oriented event. No biker event is a family event. Leave your kids at home! There were never any children present during the events I'm about to share with you—and that's the way it's supposed to be. It's bullshit that consensual adults are being put under the scrutiny of the law and of religious groups. Now, I want to share with you some of the craziest sex driven stunts I've witnessed and participated in over the years. So feel free to jerk off, hey, let's not forget...this *is* America!

Let's start with my ole trusty ice cream trike. The rule is, if want to have your picture taken on it, something's got to go! Of course,

I do deem it necessary to make up the rules as I go. After all, I am the Ice Cream Man From Hell. "Sure ya can sit on my trike, but ya got to take off your top. Sure ya can sit on my trike, but lose the panties. Sure ya can sit on my trike, just open em a little wider honey!" I'll tell you what, that trike has seen more ass over the years than a Port Authority toilet!

Know this, I never crowded the girls around my trailer for my personal enjoyment, well maybe sometimes, I've always done it

Sex Smells

for the enjoyment of my friends and fans. Hey, I have a reputation to live up to ya know! The trike just seems to have its way with women. Sometimes I swear that bike can talk…"Hey sweetie come over here and while you're at it, mention my name to Ice Cream and I'll make sure ya get a good seat!"

In 1991, I was given the opportunity to take my act on the stage in New York. At this point I wasn't quite over feeling like a jerk in my uniform but I wasn't going to let that hang me up. Frankie Baby came knocking on my trailer…

"Hey, Ice Cream!" Have you ever hosted a wet tee shirt contest before? My guy's too drunk to take the stage! Think ya can handle it?"

Of course I lied through my teeth and told him I had an extensive resume of wet tee shirt contests, bachelor parties, funerals, bar mitzvahs, strip clubs, black market trading—you know the deal.

"Just shut your pie hole and get the fuck up on that stage!"

That night, when Frankie Baby replaced a drunk with a drunk…history was made! The magic had just begun. The magic of the Ice Cream Man From Hell's uninhibited, unadulterated, sex-capades—I was hooked. Due to the crowd's overwhelming enthusiasm, I was invited back on stage every year. The louder ya scream, the harder I work. I give your energy right back. If you're screaming, those broads are shoving beer bottles up their asses! Everyone knows how notorious I am for getting chicks to bend over and show their good side.

Of course I was nervous on stage that night, it was the first time I had performed in front of a crowd since my Dylan days. Right away I realized that the girls needed guidance, they were nervous too. I knew that man handling the ladies wasn't the way to get them excited. My job was to make them feel comfortable, sexy, and beautiful. This is truly the secret to my success of stripping chicks. If they trust me, I can get them to do almost anything!

You're Next

One of the things I became famous for over the years on the stage was the ICMFH salute. After coaxing the girl's out of their panties, I'd have them all bend over for the prize winning ass shot. Yes, yes, yes, I like to get close to the exit before closing a show! The girls knew that taking off their clothes wasn't enough to win first prize. So by the middle of my song and dance I'd get them so confident that they'd be willing to do almost anything to win. The first year it all started with a cigar tube. I know you're confused, butt just stay with me. This 5' 8" smoking brunette with a new set of tits went all out for first place. She resorted to grabbing whatever resources were available. The competition was fierce! She sat her bare, stiletto-wearing ass down on the edge of the stage and spread em. That brunette pulled a cigar tube out of her pussy and jerked herself off till she had christened the stage...thank you God! As she exited the stage for her prize, I asked her to give up the tube. After sniffing it, I threw it into the crowd, and they threw it back. I put it in my front pocket.

Sex Smells

Over time you get to know a lot of the participants, they're hard to forget, and most of the spectators become repeat offenders...can ya blame them? Who'd want to miss out on this kind of action? The following year in New York, the grandstands were packed when I opened the "WHAT tee shirt?" contest by pulling that same cigar tube out of my pocket. When I swiped it across my nose, I got a standing ovation, I couldn't believe they remembered! Whether the girls on stage competing for the prize that year knew what the cigar tube was all about or not, they had better get creative if they wanted to top last year's prize winning performance.

"The louder ya scream, the harder these girls are going to work! Now, let's see if we can top last year's performance folks. Let me hear it, ya make me wanna scream!"

I have to admit, that girl on girl shit excites the hell out of me...and every other guy I know! It's a sure fire way to get the crowd's attention. There's nothing like seeing two beautiful sets of tits sandwiched between two beautiful chicks tonguing it! That same night a mighty blonde/brunette duo were hot for each other from the moment they stepped out on stage. It was like the paparazzi were out. I've never seen so many flashes going off at once.

"Alright folks, keep it together! We have one more contestant backstage. She's going to have to work pretty damn hard to top these two. Let's see what I can rustle up for you! Let's hear it folks, ya make me wanna scream!" It seemed pretty unanimous that there'd be a tie between those oh so hot, twenty something morsels that were backstage and still going at it. I walked over to introduce the last little hell cat even though I was having a hard time keeping my eyes off of what I thought was first prize.

Just before I announced the next contestant, she gave me a wicked little smile, "I believe you have something of mine in your pocket." It was the cigar tube broad—I couldn't believe it! I didn't recognize her at first. She was topless so I'd already decided who I was talking to. I reached into my pocket and handed her back what

You're Next

was rightfully hers, but then I changed my mind. She ignored me and strutted onto the stage in nothing but a thong, carrying a small duffle bag over her shoulder. She started pulling off an incredible dance. She may've been a stripper, but I'm not sure. She wasn't hired as a ringer. You can't pre-plan that kind of magic. After her thong came off, she bent over to give the famous ICMFH salute and then sat down spread eagle on the edge of the stage. The crowd was anxious and extremely excited! I kept waving the cigar tube in the air..."Ya make me wanna scream! Let's hear it for last year's winner folks!"

She got into position before opening her bag of tricks, inside her duffle bag was a cucumber the size of my forearm. No way! Maybe it was a squash; I mean it was fucking huge! The crowd was going berserk. Someone was bound to have a heart attack! That brunette spit on that giant cucumber and slowly started working it in and out of her pussy. She waved me over and asked me to silence the crowd. I got everyone calmed down; the grandstand and floor were completely silent. With one hard thrust that brunette shot that cucumber out of her pussy like a cannon ball!

The crowd was cheering like it was the World Series. She shot that cucumber into the grandstands like it was a home run and the entire section of fans scurried to catch the prize! My God—that woman could've probably crack a walnut with those lips. I'd never seen so much muscle control in my life. Need I say more? Oh yeah, by the way, she did win first prize.

Later on that evening the booze was flowing and I started my shuffle back to my trailer to catch a few zzzs. I walked past two dudes I knew, Knuckles Manachio and J. J. Steel. Knuckles had caught the prize winning produce. How do I know? Because he was coddling the thing and showing it off like it was a newborn baby! J. J. was fed up with Knuckles stupidity! He yanked the cucumber out of his arms. Then he gripped it like a bat and smacked Knuckles upside the head with it two or three times! Knuckles started screaming, it was so damn funny!

I could never have staked my claim as the "Hardest Working Man in Ice Cream" or share all of these great stories with you if it wasn't for these wild chicks along the way. I just got to say thank

you to each and ever one of those beautiful girls over the years who just like to have a little fun! All of you are beautiful in your own right. I have to admire your boldness...and trust me I do! When women get up on that stage and purposely put themselves out there for sexual attention, it should all be in good fun.

It's only once in awhile at an event when I come across a lady who truly doesn't understand that just because she has fake tits, it doesn't make her a fucking princess! There was this one blonde for example, she had just gotten a new set of tits and decided that she wanted to use the, "WHAT tee shirt?" contest to show them off for the first time. She had an ass that wouldn't quit and her new rack put her high on the babe meter. She was looking pretty hot but she definitely needed some coaching, so I encouraged her to start

You're Next

out on stage in her panties and bra. I had her parade around for awhile before I told her what to do next...by all means take off your panties! It wasn't long after that, her top was off...she was a little nervous yet doin so well for a beginner.

She was comfortable with being fully nude, so comfortable that she started undressing the other contestants and kissing them. Unfortunately for her, this wasn't one of the State Fair Beauty Pageants she was used to winning. The double bubbled prom queen didn't go home with the crown that night. Don't worry little lady, I'm sure your daddy would still be proud. That's how wild and crazy these contests get. These chicks have full blown lesbian sex in front of thousands of people and still don't win! Oh well...hey, better *fuck* next year!

I was off stage and back at my trailer while the girls were still being photographed...my job was done. I was hanging outside of my trailer schmoozing with the crowd and out of the corner of my eye, I saw the blonde push a few people out of the way. With no hesitation, she hauled off and smacked me across the face! That bimbo started clawing at me like a cat; it took two guys to get that stupid whore off of me. I was furious! What a sore loser, I told her next time to try pulling her pussy lips over her head maybe that would get the crowd's attention.

The next day she came over and apologized for attacking me, she admitted she was drunk and that's why things got out of hand. I told her if I had anything to do with the judging, she would've been the winner. Then, I asked her to step behind the trailer and wait for me. I hustled up some of my friends and explained the situation. I told them to play along so we could have some fun with this broad. The guys stepped behind the trailer and praised her butter face...I mean her beauty up and down. I told her if she took off her clothes, they could definitely let her know if she'd be the winner tonight. So she stripped down to her bare ass and posed for some hole shots. By the end of the photo session the guys encouraged her to get on the stage again that night. She left my trailer feeling like a real winner!

During Saturday night's show, that blonde bitch worked her ass off, but once again she didn't win. Hey, that's okay I thought to myself, at least the guys got their way with her. This time she didn't wait to get over to my trailer, she started stomping me right on stage in front of the entire audience! Thank God security came and took her away. I can't tell you how badly I just wanted to push that stupid bitch off the stage. She was really starting to jive up my weekend! I guess she felt like spending her old man's G's on those fake tits entitled her to something more than just sucking his cock. Ya win some; ya lose some, what can I say?

Then there's times when you're blessed with women like the Dildo Lady. The Dildo Lady would carry around a briefcase full of dildos for sale. She was a cute little thing, but her approach was all wrong and I could see she was losing sales. So I decided to play the Good Samaritan and help her out. I told her we needed to set up a live infomercial to get her product to move. I propped her bare ass up on the freezer of my ole trusty trike and volunteered to be her assistant. I held her briefcase open while she personally demonstrated every model on herself. She shifted through every speed on those suckers and attempted to talk to her audience in between long oh, oh, ohs and groans. Everyone got their money's worth and I sold a few extra tee shirts to boot!

In the early '90s, Big Dick Duke and I decided to be the founders of a charitable cause. So we hung a sign on the front of the trailer...

> **Home for Wayward Women**
> **Open 24 - 7**
> **Office and confession booth**
> **Open 9 - 5**

You're Next

Chicks started flocking to my trailer telling us about their relationship problems and asking if we had a place for them to crash. Only women were allowed to enter the trailer for topless confessions and we'd comfort them with free ice cream. The *Home for Wayward Women* grew quickly and things started getting out of hand when this skank, Suzy Swallows approached me with a proposition..."Oh Ice Cream Man, you don't know how much I truly admire you. I'd do anything for you...ANYTHING! Please Ice Cream, I want to suck your cock like a big hard popsicle!"

I tried to play it off—I mean pawn her off, but this broad wasn't taking no for an answer. She was like a cat in heat. I decided it was time to put her under my arm and walk her into my trailer. I told Suzy that she could have me but only if she sucked a few of my friend's cocks first. She happily agreed. Hey, don't think for a second I'm not a gentleman, I offered her a pillow to kneel on. Let the suck fest begin! Within a short time she was neck deep and I needed to find more friends. I was grabbing random dudes off the boulevard and offering up free blowjobs with every ice cream purchase. The

Sex Smells

line started forming around the corner and down the midway. That cum guzzling whore was sucking cock for what seemed like hours! I was running out of candidates, no one else was signing up. I think she sucked every snot stick in the place! Fuck it, she'll come out of the trailer when she's good and full.

Finally, after every flesh helmet was spit shined, she came out for her prize. "Are you ready for me Ice Cream? I'm ready for you baby! Didn't I do a good job? Aren't I such a good girl?" I put her under my arm again and walked her away from my stand. As gently as possible I said, "You are out of your fucking mind to ever think that I'd let you suck my cock. Now get the fuck out of here with your cock breath, ya stupid whore!" I know I'm a scumbag but hey, I made a lot of people smile that day!

That cum dumpster slowly sulked away and took a seat at the picnic table directly across from my stand. She pouted for awhile and kept looking over at me with her big sad cockeyes. Fuck that! I don't have time for her shit, I had ice cream to sell and guests to entertain. Man, I sure know how to throw one hell of a party. "Napkins all around!"

About an hour after I ditched the bitch…I mean sweet young lady, an ambulance came screaming down the midway and parked right in front of my stand. What the fuck is going on now? Someone must've gotten stupid. I hoped whoever it was would be okay, but this sucked for me because the ambulance was jamming up my stand.

Turns out it was Suzy Swallows, the paramedics were hauling her off in the ambulance. What could she have possibly done to herself in the past hour? Man she wasn't fucked up when she was in my trailer. She wouldn't even drink the beers we offered her? Did she try to kill herself? I knew this wasn't good.

As soon as they loaded that dirty little pig into the ambulance, the cops were knocking at my trailer door. Did they see her sucking cock from way up on the hill? Yeah, that's right, we

You're Next

know you're up there. The cops instantly shut me down and yellow taped the perimeter of my ice cream slinging stand, it was now an investigation. I pleaded my case, I didn't bullshit them at all. I told the cop that the fucking slut was giving blowjobs from my trailer like it was a drive thru. We didn't give her any drugs, she didn't even drink any booze. Her throat was so jammed full of cock—there was no way she could've gotten anything else down there. Cum to think of it…I'm surprised she could even breathe! I'm telling you, this chick wasn't whacked out, she was completely straight when she propositioned me. If she wasn't, I would've sent her packing. I didn't need any heat and no one was there to make anyone do anything against their will.

We were still shut down when the report came back from the hospital. That bitch was cum drunk! They had to pump her over loaded, sperm filled stomach. Between the alcohol content and traces of whatever else may've been in that dumpster size load she sucked down, it created a strange brew in her stomach and she needed medical assistance. The cock breath beauty overdosed on sperm. Who knew that was humanly possible? Man, I bet she had the shits for days! So, listen up ladies, the shit may be cock full of protein, but don't be a greedy cum guzzling whore or this could happen to you! I was back in business by popular demand, and luckily, they didn't kick me out after that little fiasco. They removed the tape around my trailer and left well enough alone.

In 1994, when I expanded my territory to Daytona Bike Week in Florida, I approached Billy Stevens, the owner of the World Famous Iron Horse Saloon. Iron Horse Billy has been a large contribution to the success of Bike Week. That top hat rules Daytona. I was only a few years into this Ice Cream Man From Hell gig and already my reputation was preceding me. Billy wanted nothing to do with my sex driven shenanigans, he ran a respectable joint. I was persistent though, I knew the Iron Horse would help

the Ice Cream Man get more recognition. By 1996, Billy finally allowed me to sling my merchandise at his saloon on a promise and a handshake. We agreed that I'd keep my act under wraps. He knew that I had several other qualities to help keep his guests entertained, "Thanks Billy!"

Spider is another cat who saw my potential early on in the game. Spider has been open to my stupidity throughout the years and has allowed me to do my sidewalk act in his stores. He's a good businessman, a real no nonsense kind of guy. He's the first one to tell me when I'm screwing up but I think he keeps me around so he can sniff a thong or two.

My first year pedaling my act at Spider's Store on Main Street in Daytona, three black chicks walked in like they owned the joint. They were dressed to kill and were quite flamboyant. They sparked my curiosity so I had to know what they were up to. They told me that they were working girls from Orlando and were in town to make some money. I just had to laugh, it was obvious they had never worked a bike event before. So I decided to put my two cents in, "Look girls, number one, the cops are going to know exactly what you're up to. Let me put it to you this way, you don't exactly fit in here. And number two, there's so much free loving going around, I don't know how the hell you expect to make any money!" The girls started to curse me out because they were pissed off that I was all up in their biz-nass. So to shut them up, I told them that if they needed anything they knew where to find me. With that advice I sent them on their way.

    The girls showed up about forty-five minutes later to let me know that the cops were harassing them. I had an apartment behind the store, so being the cordial guy that I am, I offered the girls a place to hide out for awhile. I knew it was probably a bad idea because I was working and I wasn't going to leave them alone in my pad. They would've robbed me blind. The luscious ladies asked me if they could take a shower and the next thing you know, I had three naked prostitutes running around my apartment. How the hell do I get into these situations? I told them to hurry up. I needed them out of the apartment. I had to get back on the streets to hustle. I heard some giggling coming from the bedroom. I had to reinforce what I'd just said, besides I needed my pimp hat. The three chocolate beauties were making out on my bed. What the fuck?

    "Come on Ice Cream, we ain't going to charge you nothin. You've been so nice and all, we just want to have some fun."

    "No thanks, I'm married. I don't go there, but I appreciate the offer." But of course, being the scumbag that I am, I stood there and watched for a moment. Wait a minute, I got to go!

    "Look girls, I really got to get back to work. Put on something sexy and I'll put yas to work. I'm not talking about selling pussy but we'll figure something out." What to do…What to do…I always know what to do when it comes to good-looking women. I decided to spread em—literally, all over the storefront for a hook, line, and sinker. I propped the whore with the twenty-seven inch waist and the perfectly round ass on the top of my trike. I told her not to stop shaking it till I said so…

"Chocolate éclairs! Chocolate éclairs!" Drrrrrring! Drrrrrring! "Come by and take a lick! Ya can't holla for a dolla! Come on over and take your tongue for a sleigh ride folks! Free photo op with every ice cream purchase! Chocolate éclairs! Chocolate éclairs!"

People were rolling in and out of the store to see what all the commotion was about. We drew quite a crowd. It only lasted a good twenty minutes before the cops yanked me aside and asked what the hell I was doing. I explained to the officer that he should be thanking me for keeping those whores off the street. He didn't seem to think I was doing him any favors. He called for backup to break up our sidewalk act. Man, we had a good thing going too.

Main Street at Daytona Bike Week was getting tougher and tougher every year. I was getting heavily fined and even arrested on a regular basis for my tomfoolery. I decided to start looking for a bike week home somewhere out of town, that's when I came to an agreement with the owners of the Black Chicken. They needed to hustle up some more business to put themselves on the map and I was just their guy!

It was my first opportunity to host my, "WHAT tee shirt?" contest in Florida along with several other outrageous ideas that I had up my sleeve. I set up the stage with a fourteen-foot tall birdcage I had stumbled upon while in Mexico. It had an eight-foot high platform and plenty of room for dancing. It brought a Burlesque flare to the show, which everyone seemed to dig. There was always a beautiful body in that cage. Even the guys participated in the cage dancing. I've had girls that were left stranded at bike week by their old men dance the go-go cage in order to make enough money to get home.

You're Next

The early days of the Black Chicken were the lost western days of bikers past that people only wish they could've been a part of. The famous, "all male buns" review started on the stage at the Black Chicken. This brilliant idea came from the mouth of a desperate girl. She was whining about how I do everything for the guy's pleasure and nothing for the ladies. Who cares? I scratched my melon and thought for a second. Then I walked up to a few guys and asked them if they were in the mood to moon the audience as a way to tell the world to go fuck themselves. Men or women, you just got to know how to talk to them. Especially if you're trying

to get them to take their clothes off! They thought it was a great idea. Good then, tonight's your lucky night!

This great idea led to even more insanity, and for the first time there'd be men and women on the stage together. The way

Sex Smells

it worked best was if I'd open the show with the, "all male buns" review. By the time the gals got on stage they were so damn horny that all hell broke loose. By the end of the event, it was a full out sex show! I'm not talking about any touchy feely shit, I'm talking about guys getting blowjobs right on stage. If you don't believe me search out the film, Daytona Bike Week '98...with your host, the Ice Cream Man From Hell.

Spaghetti wrestling at the Black Chicken was a sight to behold. Some people choose to have the ladies wrestle in Jello, mud, cabbage, or even pudding. I chose a little spaghetti and olive oil al dente. Would you expect anything less from a good ole Italian boy? After a few years, the girls got hip to the pit..."Hey, why are we in here kicking the shit out of each other when we could be kicking the shit out of the Ice Cream Man!?"

You're Next

It became a tradition at the end of the contest for all the girls to pig pile me. They'd rip off all of my clothes and shove spaghetti in every orifice of my body!

It took four years before the cops started poking around the bar. As the years went on, the locals started complaining about the high sexual activity at the Chicken. Hey, like it's my fault the girls were so competitive! The last year I performed on that stage, I was pulled aside by an undercover cop…"If you go up on that stage and pull down your pants for this, "all male buns" review bullshit you do, I'm going to arrest you on the spot, and it's going to be a long bike week for you."

I walked away and went behind stage. I knew there was no way he could arrest everyone in the joint, so of course he was going to target the leader. There was no way I was closing the show. I decided to go out on that stage and rat out the rat. But how could I get away with pulling down my pants without getting arrested? "Anna!" I hustled my beautiful wife out of her panties, slipped them on under my cape and headed for the stage…

"I wanna hear ya scream! Does anyone here smell a rat? Look to the left of you…look to the right of you…they're all around. They're infringing on our party. Don't get silent on me now. I wanna hear ya scream!" The crowd went crazy, even though they were confused.

"Don't worry, it's impossible to shut us down. They don't have the man power. I was told if I pull down my pants for the, "all male buns" review that I'd be arrested. What do you think I should do?" The crowd fell silent.

"I say—FUCK YOU, but first I wanna hear ya scream!" I dropped my cape and low and behold, I was standing there in Anna's little pink lacy panties. I wasn't nude, they couldn't do a thing, and the show went on…but I was reduced to parading around in my *Manties*!

Sex Smells

The owners told me I had a choice make. The bar was being hassled and were pointing the finger at me. There was no way I was going to change now. So rather than fight for freedom, they caved in and decided to eliminate the hassle. I got the cold shoulder, even though I had made them enough money to pay for all the beer I drank. I'm not a braggart, but it was my talents that put that fucking place on the map. If it weren't for my stage shows, that bar would've never become a bike week hot spot! Yet they took the easy way out. In the end it wasn't me they hurt, it was the spectators and fans they turned their backs on that lost out.

One of the few places left on this earth where I get to be myself is at RMC, Reading Motorcycle Club in Oley, Pennsylvania. It's the greatest party on this planet and the greatest love fest of the year! For three days, it's a little piece of heaven on earth. Every year, I bring an inflatable pool that seats six to set up next to my

trailer. I call it...the Sex Pool, and it takes precedence over all merchandise when getting set up for the big weekend. Hey, Lord knows I need to make money, but let's keep our priorities straight—anything goes in the Sex Pool. I've never been prejudice when it comes to women, that's something you've got to understand about me...I love em all! My only rules about going in the Sex Pool are, clothes are optional, and no shoes allowed! RMC is the holiest time of year, it's when everyone gets to step out of their skin and live life to the fullest while fulfilling all of their freakish fantasies.

    To set the mood, I start Friday night off with the Sex Parade. Every year I bring boxes of Halloween masks along with other props for the participants. Everyone strips down bare ass naked and marches through the midway in their masks and birthday suites. Tony I Fucked Em Two Times is always at the head of the parade. I guess you could call him the sex leader. Two Times Tony stands about 6' 2" and weighs in at about 275 pounds and is usually sporting a pair of suspenders. The only time I've ever seen him without them is during the Sex Parade.

    As always, I like to be the mediator and the referee of the weekend's activities. I'm on constant watch for people who may be in need of my assistance. Tony blew the horn one day when he noticed a young man getting a blowjob right out in the open across from my trailer. I knew this situation needed my immediate attention. So I strolled on over and tapped the little lady on her head, "Could ya please stand up for a minute dear?" Her boyfriend looked confused, but he knew who I was so he cracked a smile. I had my arms around both of them in a close huddle. I felt like the prize winning coach because I knew I had a great team...

    "Okay, now listen up, everything you're doing here is great. I want you to keep up the good work, but the fact that your standing out here where everyone can see you may cause some problems. Honey, I admire your willingness to please your man and in no way am I discouraging that. But if you stand out here in the open, some

Sex Smells

of these guys might think you're hanging around to service them too. I know you're not *that* kind of girl. Now, if those are your intentions I admire that, you're a real team player. But if this is just about you and your man, I can provide you with a small audience where you won't be harmed—just step behind my trailer."

Of course she thanked me for my concern, you know I was just looking out for Big Dick Duke's...I mean her best interest. They followed me behind the trailer and she continued to honker down on her boyfriend's cock. My crew was cheering her on like a champ. Hey, this is our kind of game, the season never ends! I had my arm around the guy while he was getting sucked dry and I kept asking his sweet little girl to look up so everyone could admire those beautiful cockeyes. RMC is just magical, we take it over the edge all weekend long, and no one ever gets hurt. This *is* truly why I love America!

I've woken up to naked bodies sprawled outside my trailer on several different occasions. It's usually due to complete drunkenness from the night prior. Once we had a guy who was still stone cold passed out by noon the following day when we opened for business. There was no moving his ass, he was down for the count. I was okay with it because at least he was safe and still breathing. He actually ended up becoming one of the best salesmen I've ever had because he drew so much attention to my popsicle stand.

In all of his vulnerability, this strange woman stumbled upon him and decided to molest him. She stripped down naked. It scared the shit out of me at first, I could've sworn I saw flies buzzing around her pussy. The curiosity of the fellow onlookers was bumping up my tee shirt sales. The toothless buzzard was doing everything she could to get his dick hard. After jerking him off for a good fifteen minutes, she resorted to a blowjob, but he still wasn't coming to. He probably didn't even know what planet he was on. We kept egging her on even though we were fully aware that nothing she did was going to work. She got herself so hot and desperate that she swarmed in and copped a squat right on his face! The crowd gasped and looked the other way. We all prayed that he wouldn't wake up. That poor bastard never knew what hit him! When he finally snapped out of it that evening, I congratulated him on a stupendous show and asked him not to get to close because his breath still smelled a little funny.

There's no other species on this planet like biker chicks. They don't give a shit about what anyone thinks, says, or does. They do things solely for their own personal satisfaction—which I admire. Hot rod chicks are pretentious, they think their shit don't stink and have no interest in having a good time. They're just too high maintenance. While on the other hand, most biker chicks are down for just about anything. They just seem to know what they want, and they get it…boy do they ever get it!

Terry Train Time is a prime example. Her objective every year is to beat her own gangbang record. There's no cash, trophies, or cameras involved. It's purely for self-satisfaction and ego. Every year she stands on the corner of the midway and starts her campaign, she's absolutely motherfucking serious about her work! I'm telling you it can't be out of desperation because she looks damn good thumbing for cock rides in a thong and heels. Best I could tell Terry would screw no less than fifty guys a day. Her weekend routine was eat, drink, and screw, eat, drink, and screw. Right on!

Now, the next story I have to share with you isn't exactly sexy…it falls under the category of bizarre. It's one of those shockers that just has to be told! This chick Wanda will forever be burned in my brain. Obviously, because I remember her name and I remember exactly what she looked like. She was by far the hottest chick on stage that night. Being that there are no showers, I always set up buckets of bubble bath for the girls on the stage, you know out of courtesy. Actually, it's so we can watch them scrub each other down. Who am I kidding? Back to the girl in question, 5' 6" 36...24...36...Perfect! Wanda was a stunning olive skinned, Latin princess with black hair all the way down to her ass. The signature prop for the, "WHAT tee shirt?" contest that evening was a swing that was mounted from the ceiling above the stage. I love watching those little ladies double saddle that twelve inch piece of wood! There wasn't an ounce of fat on her tall, slender body. Wanda was in great shape, I could tell by the way she was working that sex swing. She was able to pull herself three feet up the chains to give the cameras a full spread eagle shot. Wanda was hot, but with the magic in the air that night it was going to take more than her pretty face to win.

    For the final round, I called all of the girls out onstage to let the crowd get one more, good clean look. Things were a little chaotic, I couldn't pull the girls off each other. But who am I to stop them from sponging each other down and jamming their tongues down each other's throat? The contest could wait. The Latin beauty asked me if I'd call her up last and I agreed. When I finally got everyone calmed down, I escorted Wanda out to center stage and stepped back to jive with one of the guys from the Razorbacks Band.

    I heard someone yelling my name from the other side of the stage. "What?" I turned around; it was one of the photographers. She had a concerned look on her face and was pointing at Wanda. I was confused by her signal..."What?" Angelina, my trusty friend and road warrior, was too young to be having any kind of war flashbacks. Yet she panicked and dove behind the speakers like she knew a bomb was about to go off. I looked up at Wanda...Oh shit! No fucking way!

    That Latin skank was squatting down over a mug and was pissing in it! Wanda stood up, downed the cup of piss like a warm foamy beer and then she proceeded to spit it out all over the front row audience! It happened so fast that I'm sure not everyone who had gotten sprayed knew that it was piss! Then she proceeded to fling the mug into the crowd and whatever she couldn't swallow traveled in a steady stream and splashed a few more luckless pedestrians. She wasn't crowned the winner that year I can tell you that.

After the show was a wrap and I got ready to exit the stage. Wanda grabbed me by the arm, "How come I didn't win, I really think I should've won. Don't you think I was the best looking girl up there?" Oh no, here we go…I really wasn't up for a catfight. "Are you out of your fucking mind? If I were you, I'd crawl back into your tent and not come out for the rest of the weekend. You're lucky no one came unglued and kicked your motherfucking ass for that stunt! Maybe the smell of your breath had something to do with why you didn't win…Stanky Skank!" Man, I needed to get myself a stiff drink after that one!

It was Beetle Juice who taught me that it's reasons like this that you can't do two shows a night—you just can't do it! It's tales like these that have crowned me the *Hardest Working Man in Ice Cream!*

Chapter 8

Sidewalk Sideshow

Step right up folks and witness first hand, the confusion and bamboozlement of the one, the only, sidewalk sideshow! The freaks, geeks and strange women of the bizarre are right under your nose tonight for your viewing pleasure. The stars of the street stage are all under one big sky to feed your curiosity. So prepare to be dazzled or even disgusted! You may be laying eyes on me for the first time, but trust me…you've heard me before. My name is Doctor Tom, and I've broken every noise violation known to man at every bike event in the country. I'm not talking about the pipes on my bike, rather my windpipes! My notorious voice and ear popping, bugle blowing is why I've been asked to introduce the show this evening. So step right up and enjoy!

You'll see Indian Larry sleep soundly on a bed of nails…this rare species of grease monkey from Brooklyn, New York, is numb to pain!

You will witness the missing link of the sea…Bambi the Fiji Mermaid is alive and in the flesh. Gentlemen! Please keep your tongues in your mouths and your wallets on the table for this one!

And for the ladies, we have another special oddity…Archie, the Horniest Man in Daytona will be performing here tonight. To ensure everyone gets a good seat, only two dames at a time for this act. That way each one gets a horn!

And don't forget while you wait, please stop by the ticket booth. We have our very own boobologist on staff to tantalize those pretty titties! Pimp Daddy Pappy, President of the Crippled Old Biker Bastards, is here to fondle your fancy!

You're Next

Come inside and be amazed by the only living dead girl...Goth. This musical prodigy is alive and accurate. Observe the damsel of doom and her mesmerizing séance on the piano, but be warned—you may never behold daylight again!

You will also be thunderstruck by J. J. Steel and his death defying stunts...watch him risk life and limb for your captivated eyes. Beware of the smoldering blaze as J. J. Steel turns himself into a fury of fire!

And don't miss the California Hell Riders perform their fearless act...The Wall of Death. Watch this daring family endanger their lives inside an original 1963 motordrome. This is one of the oldest and last thrill shows on earth folks!

Behold the next rare species, she's one of the last Carney folk known to man. Her fast jive and wild behavior is something our society no longer knows. Just a word of caution as you enter her booth...Miss Chrissy the Patch Queen is notorious for running with scissors! But don't let this intimidate you from being in her presence; the word on the street is she gives good thread!

Tonight, we bring you two rare genetic defects to observe. First up is Pee Wee Davidson. This illegitimate love child is a direct descendant of Vasqual, the legendary man who has been supplying the public with motorcycles through the 1900's. Due to Pee Wee's severe mental retardation, he has been shunned by his family and barred from his inheritance. He's been diminished to spending his life collecting cans at motorcycle events as a means of survival.

Now for the second strangest wonder of the world, the Bell Boy from Hell! This eccentric phenomenon is questioned to be part human and part monkey. He is the last descendant of the genetic pool in the flying monkey family—this is no hoax! If you don't believe me, come in and see it with your own two eyes.

Smoking is permitted on the street stage, so don't be shy. That clean, lean, cigar-peddling machine, Bean're will happily get you a quality cigar served with style for you to enjoy during the

Sidewalk Sideshow

show. He's the tall gentleman in the psychedelic purple suit and his girls are always ready to serve you!

So step right up to experience the true Carney power that lurks around the streets of every bike week in the United States! File in a single line, pull out your dollar bills, pay the pretty lady on the left, and step behind the curtain please, clothes are optional! After the show, don't forget to pay a visit to Loretta the Pin Lady, who's famous for supplying trinkets and treasures to every freak and fellow biker. I promise you, she won't let you go home empty handed! Rodent the reporter will be scurrying through the crowd recording the buzz, so please watch your step. And make sure to smile when approached by this scraggly little rat with a camera, because your mug might just show up in next month's motorcycle magazine!

You're Next

Now, Ladies and Gentlemen...there has been much controversy around the world as to whether our last oddity is man or myth, real or cartoon. When you meet him, prepare yourself to laugh, be astonished, and even traumatized! Ladies and Gentlemen...The Ice Cream Man From Hell is here to perform his rough and ready magic for all to see. His street rap is not for the weak, and I promise you it's sure to be an experience you will never forget!

And now, I give you your host for the evening, The One, The Only, The Ice Cream Man From Hell...

Human curiosity and eagerness to be amazed has fed families since the P.T. Barnum and Bailey days. All my fast talk and flashy costumes would be useless if I didn't have my rap down. It draws the people to me, but that's not all it takes! You have to be a damn good performer to make the whole gig work. When I became the Ice Cream Man From Hell, I invented some timeless antics for approaching unsuspecting victims and some unforgettable lines that were sure to burn in the memory banks of all the show seekers. I'm a street performer, at least that's what they call us these days. When I roam around an event, I have a prop in every pocket and my timing is right on!

My performance training stems back to my shoe shining days, even then I knew how to get people to pay attention and reach into their pockets. Every now and then I go back to my humble beginnings and shine shoes at motorcycle rallies. I've changed my routine a bit and of course I charge a five spot now. Hey, it's called inflation muscle head! When I was shining shoes during Daytona Bike Week in 2004, I came up with a new crowd pleaser. In my shoeshine box, the same one I've owned since I was a boy, I've added an extra can of brown and some French bread. The days are long and hard when I'm a shining, and a man gets hungry ya know! Just before the second shoe, I always break off a hunk of bread for a quick snack. My customers are sickened when they witness me dunking my bread into a can of brown shoe polish like it was marinara! "Hey, don't puke on your own shoes. It'll cost you an extra five spot! I'm just trying to having a little lunch over here."

It was my crazy antics that got me called into New York City in the early '90s by some close friends to work a gig called Biker Slut Night. The Indian Larry Circus was performing in the Ole Pavilion Arcade on Surf Avenue, and they asked me to join the festivities. The show brought the bikers into the city, who at the time, were in the know about Larry's crazy antics and the underground scene of Psycho Cycles.

A good show is not gauged by how many people come through the door or how much beer is sold, not to the performers anyway. A good show is all about the vibe! If the audience is enthusiastic, the performance is a success. The more you're willing to participate, the harder we work, and that's what makes the magic! It's that simple.

Sword swallowers, fire-eaters, human blockheads, and rubber girls amaze the spectators. They create an unrestrained environment and permit the human mind to run wild. The gals were loose and more than willing to participate on stage. The Old Burlesque style atmosphere made all the women feel of equal beauty. They were comfortable and eager to show their skin. Coney Island entices the imagination, which is what makes it so special. There are no projectors or cameras, no high dollar props to feed your brain—it's just good ol' Vaudeville.

Indian Larry demonstrates his painless pleasure of lying on a bed of nails while everyone waited in anticipation for his wife Bambi, the Queen of Coney Island and the most beautiful Fiji Mermaid in existence. Larry and I carried Bambi to center stage and propped her up on a stool. She exposed her strange land diet of live goldfish and cat food to the onlookers. Being the Madonna of Mermaids, she couldn't rightfully walk around on dry land with

You're Next

fish breath. So, she grabbed the only thing available, a clear blue concoction of ammonia—better known as glass cleaner and sprayed it into her mouth to freshen up. During Bambi's performance we hung out on the fire escape and gawked at the freaks in the audience, while the audience gawked at the freaks on stage.

For the grand finale, a porcelain claw bathtub was placed in the center of the stage. It was time for the Pirza Wine Bath—a Coney Island tradition. We placed Bambi in the tub, her golden locks spiraled over the smooth porcelain and her aqua leather mermaid tail fanned over the edge. Standing eye level to the stage, you could see the tops of her glistening breasts. Bottles of wine were poured generously over her fair naked flesh—we turned into animals!

Once the tub was full, Larry and I baptized ourselves in the warm red liquid and I drank directly from the tub. The entire night was right on the edge and the grand finale was so erotic that everyone in the room had a mental orgasm.

When I'm in Brooklyn one minute and Daytona the next, I got to create illusions of myself to keep the people in anticipation. Since I'm only one guy, I keep cardboard cut outs of myself in different locations so that I can be in more than one place at a time. That way, if anyone has any questions, they can ask me directly. It's a costly prop, but the investment is priceless.

At the Iron Horse Saloon, another innocent victim was pranked by the Ice Cream Man From Hell's antics and I wasn't even there to enjoy it...but boy did I hear about it! It was free beer hour, the suds were streaming and everyone was well on their way. A little beer breath babe came stumbling down the midway and lost her balance right in front of my booth. Lucky for her, I was right there to catch her fall! As one foot twisted around the other, she reached out for my assistance. When she figured out which one was her left and which was her right, she adjusted her step and thanked my cardboard cut out for catching her fall! After burping in my face, she stumbled on down the row. Pretty good illusion huh? Next time I'm gonna see if I can get that stiff a blowjob. It's the least I can do considering he works so hard for me!

Our next hardcore performer is J. J. Steel...a man who lives the life of fire breathing, high flying, motorcycle jumping mayhem. J. J. is a live super hero exploding from the pages of a comic book — he rides fast, turns fast, eats fast, eats ass, breathes fast, and lives fast. His balls are always to the wall. I personally enjoy blowing shit up, so when he asked for my assistance with the pyrotechnics for a jump that he was gonna perform at the New England Summer Nationals in Worcester, Massachusetts, of course I said yes! The burn out pit was set in an underground tunnel that parallels the main drag of the show. The concrete walls that perimeter the pit are used as a perch for spectators to dangle their legs from and smell the burning rubber. J. J. asked me to grab the microphone and get everyone prepared for his jump...

"Ladies and Gentlemen, at this time anyone who has a pace maker, heart problem, vertigo, shortness of breath, is hearing impaired, or has any other physical condition that cannot withstand the acoustics from the pyrotechnics of this show, please make your way down Main Street at this time. Once again folks, anyone who has a physical condition that cannot withstand the acoustics from the pyrotechnics of this show, please make your way down Main Street. Now for anyone who was not listening—this is your last warning! Everyone and anyone who is sitting on the wall needs to remove themselves at this time. The bass from the pyrotechnics of this thrill show will shake the barriers causing you to fall face down. I know it's the best seat in the house folks, but for your own safety as well as the stuntman—move your ass!" No one was budging. I turned to J. J. Steel and he gave me the thumbs up, what more could we do?

One...Two...Three...**BABOOOM!** J. J. came flying out of the tunnel at a supersonic speed just as I set off the bombs. People were dropping like flies into the pit! Arms and legs were flailing while bodies flew backwards onto the street. Soda cups were spilling, popcorn was popping, women were screaming, babies were missing and the Coney Dogs were airborne as J. J. soared through the sky for hundreds of feet and hit the ramp at the far end of Main Street! You could hardly believe it—even though you'd just seen it!

"Ladies and Gentlemen, J. J. Steel has made the landing on two wheels! Folks, have you ever seen anything like this in your life?! This man has risked life and limb for your pure viewing pleasure. For those of you who missed it—I told you to get the fuck off the wall!" Some people just don't listen. "All Hail, J. J. Steel, the greatest motorcycle stuntman who ever lived!"

Bring the baby and your lady, just make sure she's under eighty because the thrills, chills, and spills of The Wall of Death

may put her to rest. This is an action packed motorcycle thrill show you don't want to miss! The Wall of Death is a wooden barrel that stands fourteen feet high and twenty feet in diameter. Inside, a team of daredevils ride classic Indian Motorcycles on ninety-degree perpendicular walls. Just like a carnival ride, the barrel is portable and moves from event to event just to thrill and entertain you. This tradition dates back to the early 1900's and today there are only three Walls of Death left touring the United States. One of the families that passionately keep this show alive, a show that is appreciated by only a handful of people who marvel in its authenticity is, the California Hell Riders. Something I've always admired about this family besides their massive balls is that they choose to compliment each other and never compete..."In our show

You're Next

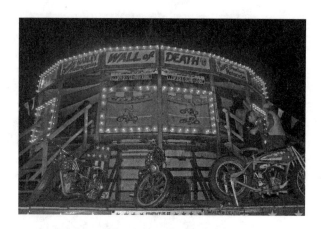

there are no stars, we are a family. Each member completes our circle." That's their motto and the loud siren means it's go time. It's show time and their rap goes a little something like this...

"We're about to start another show down here at the Wall of Death. It's a show for the young as well as the old, a show for the ladies as well as the babies! It's a thrill a minute, a mile a minute, with each and every spin of the motorcycle wheel. Just picture it folks! You're sitting in your living room, you're watching the New England Patriots on your TV. You've got your feet up on the recliner and all of a sudden—this crazy guy on a motorcycle is cruising around your living room walls! Well, that's exactly what we do down here at The Wall of Death. We just took the corners out to make it a smoother ride! You're not going to go on the inside and see strings, wires, or mirrors—there are no midgets running around the outside of the barrel with a magnet. This is not an illusion! Just real live flesh and blood daredevils that risk their lives and limbs everyday just to thrill and entertain!"

In the spirit of the new liberated female motorcyclist, there are a few women that need to be acknowledged. If it weren't for these women, Harley would've never persuaded you to ride and you probably don't even know them. Let's get real girls, it's a man's world out there among the motorcycles, but it's these women who've held a stake and laid the groundwork for the female riders of today. Don't get me wrong, it's great that more women are riding motorcycles. I just think you should know who had the guts to be players on the scene long before you and your girlfriends designated it fashionable. Sam Morgan and Sandra D are two of the hottest chicks on the earth and they ride The Wall of Death for a living. They could smoke any dude I know on two wheels! No fear resides in the hearts of these women and that's part of why they're so good at what they do!

Please prepare yourself for our next act, and if you fear the supernatural I suggest you step aside. The first time I met Goth was at a party in North Carolina called The Smoke Out. I had heard the buzz about her but never actually laid eyes on this freaky chick. I was sweating like an altar boy on my knees in the blistering Carolina sun when I spotted an army of dudes standing around this Chevy Van. Who the hell was in there—the Pope? They were guarding the van like it was an armored car. People were on their hands and knees begging to get inside and take a peek. I marched over and explained who I was and managed to weasel my way in. I didn't know who or what was inside, I was just hoping it was air-conditioned. Someone informed me there was a devil doll from the west coast inside. When I stepped into the van, there was a mountain of colorful silk pillows and draperies spread out like the fucking Taj Mahal. David Bowie wouldn't be playing a biker party, this was getting fruity. I closed the door behind me and crouched on the floor…I was silent. A milky white hand with dark purple painted fingernails slithered out from under the mound of posh pillows and I reached out to grab the porcelain doll. Oh my Goth! I almost shit my drawers. Goth sat up and introduced herself, her pale divinity caught me off guard—within seconds I was intrigued by her strange beauty. She's the kind of girl who puts makeup on to go to sleep. Her demeanor was vibrant and her fast dialogue and body language was like a shot of adrenaline and strangely comforting. I was at ease now that I realized she was among the living. Goth informed me that we'd be sharing the stage that evening. I thanked her for scaring the living shit out of me and exited the van. I was chilled to the spine and no longer needed the air conditioning.

That night when Goth took the stage, she started the show with some intense classical music. I was spellbound—it was breathtaking. She had an eerie supernatural innocence about her, like Tori Amos…she was not just another piano man. Before

Goth had a chance to move into her creepy carnival act, some stupid redneck bastard in the crowd started yelling, "Free bird! Free bird!" The people were losing interest, I could see their eyes moving away from the stage and their lip service was escalating. Goth was losing her audience and growing frustrated with the natives. I knew I had to do something—this was bullshit! I grabbed the microphone and made my way to center stage...

"Ladies and Gentlemen, do you know who this is?! Let me hear ya scream! Tonight we have the one, the only, Goth Girl, all the way from San Francisco! Have you ever seen a dead girl look so good and sound so sweet?! Let's give her the respect she deserves, let me hear ya scream! The louder ya scream, the harder this girl is gonna play, and maybe if we're lucky—I can get her to play topless! But ya gotta scream!" That got the crowd's attention and it sparked an unbelievable fire under Goth's ass! She played her heart out that night and got the respect she deserves. The only sad part to this story is, well, I never did get her to take her top off!

This next genius is mother to no man and the only thing tying her down is a hundred pound Doberman pinscher that she takes along for the ride. Holding your own in this world can be hard but Miss Chrissy the Patch Queen has beaten the path of motorcycle anarchy into submission! Moving on from town to town and being in the carnival is just a way of life, it's not for everyone, but some people can't live without it—it's in their blood. Most men consider her a bitch because her high boot, motorcycle riding, spandex wearing ass wouldn't fuck ya for practice! Her bee-bad ways and loud mouth has been pulling dollar bills from the pockets of rough and ready bikers since she was eighteen. Chrissy's

You're Next

boisterous growl is an attraction that lures you into her lair of pins and needles—it's a sight to behold! Let's listen in...

"Back off! You've gotta be smarter than the patch! That's why I'm in charge here and you're not. How many times in your life do ya have to hear that "size does matter" before you believe it? That's why I told you to go with the larger patch...a lady never lies. Now, just give me your leather and stand back! Don't try this at home and let me tell ya something else, I ain't your fuckin baby! Now shut up and pay up!" It's enough to make anyone scurry for their wallet when watching this master of mach speed sewing puncture through patches in a frenzy! You'll probably leave the stitch bitch's presence with a bruised ego but it's all in good fun. She's a true road warrior and one hell of a lady!

Our next freak is all the way from Oz. That tornado in Kansas swept his house away because it was made in Japan. He takes his sidewalk act seriously and will cater to your needs whether you're a good witch or a bad witch. So, as you can see by now, I'm not the only one that lurks in the alleys of the motorcycle rallies looking for innocent victims to make memories with!

Back in 2000, I started getting phone calls from people on the street, they wanted to inform me that a little flying monkey was creeping around the motorcycle circuit and his name was the Bell Boy From Hell. Shortly after the word was out, I received a letter in the mail from this guy claiming he had been following my antics for years and wanted to share in some of the fun! He expressed his admiration for the

Ice Cream Man From Hell and his only wish was to get out of his skin during the rallies. Lucky for him, I had just placed an ad in the newspaper for a personal assistant. You know, someone to open doors and carry my baggage. How could I say no to this guy? He was so sincere, and he is, after all—The Bell Boy from Hell! Womb Service Anyone?

    Please don't be afraid to shake our next oddity's hand. He may pick his nose and occasionally drool, but that's only because he has half a brain. I stumbled upon this retarded fuck, Pee Wee Davidson, at the Volusia County Speedway in Daytona, Florida. He wanted to trade me some cans he had collected for some ice cream. Of course, I couldn't take his cans. I gave him the ice cream and then invited him to hang around the booth so I could poke fun at him and show him a good time. I've always had a soft spot for the retards. You know, the ones with the stupid smile that walk around with one ear tucked under their baseball cap? After five ice cream sandwiches, Pee Wee asked me to take him for a ride on my trike. I explained to him that only the ladies were allowed to ride on the back of my trike because they take their tops off. He immediately dropped his bag of cans and proceeded to take off his hoodie and tee shirt. What was I gonna do...say no to the fucking guy?
    The spectators threw beer cans at Pee Wee's chubby little body as we made our way around the track. They were used to seeing only the finest bare breasts on the back of my trike and were disappointed. Meanwhile, in Pee Wee's simple mind, it was a glorious moment and he held his arms high in amazement that people would shower him with the most precious currency on earth—empty beer cans.
    I started to bump into Pee Wee at the rallies on a regular basis. I always offered him food and a place to crash, but he was too proud. He refused to take anything for free and always paid me in cans. I'd take the cans to shut him the hell up and when he

turned his back—I'd put them right back into his bag. I was humbled by his pride and as I got to know Pee Wee a little better, I realized why. He told me the story of his Davidson birthright and that's why he decided to work at the motorcycle rallies. His family refused to recognize him because of his mental retardation. But he didn't care—he was one of the few, the proud, the bastards.

Our next performer is not afraid to choke his chicken in public…the men want to be him because the ladies can't get enough of him. He's the man who has paved the way for goofballs like me hustling the motorcycle carnival and his name is Archie, The Horniest Man in all of Daytona. He has been the notorious model

Isabel and Archie

Sidewalk Sideshow

for Isabel's Body Web Wear, a trend that all of us guys are surely thankful for! Archie has been beating the streets advertising her product while exciting the ladies before some of us punks were off our mother's tit! Nudists by trade, Isabel developed the fine art of body webbing into a fashion basic for bikers. With some spandex and a pair of scissors, she can make you a cat suit so edgy that the cops have to do a double take. Her mission is to do away with all self-loathing and make every woman a diva. Thanks Isabel—Lord knows we appreciate your work!

Even for an old fuck, Archie is praised by men of all generations for his charismatic way with the ladies. In New Hampshire at the '92 Laconia Bike Week, Archie landed the hottest babe in the joint during the Jello Jump. We had filled a pool five feet tall with orange Jello and Archie was the first one in. He was trying to get the young ladies motivated. Every guy in the joint had eyes for this one hot tamale. She jumped into the pool of Jello with Archie and the bitch wouldn't get out! I leaned over and asked…

"What the hell was going on Archie? You're holding up the show!"

"I'm finger fuckin her and she likes it!"

"Enough said Archie!"

I held everyone back. They'd have to wait their turn, besides no one could see what was going on beneath that sea of orange Jello! The next morning, Archie formally introduced me to his new little cutie pie after she crawled out of his motor home. So just to let you young guys know, with your flashy 35G motorcycles, there are still a few old guys on the boulevard you could learn a few tricks from. So, make sure you're taking notes because it's time to observe a few trade secrets. It's a hell of a lot cheaper than that motorcycle you mortgaged!

Now I'm going to tell you about a real straight shooter on the street, the kinda guy that likes to take matters into his own hands.

You're Next

The kinda guy who "Knows When to Hold Em." Which is what Pappy, a.k.a. Pimp Daddy Pappy is famous for. I'd seen Pappy on the streets over the years but the first time we really connected was at Daytona Bike Week in 1997. I was pushing twenty-hour days in preparation for the event. On top of it, several visitors were coming over from Italy. I was loading the back of my pick-up with hundreds of pounds of uncooked spaghetti and industrial sized cookware for my famous Spaghetti Wrestling Contest when the phone rang.

My father was on his deathbed and I was needed in Jersey immediately to make some decisions. In the middle of pounding the bike week streets, I had to slam on the brakes and within hours, I was on a plane back to New Jersey—not knowing what to expect. During the flight, I couldn't help torturing myself about the lost years with my father. I needed to tell him how much I loved him and what a great father he was. You see—I hadn't seen him for several years because of my anxiety over visiting him in the looney bin. We never did tell my father that Heller had died a few years prior, what sense did it make anyway? Frank and Heller were in the same institution and Frank didn't even know his own son was there. As far as I was concerned, he was already dead inside. That's exactly why I hadn't seen him for so many years.

By the time I had gotten off the plane, my father was dead. I had to keep my thoughts of our relationship to myself now. I didn't even get the opportunity to whisper them in his ear. Even if he wasn't coherent, I could've at least said my peace and he could've taken my words with him. It was over now and I was standing on the inside looking out. I was all alone, my father and my brother were nowhere in sight. The white walls and fluorescent lights sent me into a fit of rage. I walked down the hall, I felt like knocking over every stretcher, every cart, and every tray. Several nurses tried to calm me down and I thought about spitting at them, but I knew they would needle me. I think they were confused about whether I was a patient or not. It had all come to a head and I lost it. I had to get out of there and fly back to my wife and finish out bike week.

When I got back to Anna in Daytona, I couldn't think straight and when I finally took a breath, I collapsed. I didn't even have the strength to finish out the event. I didn't care at that point about my commitment to The Black Chicken or that my popularity was soaring. I was hiding out in my trailer as much as possible and had no desire to be on that stage.

This sixty something year old man, with a beard down to his chest, felt the need to say something about it, "Well that's life and that's death, you can't do nothing about it. This is a big event for you. You better wipe your pussy and stay focused because this might be your last bike week if you don't!" Man, I wanted to pummel that ole fuck! Maybe beating the shit out of his wise ass was worth getting up for and would make me feel better.

"If it'll make you feel any better...I'll be your Pappy." I looked at him and smiled. I had never been so touched by a complete stranger. I gave him a hearty handshake and a hug and got my sorry ass out on stage.

"Let's hear it folks! Ya make me wanna scream!" I was back inside myself. Pappy stuck by our stand that whole week and helped me and Anna with whatever he could. Thanks to my Pappy—I made it through another bike week!

Pappy is a famous character on the circuit because of his extensive collection of "Know When to Hold Em" pictures. He has compiled hundreds of pictures from all over the country of himself holding strange women's breasts. His books are more popular than Sleezyrider. Women seek him out to get in his books because of his charming personality. Men seek him out to smell...oh, I mean, shake his hand. He's not just another dirty old man. In fact, he has so much charisma that it's immortalized him. The famous sculptor, Mark Patrick, used Pappy's unforgettable image for a piece entitled, The Story Teller.

You're Next

Here's typical dialog in the life of *Pimp Daddy Pappy*. The scene is set at the Iron Horse Saloon. Although he helps me sling tee shirts on occasion, his real motive is to expand his photo collection of unsuspecting victims...

Pappy: "Hey ladies, what can I do for ya, to ya, or with ya?"
Female Victim: "You're so sweet...I like your beard."
Pappy: "You girls getting into any trouble? Do ya wanna?"
Female Victim: "I like those little skull beads you're wearing in your beard...they're neat."
Pappy: "Yeah...well I like those!" (Pointing to the innocent victim's rock hard nipples!) "It's not cold out here, so ya must be happy to see me!"
Female Victim: "You're making me blush old man."
Pappy: "Ya know, with breasts like those, you could be in my famous archive of photos." (Pappy pulls out his photo books.) "I've got the camera when you're ready—top on or off? It's your call."
Female Victim: "You know what, let me find my girlfriend first, I think she wandered off."
Pappy: "Hey, that reminds me, ya know who was just here lookin for ya?"
Female Victim: "Who?"
Pappy: "Nobody!"

Sidewalk Sideshow

Female Victim: "You're so funny and cute! Let me see those books. You know what, you can take my picture!"
(Pappy has his young protégé, Johnny Socks, take the famous "Hold Em" shot, while Pappy concentrates on not only holding em, but also posing for the camera!)
Pappy: "Come back a little later when the boss man's gone and we'll fool around!"
ICMFH: "She was cute did you get her picture for your book?"
Pappy: "COBB Dammit! Of course I did. I'm Pimp Daddy Pappy! I used to build racecars for a living that was nothing! I'm going to the Porta John now. Ya want anything while I'm there?"

After the peak of my emotional rollercoaster with my family's mental illness that I've had pent up inside of me my whole life and after the agonizing realization of my father's death...there was Pappy. It's amazing how a negative can turn into a positive if you just open your mind and heart to accept it. From the day Pappy gave me the pep talk, I became his adopted, illegitimate, bastard stepchild. Sort of the way I had taken Pee Wee Davidson under my wing. I can't tell you how many people have approached Pappy at the Iron Horse and said, "How's your son?" It's our eternal joke!

Biker events have become tent filled streets, cluttered with cheap leathers and trinkets—a flea market of baby clothes and "made in China" stickers. The sidewalk sideshow has kept the true spirit alive of the independent, rambling on roadie biker, despite all the high dollar items you see. We are a dying breed of street performers who've paved the way for people like Jesse James and Orange County Choppers. The truth is, Jesse was still in the sandbox while we were beating down the path. This may be the first time you've been introduced to The Sidewalk Sideshow and the people in it. The one thing you really need to know is...We are the lifeblood that

You're Next

flows through the veins of the rallies, the circus, the subculture. However you chose to label it. We are the beat of the road and the pulse of the street beneath the rumble of your big motors. We've been out here trying to keep this thing alive and feed our families long before it ever invaded your living rooms. Don't get me wrong, it's nice you've decided to join us. After all, life should be viewed through the eyes of its beholder and not a television screen—I admire anyone who has the desire!

Chapter 9

Misadventures and Half Truths

I think the guys would agree that the best sanctuary for insanity all year long is Oley, Pennsylvania—what we can recall of it anyway! This best kept biker love fest has manifested over fifteen years of great memories for me and my fellow road warriors. It's all about celebrating why being a free wheeling motorcyclist is so damn great!

The first time Anna and I stepped into those sacred corn fields in Oley, we parked our rig a hundred and fifty feet away from the free beer so there was no way you could miss us. We had a decent afternoon of slinging frozen cow's milk. When the sun faded away you could smell it in the air—this was going to be one wild party! I got a gut feeling that I needed to prepare myself for a very rare sight called the Puerto Rican temper. The drunks were leaning on *Anna's Ice Cream* wagon and puking on the rubber—she wasn't having it. I covered my eyes in fear of what was about to unfold. I knew those poor bastards were in for it and there was no way I was getting in the middle—they were on their own! A few minutes later when I didn't hear the wrath of Anna, I peeked out from under my vest and she was laughing. The bikers were actually being cordial to her requests, I couldn't believe it!

Yes, yes, yes, this is an ever so touching tale, but let's be honest here—if that's the best I could give you, they wouldn't call me, *The Hardest Working Man in Ice Cream*. When I'm out on the road working, I have a good time, and believe me there are always opportunities for me to have a hell of a lot of it. You see, I'm on the road for over two hundred fucking days and nights out of the year. I've seen and done a lot of shit, but having all this fun really isn't easy on the brain or on the sack. Road life is hard and I just can't help but miss the hell out of Anna.

Once I get home to her, it usually takes me a good two weeks to screw my head on straight. After I've had the chance to wash my brain and ring it out to dry, I look forward to sitting in the basement shooting the garbage with the guys and sharing the *Misadventures and Half Truths of the Ice Cream Man From Hell*.

On that first night in Oley, we set up camp behind the beer trailer—what were we thinking? Talk about no shut eye! Those cats stayed up twenty-four/seven and marched back and forth for the all you can guzzle special. The empty keg pile literally reached the sky! I stuck it out and scoped the scene even though I knew this wasn't a place to be selling ice cream. When people are boozing the last thing they want is dairy.

The next morning I suited up, packed the trike, and headed for the hillside of sexpods to witness the aftermath of the free beer. The fields looked like Gettysburg, limp bodies lay scattered next to beer mugs emptied of ammo, and all the campfires had been left unattended. The unlimited suds had claimed their victory—everyone was kicked! The few stragglers that weren't inside their sexpods, I mean tents, revealed themselves from behind the pines while I cruised by and rang my bells. The survivor's body language was eerie, they were too strung out and geeked to speak but I did hear a few people mumble…"Who the fuck is this guy?" So I started shouting my sales pitch…"Ice Cream! Ice Cream! It'll make your motha scream! It's better than Maalox in the morning!" Drrrrrring! Drrrrrring! "Ice Cream! Ice Cream!"

Heads started cocking to the side, limp wristed arms were pointing towards the sky craving the nourishment of an ice cream sandwich—my bells had awoken the dead. I scooted feverishly back and forth from the trenches to my freezer all day. Everyone was

hung over and wanted my sweet treats—I couldn't keep my ice cream stocked!

That evening, Anna and I got several invites to party in Podville. I was unsure at that time if the RMCers were thankful for my rise and shine routine, or if they just wanted to kick my ass for ringing those bells so early in the morning. Or maybe it was my incredibly good looks and fast talking that got us all those invites!

I parked my trike and we took the shoe leather express through the fields. Every camp we passed by had their hands out offering up their rations. People just wanted to make sure we were having a good motherfucking time. From foot long fine ones to firewood, beers to bongs, hamburgers to head, it was a weekend of freedom and indulgence at its best! It's nice to know there's still a place on this earth where people can Party in Peace. It felt like I had

You're Next

closed my eyes only for a second before I was back to slinging ice cream, and now I felt like I needed to take some of my own advice!

"Ice Cream! Ice Cream! It's better than Maalox in the morning!"Drrrrrring! "It's seven a.m. Bring out ya dead! Bring out ya dead!" Drrrrrring!

I couldn't praise my trusty ole trike enough that morning. My skull was cracked wide open from the booze, so hoofing it wasn't an option. The love was flowing like mother's milk and the bare breasts were looking just fine, so I couldn't complain. By dusk I was ready to climb under a rock, I had done a good job of pacing myself but the lack of sleep was wearing me down. I decided the right thing to do was not to repeat last nights performance. Who was I kidding, I was having too much fun—I'll sleep when I'm dead!

That's where it all began, the RMC Anniversary Bash, it was the first place I was accepted as the Ice Cream Man From Hell! Every year since, I've been warmly welcome with open arms and open legs. Whether I decide to sweat it out for fifteen hours pushing popsicles or lay in a pool of my own vomit, the song remains the same at RMC. No matter what the circumstances, I always get…"We love you Jimmy!" I'm so thankful for all the worldwide love I get as

Misadventures and Half Truths

the Ice Cream Man From Hell, that's what keeps me going, but it's personal at RMC because thousands of people call me Jimmy.

"Whether I'm a rock in the street or a leaf on a tree,
When I die, I want my soul to rest at RMC!"

"Hey, Tony I Fucked Em Two Times, being that you're in the club, why don't you tell the guys a thing or two about RMC."

"RMC stands for Reading Motorcycle Club. We're over ninety years old and have more than 1,100 members. We're the second oldest motorcycle club in the country, although there is some debate over that. Every year we hold our anniversary bash on our club's property in Oley, Pennsylvania. There's no debate though, that we host the best party on the planet! Our main focus has always been the sport of motorcycling. We've got a track on our property that's 500 from starting line to finish, with another 500 of shutdown. Jimmy, tell Dominick about that time Brooks had the run in with the KKK."

"Oh yeah Dom, you're going to like this one, but first I got to tell you about Bimi. He was the president of RMC, and he

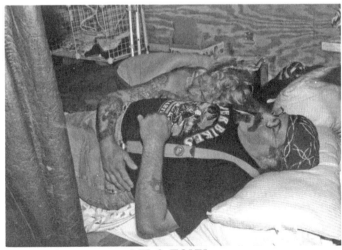

ME & TONY

unfortunately left us in 2004. Bimi never busted my balls, he always insisted that we have fun. Bimi, I hope you enjoyed the sexpool as much as we all did."

I've seen the KKK make several appearances at biker parties in search of some real down home, shot gunning, beer drinking, pussy eating, wonder bread bagging, all American good time. One year Brooks was really hot on meeting the Grand Pooba, you know, the one in the red cloak. Of course, I offered him my assistance. After all, help would be needed in preparing for such a grand introduction. Brooks was so hell bent on meeting this guy that I just wanted to make sure he left a lasting impression. Actually, I recall the first time I met one of their crew, I stuck my head under his robe—I knew something had to be going on under that bed sheet!

Anyway, as Brook's KKK advisory, I suggested that he strip down to his bare ass except for a leather belt around his waist. The blacktop was hot, so I gave him my buckskin slippers and let's not forget about the gargantuan Viking Helmet. Man I got to tell ya, he looked fucking great, like a real whorior—only naked!

Now that Brooks was all suited up, he hopped on the back of my trike and we putted off to the KKK headquarters. I nonchalantly introduced him to the king cone that looked exceptionally tall in that pointy hat. After all the how-do-ya-do's, I stood back, watched, and waited. I knew this ridiculous situation would take care of itself. I was bullshitting with his bodyguard when the Grand Pooba says to me…

"Hey Ice Cream, does yer friend here know he's naked?"

"Yep, he sure does!"

So there was Brooks in his birthday suit surrounded by a bunch of men in sheets. We were all sitting in front of a run down pop up camper that was draped in confederate flags—can you picture it?! What the hell can you do but laugh? The gracious ace gave Brooks a pewter pin of hate and he scrambled for a place to put it so not to be rude, but he was all skin!

Misadventures and Half Truths

    The King Klan's bodyguard grabbed a camera and started shooting pictures of our trailer side chat. For a high hat wearing guy, he was so damn happy to be getting those pictures and I was happy for him…"Gosh man! We live in such a small town. The minute I git dem dare photos developed, you bet the whole community's gonna have a good laugh. Yep, you betcha! Yep, yep, we ain't never seen nothin like dat dare before, I'll tell ya what!" Isn't that the truth? We were all laughing at each other's expense, but hell, live and let live right? Hmm, it's moments like these that make it all worthwhile.

    Stress is a true ailment in this country and we all could learn a thing or two about the road to enlightenment. We all need to get the lead out and freak the fuck out once in awhile just to stay sane. The everyday bullshit drags us all down. I know a lot of guys breaking their backs and busting their humps all week and it's never enough. They come home drenched because the boss man pissed on them only to find out their pretty little wives have been spending their afternoon's gang banging their son's friends. It never ends, life is full of pressures when you're trying to suck the snot stick of the cooperate bulls and still in debt up to your eyeballs!

    Instant idiocy builds character as well as people skills, which are important to ensure success in the working world. When Johnny V is sporting the collar and baptizing women's shoes, he always practices good posture and radiates self-confidence. That's why no one ever questions his credentials. Due to his poise, innocent victims overlook the fact that from the waist down he's wearing Bermuda shorts, black ankle socks and loafers! If you choose to be a go-getter in life, it's advantageous to emulate successful men who've come before you. So take it from the Padre and freak the fuck out once in a while—it'll do ya some good!

    I got to tell you though, the Home for Wayward Women wouldn't be where it is today if it wasn't for the Padre. His kind heart has never been tainted by strict dogmas and he's always been willing to let any women receive confession. Lost holes—I mean lost souls, stumbling around topless feel instantly guilt ridden when in the Padre's presence. But with a little reassurance, they understand that unless open and relaxed, the full benefits of confession will never be received—in other words keep your top off!

"Okay my child, what seems to be bothering you?"

"I thought being a career stripper would be a good idea. I mean, that way I wouldn't have to sleep with anyone for money I could just take my clothes off. But it's so tempting because I'm so pretty! You see, my husband caught me cheating on him. When he walked in, I had a smile on my face and a dick in each hand. Padre, do you think this has anything to do with my father touching me when I was a little girl?"

"Have you been drinking this evening?"

"Yes…why, is that bad?"

"No, of course not my child. Fortunately for you, God doesn't punish the stupid. Now for your penance, it will be a bare hands, bare bottom spanking, while I drop my pants and stand here commando!"

"Oh, thank you Padre!"

As if she had just received a miracle, she gave Johnny the warmest hug and pranced away. They kept coming and the Padre keeps smiling! Priceless isn't it? You know one of my goals as the Ice Cream Man From Hell has always been to do what I can for others. Just like the Padre, I like to see them smile!

"Talking about making people feel good, do you remember the Can Man Jim?"

"Are you kidding me Duke? Of course, I remember that red nosed Polish bastard! We went out to his gravesite last year after RMC to say our farewells and leave him a few cans. He was always one of the guys I'd make sure had a smile on his face when we'd cross paths."

"Are you talking about Pee Wee Davidson?"

Misadventures and Half Truths

"No, I'm not talking about that can collecting retard Pee Wee Davidson, keep up Pappy! I'm talking about that fella who collected cans for some extra jing-aling at RMC's Anniversary Bash for years."

I believe the cash from those cans was his alibi just so his wife would let him hang out at such an outrageous biker party. Like clockwork, she'd drop him off and pick him up in a red Cavalier at the front gate. All the bikers would bag their cans to make his work day go a little smoother. Mostly this act of kindness was committed so that The Can Man could have some extra time to enjoy the scenery. Everyone dug him and he was fun to have around.

The first time I met The Can Man he approached me with his bulldog like jowls and said, "Ice Cream, give me what I like!" So I showed him my selection of ice cream but he shook his head, "No, no, I want one of those girls to let me suck their titties. I just want a little suck you know. I'm an old man—yes?" How could I deny such an honorable request? I had no problem accommodating him, it

You're Next

was that kind of party and I'm that kind of guy. Besides, I got a good laugh watching him gum those big ole titties like a blowfish gasping for air! When all was said and done, he kissed my hand like I was the Pope and in turn, I hugged and kissed him back.

The last year I saw The Can Man at RMC he had a sense of urgency in his handshake, "Ice Cream, you know, I'm not doing so

good. You know, I'd like to ask a favor perhaps." I said sure man, if it's at my disposal. I'd be more than happy to help. "Oh, the doctors, they bug me you know. They say I got the cancer or something—you think you can get one of the girls to suck the cancer out of my prick?!" What am I a doctor now? Of course, I told him I'd see what I could do and if the cancer didn't kill him first, I knew I could find a little lady who'd be happy to give him a heart attack!

Jack the Wack was another one of my favorite people at RMC who had a way with the ladies. Jack had the heart of a lion and the thirst of a camel even though he was confined to a wheelchair. I did my best to make sure he never felt left out. Man, did Jack know how to have a good time. Rest in peace you dirty ole bastards!

Misadventures and Half Truths

"Hey, Tony I Fucked 'Em, did I ever tell you about meeting Ed Roth for the first time at the New England Summer Nationals?"

"No man, what the fuck is the New England Summer Nationals?"

"One of the biggest car shows in the country. It's held in Worcester, Massachusetts and it's put on by this great cat named Bob Moscofian. Ed Roth used to sign autographs at Green Hill Park. It was early in the game for me when I met him back in 1992."

"Ratfink Rules!"

Damn straight Ratfink Rules! That's why I shit all over myself when I met him, I couldn't control my excitement. I was tooling around on my puttsicle when I spied him signing autographs, so I slammed on my brakes. I was having flashbacks of my school days when I used to color in the Ratfink and the Junk Yard Kids coloring

You're Next

books and impressing Triumph Mike with my Ratfink keychain. I cut in the front of the line and started acting like one of those little rat bastards that stands around *Anna's Ice Cream* truck. "Wow man, look, do you know who this is? Big Daddy Ratfink! Man, I can't believe I'm standing right next to you!" Ed pulled me aside and told me to calm the fuck down and stop acting like an idiot. He told me that he admired my rap and that he thought I really had something going, but he didn't have time to talk to me right then and there. He asked me to meet him later that evening at the hotel he was staying at downtown. Wow! Ed Roth wanted to hang out with me. This was one of the best days of my life. So I wiped the stupid grin off my face, gave him a hearty handshake, and told him I'd see him later.

I met up with him that night in the lobby of the Crown Plaza Hotel on Main Street. We sat in a small bar and I sipped a cocktail while trying to keep my composure, but I was too damn excited! I was looking rough from weeks on the road. Actually, I looked like I always do, but for the first time I felt self conscious because Ed had something to say about it. He told me again that I really had something going with this whole ICMFH concept but that I looked dirty…I knew that…I always look dirty!

Ed was just trying to give me a little business advice. He told me flat out that even with my winning personality, I looked like a walking billboard for trouble because of my dirty duds. A stereotypical rough and tough biker, which wasn't necessarily a good thing for my image in his opinion. He kept saying, "You look dirty. You just look dirty and I can smell trouble all over you." He suggested that I clean up my image a bit in an effort to be a more approachable guy to the general public. I understood what he was getting at, but if that statement had come from anyone else, I would've told him to fuck off. For years, Ed sported a tuxedo and top hat to draw attention while he was airbrushing and it worked for him. Unlike me with the long hair and dirty ass cum stained

Misadventures and Half Truths

Ed Roth (center left)

vest. So I finished my drink while we bullshitted about building cars. Right before I split, I gave him my card and told him to call anytime.

    A year later, the phone rang and to my surprise the voice on the other end was the one, the only, Ed Roth. I didn't know if I'd ever see him again and now he was calling me! Ed said he couldn't get me out of his mind, so he decided to draw me. He wanted to fax some artwork over and if I liked it, I could do what I wanted with it. He sent the drawing over and I immediately called him back. The first thing I wanted to know was why I had short hair in the picture and he said, "I told you already Jimmy, you look dirty and I'm trying to clean you up a bit for the kiddies." I just kept my mouth shut, Ratfink was doing sketches of me and my classic '54 Chevy Ice Cream Truck...how could I complain?! I can't even tell you guys how honored I was, but being the rat bastard that I am, before I put his drawing into production for a new tee shirt design, I drew a ponytail. Hey, I've always had long hair!

Actually, that drawing was the spark that lit the fuse under my ass to build my '54 Pro Street Ice SCREAM Truck that was featured in the *Discovery Channel's* Monster Nation Series—Hot Even When it's Cold Baby! I used Ed's artwork as the first blueprint for the project. I got the opportunity to share the idea with Dave Cronk, one of the best classic automobile fabricators and creators in the USA! I met Dave at Lead East, another big car show in New Jersey where Anna and our crew used to sling ice cream. Dave dug the

Misadventures and Half Truths

My '54 Chevy Pro Street

idea and the artwork so much that he took on the project of building the Pro Street. It was a labor of love because he believed in the Ice Cream Man From Hell. Dave is the guy who deserves the credit for that badass creation. Even though Ratfink never got a chance to see the Pro Street completed because he passed away in 2001, I put him in my dedication on the side of the truck for helping us make it happen.

It's actually because of Ed Roth that I got to meet Karl Smith, another legendary motor head artist. We had a strange introduction...the first time I met The King of Carney, a.k.a., Big Daddy Rat (not to be confused with Big Daddy Roth), I barged into

You're Next

his airbrush shop on Main Street in Daytona Beach on a mission. I wanted to know who the hell this airbrush artist was that was strutting around the east coast calling himself Big Daddy Rat. Nobody fucks with Big Daddy Ratfink on my clock—how dare he disrespect Ed Roth! I got in Karl's face and laid it on the line. I thought he was ripping off a legend. Karl claimed that he'd been on the block just as long as Ed had and if I had a problem with it, I'd better go directly to the source.

The next day I put in a call to Ed Roth, he was calm and reminded me again not to act like a dirty little punk—it wasn't necessary. He explained that Karl's East Coast, and he's West Coast and even though their artwork was similar, he'd never taken offense to it. Ed told me that there was more than enough room for both of them and after all, there's only one Ratfink! That's all I had to hear. I put my tough guy attitude away. If Ed was okay with it, then so was I.

You see, I was still new to the game and had just started showing my face around the Daytona Bike Week streets. Daytona Beach was Karl's turf and his airbrushing was not only a cultural icon for bikers, but he also started the most prestigious bike show in the world called the *Rat's Hole Show*. His show got so much recognition and was so heavily publicized, that it eventually became a traveling biker circus and one of the stops was Italy. Karl asked me to go along for the ride because he would need a baggage handler, someone to open doors for him and act as an interpreter. Lucky for me, I speak fluent Italian, so I was the right man for the job. I was brand new to the scene then, so I had no beef acting as Karl's assistant. After all this was a huge opportunity to get the Ice Cream Man From Hell some international exposure. We all have to pay our dues and I was just grateful that Karl took me along for the ride!

The *Rat's Hole Show* was a hit over there and we were treated like kings! The event is hosted by Italy's famous *Bikers Life Magazine* and, man, did they sure take care of us. I have to say that I dug the

Karl Smith in Italy

bike scene in Europe more than the States. Don't get me wrong, I dig the American scene but you got to see the crazy rides they're building over there man!

The major difference between the American and European bike shows is that in Europe, the motorcycle culture is predominantly male and their builds reflect the '60s and '70s style of bikes built in America. The look is rough and ready and anything you can chop, you can ride. It doesn't matter what it is. The bikers over there look like warriors of the lost days because of their crazy

You're Next

Mad Max style creations. It's a trip to experience. I wish the US would switch back. Somewhere along the line our motorcycle culture had forgotten that the core is riding—not how fucking good you look. In Italy, their creativity overrides the dough!

When I got back from Italy, my face started popping up in foreign publications all over the world. Which opened the international floodgates of media exposure for the Ice Cream Man From Hell! Camera crews from overseas, particularly *Bikers Life*, started hunting me down at American Bike Weeks to bring back updated reports to their countries. I got several invites back to Italy after my trip with Karl and I got instant acceptance from the culture. They loved my shtick. It probably had a little to do with the fact that I'm a guinea myself.

"That's a great story Jimmy, but it isn't the best you got. Tell them about Karl's funeral."

Roger Lohrer, International photographer

Misadventures and Half Truths

One of the only funerals I ever went to was Karl Smith's. His untimely death occurred during Daytona Bike Week in 2002. It was the 30th anniversary of his World Famous *Rat's Hole Show* and that's where the service was held. I don't know what it is about people dropping like flies around bike week, but I do know that I hate going to funerals. I'm extremely uncomfortable with the whole concept and I usually skip out. It makes no sense to me why I should be cooped up in a hot building waiting in line to look at a dead guy—no disrespect! Although I was uncomfortable with the thought of standing in front of thousands of people and talking about Karl, when asked, I accepted. I didn't know what I was going to say, so I had to stop and think twice. After several hours of pacing Main Street, the answer came to me. I'd say exactly what Karl would want me to say.

The day of his service, I held my composure, no one needed to know how uncomfortable I was. Besides, this wasn't about me, or them, it was about Karl. I was last in line to speak and I paid close attention to my surroundings when nearing the microphone. Sometimes I'm like a bull in a china shop and I didn't want to take out any flower vases, or bump into any of those custom bikes! I was so damn nervous but like the Padre always says—God doesn't punish the stupid.

I reached for the mike and thanked everyone for coming to honor the life of such an admired man, Karl Smith, Big Daddy Rat. In the midst of a deep breath, my cell phone rang. I excused myself and turned my back to the group of mourners who were appalled and impatiently waiting for an apology. There were TV cameras and journalists all over the joint. It was bike week and I had to answer the phone, for all I knew one of my people might've had a problem. This wasn't good. I spoke for a moment with the voice on the other end while the whispers behind me escalated and I started to break a sweat. I turned around to face the fleet of fuming eyes that were all fixated on me. I opened my mouth in an attempt to make an

You're Next

apology, "Ah, sorry for the interruption folks, but that was Karl Smith, so I'm sure you understand why I had to answer it. He asked me to convey a message to you. Karl would like you all to get the hell out of here. Get off your cell phones, get on your bikes, and go for the ride of your life!"

After conveying the message, I smashed my phone on the ground. I waited nervously for the crowd to register what I had just said, or to take a punch in the throat, and in no particular order. Instead, the crowd exploded into applause! Most importantly, the distressing vibe that lingered over the *Rat's Hole Show* dissipated. The international camera crews stopped grinding and started grinning. Everyone went back to celebrating the show and soaking up the Florida sunshine.

As I get older, the topic of death really fucks with my psyche, but it was pointed out to me that the more people you know, the more deaths you're going to hear about. So where do you turn when contemplating deep philosophical questions about life and death? You turn to the Pope Mobile bro.

"The Pope Mobile, of course!"

The Pope Mobile, better known as the Oley Kow, was part of a little gathering called Italian Day that I orchestrated for my fellow WOP-azoidians at The Black Chicken during Daytona Bike Week 2000. I felt compelled to make sure they were warmly welcomed and felt right at home. So I decided to re-create a little piece of the Vatican. Seeing that Pope John Paul II had just come to America and didn't get a chance to swing over to Daytona Beach—I thought he'd appreciate the gesture. So I hooked up with Outrageous Rick, and old friend from West Virginia. I purchased a Chevy Cargo Van and got to work. The first order of business was to strip it down and paint it white, metal blue wasn't my vision. We installed a four by three foot Plexiglas box top that had a two-body capacity. You know what I mean, we'd be able to fit two broads in there. We cut a hole in the roof of the van so that we could crawl into the box, I like to call it The Pope Dome. We reinforced it with a slider that was sturdy enough to stand on. We stocked the van with cardinal hats, matching drapes, nun's attire, black shirts, white collars, compliments of Padre John, and a few sex toys. Thus...The Pope Mobile was born!

We piled in the van along with Duke, Anna, and a few other guys and headed towards the beach for The Pope Mobile's maiden voyage. I didn't know if we'd make it to our destination or not because the vehicle wasn't street legal and The Pope Dome wasn't exactly up to code. It was bumper-to-bumper traffic on Main Street when Anna climbed into the driver's seat. I had her take the wheel so I could get into costume. I was on top of the world. This was going to mark my most outlandish prank yet! I climbed into The Pope Dome and Duke rolled down all the windows and started chanting… "The Pope Smokes Dope! The Pope Smoke Dope!"

Bikers started swarming the van to join us in song and Anna passed out black markers so everyone could autograph the white paint job. Our buddy The Jello King, was dressed like a nun. He was hanging out the window blessing the innocent when he decided we weren't taking it far enough. He climbed in The Pope Dome and stuck his head under my robe. The Jello King was bobbing his head up and down. It must've been the nun in him that made him do it! Everyone outside started rocking the van and I knew we were on to something, so I decided to grab some more recruits. I climbed out of The Pope Dome and left The King to entertain the congregation, while I swooped up a few more luckless onlookers. Two perky souls happily volunteered, they were open to enlightenment and easily persuaded.

"Broads?"

"Of course Redman, why do you think I built The Pope Mobile in the first place?"

You're Next

The Pope Mobile

After a few Hail Mary's, the tasty little morsels had converted to nunnery. I had convinced them to undress and slip into the extra nun robes I luckily had with me. Once we got them into The Pope Dome, they immediately started working each other over while Duke was rubbing one out in the back seat.

"Blow me Jimmy!"

"Okay, okay, but don't tell me you weren't thinking about it Duke!"

Those nuns definitely gave back to their community that day. Their random acts of kindness included making out and going down on each other in front of thousands of people! I can't tell you how much I enjoyed making their fathers proud. What more could a man ask for than to see his daughter carry on like a true Bride of Christ!

Misadventures and Half Truths

I was passing everything I could through that hole in the roof. Dildos, rocket pops, prosthetic parts, silly string, anything to keep the girls amused. Occasionally, I'd pop my head up under their robes just to remind myself they were naked under there. The authorities had no choice but to let us continue down Main Street because we were causing a traffic jam. All the side roads were blocked off so pulling us over would've just created more of a mess. It seemed like it took us forever to get down that quarter mile stretch.

When we split Daytona, our goal was accomplished and the van was adorned with signatures. So we headed to the Black Chicken to prepare for my evening's performance. I parked The Pope Mobile alongside the stage when we got there and left the doors open so my fellow WOP-azoidians could continue their religious experience.

"I'll tell you what Jim, you sure have quite an extensive resume. "WHAT tee shirt?" contests, terrorizing townships, exploiting the Catholic religion, spaghetti wrestling, painting bikes for Trik Daddy with spray cans and dental floss, and I've heard you've spent little to no time performing stunt work. Didn't you ride the Wall of Death?"

"I sure did Pappy, I sure did."

Back in '98 when I was filming a video on Daytona Bike Week, I got the bug up my ass to ride the Wall of Death. I really wanted to impress the film crew and let them get a feel for how diverse I could be. Thanks to Donny Daniels Sr., of the California Hell Riders, I made it through the demanding training procedures that required a lot of mental concentration. Which frankly, I'm not too hip on. I mean the fact that I couldn't have a beer or two before rolling up my sleeves and riding the wall was frustrating enough. I said to Donny, "Who's risking his life, you or me? I'll take my chances!" Riding in circles on a perpendicular wall is tough I tell ya, my equilibrium was shot and I don't like the feeling when my balls

You're Next

hang to the left. When it came time to shoot my Wall of Death segment I felt unprepared, so I opted to have the midgets run around the outside of the Motordrome with magnets to keep my bike upright.

I've also been known to dabble in dummy sky diving. I needed to make a grand entrance to kick off Saturday night of Daytona Bike Week because it was going to be hard for me to top The Pope Mobile from the previous year. After completing my training, I met with the band to go over the plans. I asked them to announce me as I dropped in. Man, I made sure to carefully calculate my landing and got my parachute in order before my jump. I was a little nervous, the slightest miscalculation and someone could get hurt. It was 6:45 p.m. when the plane was zeroing in on the bar. I looked at my watch, if the band was on schedule, now was my cue. The co-pilot opened the door, held my chute, and let go. My heart was screaming as I soared over Flagler County, it looked like a spec of dirt, but I kept my cool. What choice did I have? I was already out of the plane!

"I ain't buying it Jimmy."

"Well good because I ain't trying to sell you nothing Two Times."

One...Two...Three...I pulled the cord—nothing. I was still gaining speed and I pulled it again—nothing. I started tugging at my side and kicking my feet, my parachute wasn't opening! I was soaring straight down at a catastrophic speed...who was going to catch me? Plan B, Plan B, wait—I had no Plan B! I could hear the applause and the rumble of the bikes getting closer as people were being pushed back to make room for my devastating landing. I was helpless—my feet were lead weights—there was nothing left to do but close my eyes! My body hit the ground at full impact.

"That's impossible!"

"COBB Dammit Tony, would you let him finish the story!"

The crowd was silent. Security created a tight circle so my fans wouldn't get hysterical over my unconscious corpse. The people wanted to see it for themselves and security was having a hard time keeping the area clear. Help was on its way. I put my radio away and walked into the bar. I pushed my way to the accident scene. I asked a few people, what the word was—the Ice Cream Man From Hell was dead. A weird beard with a record number of facial piercings gave me the elbow and said, "Hey aren't *you* the Ice Cream Man From Hell?"

"I sure am. What gave it away?"

"Then who's that guy?" He was confused so I explained to him that it was a hunchback bastard who wouldn't straighten up and pay his bills. So I filled his shoes with bricks and sent him for a ride!

As I made my way to the front of the crowd, the shockwave roared down the line and back again before the humor set in. I thought a few of my friends were going to whack me up side the head for freaking them out. I headed for the stage while the dummy was recovering. Once he was back on his feet, he spent the rest of his evening crowd surfing!

"COBB Dammit Jim! I don't know why I hang out with you sometimes! You're an ass wipe!"

"I know, I know! I have focused so much energy into the Ice Cream Man From Hell that I have to tap into my creative imagination and freak people out in order to top myself!"

"Creative imagination, you mean your single brain cell?"

"Exactly! Re-invention of my one-man band is key. When you've been around the block as much as I have, people start to overlook you. The newcomers to the culture, the fashion victims who like to call themselves bikers, are more attracted to the shiny objects and logos then the laughs. Hey Tony, do you remember the Crapper Drags we used to do?"

"How could I forget?"

You're Next

Let's get one thing straight. Long before the re-birth of the chopper craze, before building bikes became a check box under careers, before motorcycles were part of your regularly scheduled programming, guys like me and Two Times Tony were getting our hands dirty drop-sectioning fiberglass Porta Shitters. That's right—I'm talking about chopping and sectioning crappers! Maybe I should put that on my resume so it's clear that I know my shit! Actually I can't take all the credit for this one, the Crapper Drags started at Roscoe's Chili Challenge in Florida but I just took it a step further. Geoff White of Geoff White Racing, who had the fastest Iron Head Sporster on gasoline in '97, was the guy who taught me how to chop a crapper.

"How the hell do you get a Porta John down a drag strip?"

"It's simple Dominick. We use tow straps to attach the Porta Shitter to the bike. You know, like a toilet in tow. You should try it with your kids sometime. Instead of dragging them in a sled behind a four wheeler, hook a Porta Shitter to your bike and take them for a ride!"

"That ain't ever happening, you think the wife would agree to that?"

"Two Times Tony, put the bottle down and give these boys an intro please."

"Today at the Ice Cream Man From Hell Crapper Drags, our team of specialized builders have taken an ordinary, low rate, fiberglass Porta Potties and turned them into real bonafide rides! That's right folks, the first challenge for these builders is chopping and sectioning the tops for the needed material to reinforce the undercarriage. This is just a precautionary measure in case the rider shits his pants, there is only a 20% chance of it misfiring on the viewers! These sleigh rides from hell would have to do a 360 for us to witness a maneuver like that. We can only hope to see this kind of action on the drag strip today! Windows have been cut out on each side of the shitter, so folks standing drag side can witness the sheer terror of the mindless co-pilots that are confident enough to take the slide of life. Our viewers can experience the up-close footage from the shit pipe cams that have been installed in the seat. A quick fact about the Crapper Drags Jimmy, it's only recently that seat belts have been installed for the rider's safety. I'm telling you these competitors are balls out and assholes up, they've put up a fight to get rid of the regulation! The door of the Porta Shitter has been removed for two reasons, for the hell of it, and to ensure that the guy in the crapper will be chewing rubber! Now that our builders have their shit together, and with only minutes to spare, it's time to secure their crappers to the bikes. What these builders must keep in mind is the distance factor. Being side swiped by a crapper would be a really shitty way to go. So keep your distance and let the Ice Cream Man From Hell Crapper Drags begin!"

"What a ride, huh Two Times?" But of course, there's always some right wing fuck that's got to ruin a good time. Much like my sex-capades, insurance companies started banning the Ice Cream Man From Hell Crapper Drags due to high liability. I must be in the wrong business, now that I've laid the groundwork maybe I should be writing insurance policies against myself. In a society bounded by red tape and caution flags, where does a man of my caliber drift to follow through with his visions?"

"You got to go to Hewlett bro."

"Yes, yes, yes, that's right Brooks—Hewlett, Wyoming."

The first time I ventured out west to experience Hewlett, Spider informed me that no matter how much chaos I created, bail would only cost me a hundred bucks a whack. The only strictly enforced laws that are subject to further punishment are of the ole western code, offenses like livestock thievery and trespassing. So, I headed out west with a pocket full of bills, because if what they were saying was true, I had enough to get me through a few days!

You're Next

The first order of business when I arrived in Hewlett would be the local laundromat. I'd been on the road for several weeks and the flies were starting to fester in the laundry bin I like to call the back seat of my motor home. Well I slept in it, and seeing how it's a car, and it has a motor—I called it my motor home. I stopped at the first soap opera I found, grabbed my clothes, and headed for an open machine. I stripped down to my union suit, took one whiff, and realized it needed washing too. Naked, I strutted back to the rental for a place to put my bare ass and popped a hot bottle of rum that was rolling around in the trunk. Indecent exposure and an open container, I'd pay two hundred for that. The few locals that strolled by stopped to ask for a pull off my bottle, but never commented on my attire. The biker carnival was in town so they might as well enjoy the ride, and if not...I'll pay the hundred. As the sun scorched my sack, I realized this could be the land of

Misadventures and Half Truths

opportunity for me. When my laundry was done, I dug through the dryer for something appropriate to wear.

"Let me guess, one of Anna's nightgowns."

"You know me so well Redman, and being that this was such a special occasion, I wore the pink one."

I slipped it on with a pair of clean socks, laced up my boots and threw my ICMFH cape on. It was time to go to work. I drove to another one of Spider's stores and picked up my buddy Reggie Bob. You know Reggie, that Thai fella with a rolling southern drawl, "Shoot Jimmy! Where the hell ya goin dressed up like that there for? Ya got yer self a date or something?" I told him, I sure do Reggie Bob—I gots a date with you! I asked him to escort me down the street because I wanted to freak some people out. With no hesitation, Reggie agreed to be my escort. We walked arm and arm down the main strip of Hewlett unable to contain our laughter. I started to wonder if I was doing this for my own amusement because I was having too much fun to notice anyone else's reactions. Who am I kidding, of course I do this kind of shit for my own entertainment!

As we turned the corner, a cop cruiser was headed in our direction. The approaching car slowed down and the female cop had her eyes fixed on me and Reggie. I gave her a salute to ensure her we meant no harm and that's when Reggie Bob pushed me away. "Man, yer on yer own, you crazy sons a bitch! I ain't got time to be gittin arrested and all!" With that, Reggie stormed back to his post.

I walked a few more feet in search of a place to take a load off. There was a bench in the sidewalk so I set my boot on it to get a good clean dig at my nuts from under Anna's nightgown. I let out a couple of yawns and waited. If that cop was coming back to arrest me, this was worth a hundred. I've never been a gambling man but this was a game worth playing and just as I had suspected, the cruiser was headed in my direction again.

You're Next

I stood there like the Statue of David with my nut sack in the wind, either way I was going to pay the penalty. So I figured I might as well keep my composure. As the car got closer, I noticed there were two people in it. The car slowed to a crawl and the two female officers pointed and giggled at the crazy guy in the women's nightgown. I guess she had picked up her co-worker to show her the sights.

I walked back to camp to change into something a little bit more or less appropriate, it was hard telling around these parts. I put on my street clothes because I needed to search for provisions, but I wasn't getting far because I had lost my car keys. I don't know how women do it, my pants pockets are my brain bag, I keep everything in them.

"Next time you should bring one of Anna's handbags with you."

"You're right Redman, and I know just the one!"

I asked one of the local police for directions to a locksmith and he told me there was no such thing in Hewlett. He assured me that my keys were in the lost and found at the saloon—a lost and found at a bar? Yeah, right! I decided the easier answer was to punch in the back window and hot wire the motherfucker, but the officer insisted that I give it a shot.

The lost and found had worked for over a hundred years and that's why it still exists. I wasn't convinced but I started walking. When I got to the bar, the flies were anxious to report that some lunatic had been running around in a women's nightgown all day claiming to be the Ice Cream Man From Hell. I informed the barmaid of my misfortune and she grabbed a weathered derby from behind the register and told me to help myself. I couldn't believe it—my keys were in the hat! I put back a shot of scotch, thanked everyone for the heads up, and left on my newly appointed mission. To find that queer who had been strutting around in my cape!

No Panties Wednesday is another sight to behold in Hewlett. It's self explanatory, everyone runs around town with no drawers on! After it was established, we started a tradition called The Panty Tree at Spider's store. You know, a place for the ladies to hang their restrictive undergarments. When the Panty Tree is in full bloom, its perfume is so intoxicating that you wanna eat it. I slept under that damn thing all weekend! As the popularity of Hewlett grew, the township got nervous about all the public nudity. Yet every year, The Panty Tree blossomed even bigger…"Want a panty? Take a panty. Need a panty? Give a panty!"

Me and another fellow thrill seeker were hanging with this sex therapist Connie the Contortionist, whose hobby happened to be exposing herself in public. She was down for having a good time, and I just couldn't resist treating her like the bad little girl she thought she was. She was prancing around in a slutty Catholic school uniform and we all felt like she needed to be taught a lesson. That tiny brunette had a tight little ass and weighed in at a C. Seeing we were all professionals, she agreed to be part of my sidewalk act and I put her straight to work. I had this broad twisted up like a pretzel for the cameras. No amount of money can buy that kind of therapy. Maybe I should consider raising my rates. A few of the local cops had already given me several stern warnings as soon as I got into town that year about the dress code. They didn't want my money, just my cooperation. Someone must've tipped them off to my monkey business on the corner because I saw them coming…

"What did we tell you last night Ice Cream?" You're really pushing your luck now! I don't know how we can go back to the barracks without you in cuffs. The only way I can see appeasing the boss is, well, to go back with some evidence."

The cop pulled a camera out of his top pocket…I got the jest of it. While the men in uniform looked the other way, I put my Jacques Cousteau hat on and went to work. I had that sex kitten, I mean sex therapist squeezing her tits together and shoving beer bottles up her pussy! I was on my hands and knees, and in order to get the job done right I'd need some internal shots! I handed the camera

You're Next

back to its owner and split. I stopped to take a breather and wipe my brow, no matter what the demands—we all got a job to do!

"They didn't even fine you?"

"Hell no, those pictures were worth more to them than my measly hundred! I thought it was a good call on their part, I would've done the same thing if I was in their shoes!"

One of the only crimes I've seen committed in Hewlett involved some livestock. Most of the police officers still man their posts on Quarter Horses because there's only one squad car and no meat wagon in the whole town. I'm telling you, it's like the Wild West out there. The two drunks must've been caught up in the spirit of things because just like outlaw cowboys, they mounted two unattended police horses and bucked their way through the crowd. The guilty were no John Wayne, and they didn't gallop off into the sunset victoriously. The cops caught up with them quick and jerked the fools off the horses then cuffed their hands to the stirrups. The officers got back on their horses and with the crack of their whip, started a full canter for town—the outlaws were eating dirt. They struggled to keep their feet on the ground in fear of bone crushing weight of the horses.

"The guys were handcuffed to the stirrups?"

"Yeah, can you imagine it?"

Everyone moved in unison towards the Town Hall to witness the fate of the two amigos. The cops dismounted and secured their livestock and grabbed the teenagers by the collar to give the cowboys a good ole American scorning right in front of everyone. That'll teach them to mess with the west!

"Oh really? I can recall you messing around with livestock Jimmy. That Christmas card you sent all of us one year, wasn't that picture taken in Hewlett?"

Man, I was really pushing my luck that time! A popular beer label set up a promotional display on the main drag that was an absolute ingenious tourist trap. Their time honored logo of the

Clydesdale Horse and carriage came alive against the background of Hewlett's stone architecture. It was such a cool photo-op that I decided to make it a Christmas card. Plus, I happened to be running around in my Cardinal suit, again, so why not? It was picture perfect. Out of courtesy, I approached the horse hand to get his permission to take the photo. He gave me the nod of approval while gorging his lunch. I don't even think he looked up at me, that fat little man never missed a bite. I knew this was going to have to be quick and I couldn't waste a minute. So, I made my way to the horse's good side and lifted up its tail...I stuck my big ass tongue out and rested it dead center in the horse's enormous brown star!

"You're fuckin sick dude! But it *was* the best Christmas card I've ever gotten!"

"Hey, anything to make my friends laugh but wait a minute, I'm not done!"

The fat man had caught me in the act! Food and spit came flying out of the corners of his mouth and he could barely catch his breath as he waddled over to the horse's ass and started barking at me, "Are you sick in the head or something?! What the hell are you doing? I should have you arrested for molesting my horse. Get out of here right now before I call the cops you weirdo!" I told him to say no more. I had gotten my prize winning shot and there was no reason for me to hang around because a hundred dollar bill wasn't going to clear my name that time! I got the hell out of there fast and changed my clothes. If that fat little bastard told the cops that a guy in a red Cardinal suit had molested his horse, they would've known it was me for sure. So I immediately ditched the evidence!

"Jim, are you aware of the *stupid* things you do sometimes, because I got to tell ya, its times like that I'm embarrassed to say I know ya!"

"That's okay Pappy, as long as I brought a smile to your face. That's all that matters to me!"

You're Next

Let me just leave you with this one last thought. Everything I've told you containing random acts of stupidity, violence, molestation, self infliction, intoxication, public nudity, stunts performed, brain farts, eulogies, demolition of government, abomination of church and state, defacing of property, dismissal of rational thought, and all other liability falling under the heading of confusion and bamboozlement were performed by professional jackasses in front of thousands of luckless pedestrians! These events were all executed on the road and could *never* be accomplished from the chair you're sitting in. So, get out there and live a little!

Chapter 10

Price of Independence

From gangsters to guardians, criminals to Christians, and the rest of you all: I would like it to be known that the Ice Cream Man From Hell is not a member of any motorcycle club past or present. Unfortunately, there has been much confusion regarding this matter. Some years ago when the concept of the ICMFH was conceived, it was everything from hell, grandmother from hell, dog from hell, kid from hell, Mel from hell, teacher from hell, doctor from hell, and of course, the Ice Cream Man from, well, you know where. So, the concept works!

My intentions have always been to make a living and have some fun. Nowhere on any Ice Cream Man From Hell merchandise do the letters M.C. appear. I'd like to clarify that there is only one, Ice Cream Man From Hell and that I do not support any one particular cause. The Ice Cream Man From Hell is a registered trade name and **not** an organization of any kind. Peace!
1999 ICMFH Press Release

This press release was written after years of harassment, black eyes, interrogation, and distorted facts. Like I've said, I'm only one fucking guy and I mean it! First of all, I'm not much of a team player and I've never been able to follow the leader. Now don't think I'm a hypocrite because I was part of the first limo club back in the '70s. You know, the Night Raiders or because I was in the boy scouts. Even as a child in Catholic school, the wrath of God and his penguin army didn't stop me from thinking on my own! Now let's start at the beginning of this Ice Cream Man From Hell confusion and I'll explain yet again, why after all these years, I still have to explain myself.

Price of Independence

The concept of service with a smile has left me with a bloody mug more times than I care to remember. I had been riding since I was a kid but had never hung around any biker parties till Pulsating Paula and Jeff hepped me to the scene—I was hooked! I was naive to the club culture side of motorcycling when I first started slinging ice cream out of the back of my trike. In a year's time, I was bringing my trike to every party I could find in the Northeast. It was working, so I created the one, and only, *Rugged Original* full back patch to give the Ice Cream Man From Hell some identity. I modeled the color scheme of this logo to match my classic red and white ice cream uniform. Shortly after my first appearance on the scene with my one of a kind patch, I was hand delivered a letter by a friend. The letter had been given to her by a member of a motorcycle club. It stated that I needed to change the colors of my patch because it resembled their club's patch. They felt I was mocking their logo by copying their colors. They didn't have a problem with my traditional ice cream uniform—just the patch. The club insisted that I change my colors immediately. It was a warning—not a request! They made it clear that if I didn't respond to their wishes, I'd end up like Tom Carvel. Did I mention he died that same year? Enough said!

I immediately retired the vest and had my *Rugged Original* patch embroidered in a new color scheme. I had never created the patch to intentionally step on anyone's dick. Why do you think the traditional ice cream uniforms were fashioned in red and white? Why did Betsy Ross sew red and white stripes on the American flag? Look at a stop sign lately? There's a reason why this color scheme works so well. It's the most noticed, in your face, stop and recognize me color combination that reaches the subconscious mind. That's why! They beat me to the punch on the colors, that's fine, but I wasn't giving up my logo!

You're Next

All subcultures express their nonconformist views in different ways, in the biker world it's a patch. The patches a biker believes in and holds dear to him tell the rest of the culture what you stand for or who you're running with. It's a tribalistic way to let others know your views among a society of people that believe in governing themselves. The patches a biker wears are as permanent as his tattoos and are taken very seriously. At least that's the way it used to be, now everyone's running around looking like a billboard for the factory. Fuck the factory! The reason I chose to go down this road and create an identity for the Ice Cream Man From Hell is because I knew it would get people's attention and confirm that I was a Lone Wolf. What I hadn't anticipated was that my creative and independent idea would generate so much controversy! Here it is plain and simple for those of you who may not understand…it's because of the look of my patch that novices stereotype me.

To this day, no matter where I go, some people think I'm an imposter while others praise me for the wrong reasons. The rumors of any club affiliation have been nothing but a thorn in my side since day one because that's exactly what they are…fucking rumors, and it all started with my *Rugged Original* back patch. Believe me when I tell you, I'm not whining about the beatings because I've been trained my whole life to take them—thanks mommy! Unfortunately, the myths that've surround the Ice Cream Man From Hell have had a negative impact because some fear that I just might be the guy they imagine me to be.

If there's one thing I know for sure, I need to make it clear that I stand alone. I respect almost every motorcycle club that I've come to know on this planet and I look up to the elders who started them, but I've never been part of the herd—nor do I care to be! I made the right decision to stand on my own because I wouldn't be where I am today if I had done it any differently.

The rumors have been so intense at times, that innocent people were getting their ICMFH tee shirts ripped right off their

Price of Independence

backs! Club members were harassing the beautiful people who've supported me and my way of life because they assumed that I'm part of a rival club. It's kind of like the game of football. You don't go into Raider's territory wearing the opposing team's gear unless you want to get your ass kicked! The problem is, a lot of these guys have never believed that I *am* a one man band—season's over, faggot! Hey, have you ever heard of a motorcycle club that has only one member? The best way to handle the club situation is not to preach, keep your opinions to yourself, and keep the peace.

Around 1989, I started hanging with the crew from Psycho Cycles. When we started palling around it created even more confusion and heavier questioning from the clubs. We didn't care! I loved those guys and the feeling was mutual. We were just a bunch of fuckheads who liked breaking balls and riding motorcycles. We became a team and hung around the local circuit together. Being

Psycho Cycles Crew with Moto Guzzi Rep.

that I wasn't a bike builder, it wasn't about that. It was the Psycho's insatiable appetite for the ladies that sparked our friendship. "You bring the bikes and I'll bring the whores." Now that's the way I like to work! I got so drunk and stupid one night with the guys that they witnessed me fist fight a bum in Brooklyn for some fast food leftovers in a dumpster! I have an uncanny ability to make people laugh so hard they drop to their knees. Meanwhile, all I'm doing is being myself.

We had managed to land a major invitation for Bike Night at The Hard Cock Café, in NYC. Me, Duke and the Psychos rolled up our sleeves and got ready to work our magic on the crowd. After the evening's events, the manager tapped me on the shoulder while I was sitting at the bar. Supposedly, one of his staff members had a problem, and his problem was with me—calling him a stupid cocksucker!

"Not me! He must've mistaken me for someone else." I turned my back to the pencil neck geek as he started giving me his "no tolerance" speech. So as usual, when the heat was on, Duke stepped up to the plate and took over.

"Everyone says cocksucker—you've never said cocksucker? Listen, my friend didn't call that guy a cocksucker. Someone else must've called him a cocksucker! Besides, that kid doesn't look like he sucks cock, so why would my friend call him a cocksucker? Do you even know what a cocksucker is? Actually, you look like you suck cock so you probably do. Look, don't come around here accusing my friend of calling anybody a cocksucker. Man you're obviously talking to the wrong cocksucker. It must've been some other cocksucker who called that guy a cocksucker—so move on."

Every time that word rolled off the tip of Duke's tongue, it was like a dagger in the eye! Meanwhile, across the room the guy that accused me of calling him a cocksucker accidentally spilled a drink on one of the Psychos...

"You stupid cocksucker!" Stegmeyer's growl made every

fork in the place drop. He was getting ready to go off like a mental retard! Security bum rushed the scene to break up a potential spitting match. I've said it before, and I'll say it again, "Don't Trust Whitie"—he'll be the first one to give ya the boot!

Outside the bar, a golf bag carrying tourist wearing his Hard Cock apparel stopped us. He wanted his picture taken with American Bikers. We quickly scanned the crowd over that was sitting in the outdoor cafe. Then, like a squad of cheerleaders, we pulled down our pants for the camera—another luckless pedestrian served! "Here's your American Biker, ya faggot!" Man, even back then, as much as we all needed the recognition, we needed the laughs even more! No one was going to tell us how to act...all we wanted to do was have fun and break some balls!

A year went by and we were asked to appear on the Charles Perez Show. They were doing a segment on biker bitches. The purpose of the show was to depict all sides of the biker culture and the women who were involved, from whores to "properties of." Back stage was a circus of half naked broads blasted out of their minds. One of the stage directors was going over some dos and don'ts with us. I turned my back to the conversation, jerking around with the whores was much more fun. I was giving them the Ole New York Inspection if ya know what I mean, just taking a good look to see how clean they were! The noise level in the green room kept escalating and I heard an unfamiliar voice call my name.

"What? Can't ya see I'm busy working over here?" I turned around, it was one of New York's finest motorcycle club members who stopped in to check on me and the screw crew. I was approached by this major player to keep my mouth shut and not to fuck with any of the unspoken laws of the street—just bring the whores. Well who am I to argue with that, besides, I was more interested in the whores anyway! So now that we had cleared that matter up, it was show time. My heart was ready to explode because of the conversation that had just transpired.

You're Next

Three...Two...One...Action. The most memorable moment of the show was this scantily dressed gal who came out of the audience with a dog collar around her neck that read, "Slave." There was a guy on the other end of the leash that looked like an axe murderer. Oh, and another memorable moment was the fact that I didn't get my brains kicked in this time. In the end, the only ones who were humiliated were us jackasses who willingly went on that trashy talk show! If only Jerry Springer was on the air back then, I would've been in my glory...we love you Jerry!

My burning desire for success is what guided me to be a Lone Wolf and the Psychos and I were all on our own trip. We didn't have time for anyone to hold us back. As time ticked away, Psycho Cycles gained recognition because there were too many bikes and not enough talented wrenches in NYC. They blessed the world with some of the most outrageous custom bikes and The Eternal Legend of Indian Larry.

Price of Independence

The original members of the crew eventually parted ways, not due to anybody's fault, just because of life's circumstances. Some have gone to the grave, some have joined motorcycle clubs, and some have moved to other continents, but me, I'm still on the road headed for another joint. Our friendships are everlasting and I love them all equally.

Through the price of independence, I was fortunate to be introduced to a man named Coco. It seems like a lifetime ago that I had the honor and privilege to be in his presence. Coco is the oldest independent European biker known to man, and he lived in Northern Italy in a small town that was abandoned after a devastating earthquake in the '60s. As the legend goes, he was a hermit by choice, a genius by nature, and he had the ability to put a pile of parts together and make them run.

Coco is known to be the first man to ride through Europe on his motorcycle with a patch on his back. He wore two crossed motor pistons cradled in a pair of wings embroidered with blue and black thread. He was an independent long before motorcycle clubs started moving into Italy, so where the original concept of his patch came from no one really knows. Coco never melted into any of the clubs as they started to gain power. He stayed independent and never changed his patch. As a respected elder, he became the mediator of the European motorcycle world in order to keep the peace between the clubs. Coco *is* The Godfather.

The first time I went to Italy with Karl Smith, a close friend suggested that we meet with him. Coco knew of Karl and his World Famous *Rat's Hole Custom Bike Show* and had seen pictures of me in the biker magazines. So, it was arranged for the three of us to meet, he sent someone to pick us up the next morning. I didn't know what was fact or fiction about this estranged biker, but I was hoping I'd soon find out.

We spent all of daylight driving up and down winding dirt roads that were no more than sheep trails. As we climbed higher and higher through the mountains, the elevation and the extremely long journey was getting to me and I was feeling agitated. I had to stop and remember where I was and be careful not to get out of control. Or should I say, act like myself? I kept asking the driver if he knew where he was going and if Coco would even be home. He told me that Coco was always home. There was nothing around for miles and I just prayed that this guy wasn't going to pull anything funny and leave us out there to die. I had no idea what the fuck to expect so my mind was all over the place and I became anxious.

When we arrived at the small abandoned town, I was completely fascinated by everything around me. I had never experienced such solitude. Every aspect of Coco's life emulated independence. He had limited amenities, no phone and the only electricity came from a generator that was reserved for his creations and special occasions. The running water rushed straight down the mountainside and was collected in basins then carried to the house. Coco's only dependence was the soil beneath his feet. I was in awe to witness Coco's way of life because of my own desire to be an independent...it appeared like a perfect set up. In my eyes, this guy was a role model.

Karl and I received a warm welcoming and the food was out of this world! The meats were hand raised and slaughtered and we watched the bread rise as it baked in the enormous brick oven. Coco seemed exceptionally pleased to have Karl Smith in his home. They were two legends breaking bread. This was my home land so I only spoke Italian, except for when I was interpreting for Karl. I wanted to know who the real man was, not the myth. I was so excited to be in Coco's presence—I had so many questions and I wanted to get inside his head but I had to go slow. I didn't want to make him feel uneasy. There was no strange air in the room, it was a relaxed atmosphere so I was comfortable getting my answers. Karl and Coco were two great men roaming different

Price of Independence

ends of the earth and I got to witness their joy for each other firsthand.

A year later, I was invited back to Italy for another bike event. I took Anna with me this time and Coco invited us to his place afterwards. I couldn't wait for Anna to see the beautiful mountains and share in my humbling experience of being in his presence. We spent our days in the wide open field shooting pistols at mock targets and bottles. Coco and I fumbled around while Anna hit every mark with her first round, so we called her Annie Oakley for the rest of our stay. His time was growing short and eventually he'd have to split the scene for reasons I was unaware of at the time. Unknowingly, this would be our last meal together. Before we left, Coco presented me with *his* original back patch. It would no longer be of use to him and he felt if anyone should have it—it should be me. I was extremely honored by his gesture. He understood that we both knew the price of independence.

Only the one who empowers the true heart of a biker would understand the importance of a man's patch. Like I said before, when you wear a patch independently or with a club, it's like your skin, it becomes part of you. You do everything from sleep in it to rush into the mouth of hell with it. I could never put into words what an honorable moment this was in my life. It encouraged me to stick to my guns and stay independent. I'm my own man, independent just like Coco and I'm damn proud of it.

You're Next

One of Coco's life long dreams was to drift into Mexico and live out his life as a Comanchero. He gave me a picture of himself sitting on a horse draped in beautiful embroidered garments and tapestries outlined in a sash of bullets. Shortly after our last visit, Coco spent the rest of his life in exile for reasons I will not go into. It's more important to me that I leave you with the legend of an independent man. Thank you for everything brother, I hope you make it there some day.

When we arrived home from Italy, I was awoken early the next morning by an animalistic scream. I nearly broke my leg barreling down a flight of stairs to get to Anna. She looked at me with tears in her eyes and hit play on the answering machine. While riding his bike, Jeff the Axe got hit by a drunk driver—he was dead. Another Lone Wolf was gone. Fuck! The devastation was overwhelming and my head was in a tailspin. Flat Black Jeff and Pulsating Paula stuck by my side since that first gig in New York. Jeff was one of the few people who were standing on the same side of the fence as me.

Even with Coco's blessing, my problems with the clubs were escalating. Magazine covers and party invitations couldn't cure Anna's pain. It's never been her style. Anna's anxiety over the Ice Cream Man From Hell coming home with a battered face put pressure on my heart. I could feel her tension every time I'd leave for a show, but like a good woman, she never said a word. When I'd come home all busted up, not wanting to leave the solitude of my room in order to re-group my thoughts, Anna would slide plates of food under the bedroom door and let me be. She always knew I'd come to her when I was ready to talk, but right now another brother of mine was gone and I wanted to be alone.

By the mid '90s, it was apparent that my job involved a lot more than selling ice cream. The more my face popped up in the motorcycle rags, the more explaining I had to do. The more publicity I got, the more heat I got. The more everyone got to know my face, the more static I got. I couldn't back down—it was way too early in the game. So I kept myself on the streets and stayed in the public's eye, even though I was in fear for my life. Fuck It! Fuck Me! Fuck You! Fuck em! What scared me even more than the realities I was faced with was the demise of the Ice Cream Man From Hell. It was my purpose, it was my means to spread my message...I was the only one who could ensure that the Ice Cream Man From Hell would be an eternal legend.

Quitting this gig for my own safety wasn't an option, so I found comfort behind a pair of shades. Confused? Well, let me explain. If you look through the photographic history of the Ice Cream Man From Hell, in most of the pictures I'm wearing sunglasses. This has nothing to do with the sun, because I prefer the daughter, and you know I'm not a rock star! My signature sunglasses became a prop to cover my constant black eyes. Ya got to look good for the cameras ya know! Actually, I could give a fuck about that, as my Popeye tattoo reads, "I yam what I yam!" I wore those glasses because of my concern for my loyal fans and friends, and I'll tell you why. I didn't want them to be concerned *for* me and I didn't want them to be frightened *of* me.

I'm not a whining faggot, nor am I a high maintenance kind of guy by any stretch of the imagination. Once again, my relentless fuck you cocksucking attitude is what has kept my head above water, that and my fast-talking WOP-azoid mouth of course! Understand that at no point during these stories am I going to pin any particular motorcycle club for these actions, because the truth is there's no reason to. There isn't a single motorcycle club that hasn't questioned me for one reason or another. They all have their opinion about where I stand and no one more than the other.

After all these years, only a few of the old timers have understood where I stand. I believe it's because they embody the true

You're Next

heart of an independent and that's why they respect the fact that I'm not backing down in the pursuit of supporting my family. When I first got out of jail, I got a tattoo on my forearm that reads, "If they ever outlaw freedom only outlaws will be free." I embrace this statement to the core of my soul and I live by it. I'm not talking about the bad guys with guns and knives. I'm talking about free spirited, free thinking people, which in my eyes, is the true definition of an outlaw.

In the end, it always comes down to the green. Yes, yes, yes, the almighty dollar! Which I believe started this bullshit in the first place. Back in the day when I was still the new kid on the block, some people felt they were entitled to a percentage of my sales because I was working in their town. Fuck that! Because Johnny needs a new pair of shoes and mama wants a new dress? The only person in this life I got to answer to or empty my pockets for is my wife Anna!

It was just another weekend for Anna and me slinging cones and clothes when a group of guys surrounded our stand—and I'm not talking about the cops! I came around to the front of my ice cream sled and moved the conversation into the midway to get them the fuck away from Anna! This one guy, I guess you could call him the leader, though hardly competent, grabbed hold of my vest and started asking questions. The men had an issue with the square patch containing the number thirteen that was sewn on the bottom right corner of my vest. A patch containing the number thirteen is pretty common and can hold several different meanings, it depends on who's wearing it, but this one was unique. Thirteen symbolizes the thirteenth letter of the alphabet, "m" for murder, "m" for marijuana, "m" for mommy. In my case, the significance of thirteen is "m" for money...that's my story and I'm sticking to it!

The leader of the pack decided to pull out a box cutter and cut off my patch. I didn't know what the hell he was thinking or

Price of Independence

why it offended him, but this time I wasn't going to argue—Anna was no more than a hundred feet away. One of the fellas in the welcoming committee piped up, "Hey, aren't you Jimmy from Jersey? Wow man, long time no see! Don't ya remember me? We went to vocational school together, how you doin man?" Before I could answer him, I tried to jog my memory. Did I beat the crap out of this guy, or did he beat the crap out of me so many years ago? Maybe that's what this was all about? "Yes, yes, yes I remember you now. Yeah, life's been good, thanks for asking. Though I got to tell ya, truthfully, I've been better. This is a little awkward as you can see."

The guy in charge pulled back his blade, stepped to the side, and smacked his brother right across the mouth! "This isn't no fucking social call asshole!" After treating his brother like a bitch, he went back to wrestling with my vest, stitch by stitch till the patch was off. I was left with a warning and they walked away with their victory patch. Little did they know it was because of my beautiful wife Anna that they were able to get the damn thing from me so easily.

Well I'm here to tell you that the joke was on them. What the thirteen truly stood for was, the Long Island Boy Scouts Troop #13! I thought it would be a funny novelty to have on my vest because I was only a member for about two weeks before getting the boot! So you tell me, what was so offensive about that patch to have rustled the big boy's leathers? I couldn't make it in the boy scouts, so how the hell could I ever make it in a motorcycle club. Like I said, it's not my bag—I walk alone.

The only thing that cures the negative thoughts from rattling around in my head is a long, hard ride. Don't get queer on me. I'm talking about my bike! After my brutal weekend of being demoted from Troop #13…again, I went for a ride to get my brain in check. I was cruising through the countryside on a 1937 flat black, seventy-four inch Flathead…Sweet!

You're Next

I was miles away from home when I started feeling a little anxious. There was a van in my rear view mirror that had been following me for awhile. My instincts told me something wasn't right, but I tried to rough it off. Fuck em! I couldn't shake the feeling because that same vehicle had already passed me and now it was right up my ass. The blue cargo van pulled out into the left lane to pass me. I was relieved, whoever was driving was just in a hurry. The van was nose to nose with me when the large side door slid open. What the Fuck? Now I was really concerned, somebody was fucking with me! Inside the van was a group of strangers and I could feel their eyes on me. I took a deep breath and cocked my head to the left. Maybe they wanted a picture of my bad ass ride? There were three men kneeling on the floor of the van ready to point and shoot. They had motherfucking shotguns in their hands!

Before the barrel had a chance to smoke, I slammed on the brake, down shifted, and threw my body weight to the right side of the bike. I heard the blasts as I leaned it off the road into the ditch! I let go of the handle bars and closed my eyes in hopes that when the bike dumped I wouldn't get caught underneath it. My body rolled over several times before my momentum slowed and I was flat on my back. I wasn't knocked unconscious, but I was at the point of hyperventilation before I realized I was breathing! My heart was pounding so fast that it was distracting my concentration. I was trying to listen for passing cars on the road but my heart was beating so loud that it was all I could hear and I was seeing stars. "Jimmy pull it together!" I scanned my body with my hands—did I get hit? My brain was racing! Are they waiting at the top of the hill, are they coming back—don't panic! Don't panic! I pleaded with myself. I knew it would take a couple of tries to kick start the bike. Fucking Flatheads—Fuck Me! Somebody wanted to kill me and I needed to get the fuck out of that hole! A rush of adrenaline came over me that was so intense, it felt like I had the strength of ten men. I didn't know if I was injured and I didn't care at that point. I jumped up and went for the bike. I stood it upright and I thrust all my energy into that fucking pedal—the bike fired first kick. I cracked the throttle and high tailed it out of there! No speedometer—no problem, broken mirrors—no problem, blue cargo van—big fucking problem! Parts were flying off the bike but I didn't care, I didn't stop till I hit my driveway!

Even though the van was nowhere in sight, I knew my first course of action was to sell that bike immediately! Back then, a flat black paint job really stood out and the bike was marked for sure, making it too dangerous to ride. It was a hard one to part with because at one time it had been Flat Black Jeff's. If anyone would understand that sometimes you got to base you're decisions on whether it'll catch ya some lead—Jeff would!

I didn't tell Anna about my little run in that day and she never questioned me about selling Jeff's baby. She was used to my wheeling and dealing when it came to rides, so nothing seemed abnormal. I decided to take Anna and a few of the guys out for beers and wings to celebrate the victory that only I knew about. We piled into a friend's van and made our way down to one of our local hangouts. When our crew stepped foot in the joint, all eyes were on us, maybe they knew something I didn't? Man, the stress was really starting to get to me! Everywhere I went I felt like I had to watch my back, it was probably all in my head. Or was it? I was off kilter but in good company, so I had no reason for concern. It was the end of my summer tour and it was time to share the adventures of the Ice Cream Man From Hell with the boys. We laughed and ate for hours like we were going to the grave, it made all my pains seem worth it. I was half in the bag by now and it was time to have Anna take us home, I could barely stand.

We paid the check and headed out the door, Anna gasped when she reached the van. I thought one of the boys was razzing her a bit, so I made my way to the driver's side to get in on the action. All I could do was shake my head, the side of the van was splattered with bullet holes.

Someone must've put a phone call in from the bar, that's the way it works. I can't even put my hands down long enough to enjoy a fucking meal! I'm not a cop caller...so, what do I do now? When we got home, me and the guys pulled the door panels apart, the slugs were still in it. "Fuck it! Get rid of it!" Two vehicles in two days, I should've saved myself a few beans and bought my own damn crusher!

That night I lay in bed with Anna and told her about what happened during my ride the day before. She lay there silent, without a single tear in her eye. Anna is strong but I know her too well, I could feel her insides trembling as we spoke about what to do with this fucking guy...the Ice Cream Man From Hell.

That night my dreams were consumed with thoughts of someone harming Anna on her ice cream truck. We were being watched and Anna was well known around town. Her ice cream route was the same everyday and it wouldn't take much for someone to track her down. Up to this point Anna had never gotten harassed.

The next morning when I woke up, I begged Anna to take a gun with her. We argued and she refused, she didn't even want them in the house. Anna knew how to shoot a gun but she hated them. Under no circumstances would she agree to carry one on the ice cream truck. I pleaded with her, but it just caused more argument. I left it alone because it wasn't open for compromise—she made that clear! I was becoming tender to my fears for Anna's safety and I didn't know what else to do.

Even with the constant problems and harassment the Ice Cream Man From Hell has been faced with, I'm still back on the scene year after year to prove a point—that I'm not an imposter and I have the right to make money just like everyone else! I've never stepped on anyone's dick or taken money out of anyone's mouth. There's only one Ice Cream Man From Hell, so if I'm stepping on anyone's dick, it's my own! The older I get the more it physically hurts taking a punch, but I got a job to do just like everyone else. With a popsicle on my eye, I still barrel through the campgrounds at sunrise, ringing my bells and carrying on.

"Bring out ya dead!! Bring out ya dead!! Cure that hangover with something cold!" Drrrrrring! Drrrrrring! "Bring out ya dead!"

A sane person would've split at the first possible sign of his own demise, but if that were the case, I wouldn't be the Ice Cream Man From Hell! So if drunken days and unconscious nights is what it takes to never bow down—I think I'll manage.

It's the death of guys like Johnny Jet that can cause sleepless nights for a guy like me. I spent some of my summer tour of 2004 on the road with Johnny Jet because we shared a common interest—Fire! Johnny had a 1957 Chevy pick-up with a motherfucking turbo jet engine on the back of it! Wow man—talk about a show! The blue blast that belched and whistled from that engine could set a building on fire. That barrel could cook up some mean human s'mores! He was a bullshitter and our long winded conversations fed my grease monkey with the desire to turn one of *my* Ice Cream Trucks into a fire breathing machine. Hot, even when it's Cold baby! We were going to be in the stunt business together with our trucks and we were going to fill stadiums.

Our day dreams were cut short—real short. In 2005 Johnny was shot point blank in the chest numerous times coming out of a local bar. He got murdered for voicing his opinion. As usual, the papers had it all wrong. They claimed Johnny was a member of a motorcycle club, that's the fucked up thing—he wasn't. He became nothing more than another casualty, an innocent by-stander of someone else's war. Why would I ever question why I can't fucking sleep at night? Everyday of my life I have to think about shit like this. Walk in my shoes for a day and you'll understand.

Attempts have been made by the clubs to keep these wars at bay. A coalition of colors was formed to keep the peace. It was a treaty situation between all the different clubs across the State of Florida. "Live and Let Live" was the motto. I showed up for the first run to confirm my independence as the Ice Cream Man From Hell and to hand out ice cold water to the riders. I was warmly welcome by some, while others were still confused. That's why I was there, to clear the air and answer anyone's questions in hopes to finally put the distorted rumors of any club affiliation behind me.

I left the run with a feeling of victory! After fifteen years, I felt my position in the motorcycle culture was finally understood. A few months later, photos started popping up on the Internet of me posing with different club presidents at the coalition run. Great, I thought, now the general public will understand my mutual respect and that I dig everyone. My warm feeling and good intentions quickly blew up in my face. When the pictures started to surface, I was getting harassed and questioned again…even more heavily!

On his dying bed, Anna's father, a.k.a. Mr. Puerto Rico told me that when you build an empire you create enemies. He was right! I could've been the Ice Cream Man From Heaven, it wouldn't matter. I can't separate myself from the Ice Cream Man From Hell…to do so would kill me in a different way.

Look! Here's the way it is once and for all…I choose to come and go as I please, work where I please and associate myself with whomever I please. I make up the rules of my life as I go, because I am The Lone Wolf. The one thing that is out of my control is what the newspapers are selling you and the rumors people are telling you. So just like the rest of the world, you'll have to

Price of Independence

decide on your own. I hope you understand that the price of independence requires independent thinking! It's an endless cycle but no matter what the status, I'd rather die in my footsteps, despite what anyone believes, and I'll ride till I rot!

Live Free...The Rest Will Follow!

Chapter 11

The Full Circle

My power struggles on the scene had made me submissive to my environment and I started losing sight of the Ice Cream Man From Hell's vision. After so many years of being on the road, I was getting older and the road was getting tougher. Negative thoughts began to dominate my mind. But for now, I did what works best...I started hitting the bottle pretty hard...again. It was the only way I could function. My anxiety molded a painful knot in my gut, so painful that it would make me spontaneously vomit and *trust me* it wasn't the company. Eating, sleeping, and making love to my beautiful wife became out of the question. It was getting too fucking hard to just keep doing what I was doing just because it worked. I was desperate, so desperate that for the first time in my life I turned to a doctor for help.

There was only one doctor that *I thought* I could trust. I'd known him for over twenty years; he had taken care of my family and knew our history. When the insomnia began to make me delusional, I came clean with the doctor about the Ice Cream Man From Hell's unnerving situation. Well, not completely clean, just clean enough to get his attention. I've never trusted doctors and for all I knew, he was just another fucking rat. So, I gave him just enough information in hopes that I wouldn't have to beg for a prescription of Valium. I just needed a temporary fix for my nerves till I could get this situation under control. I figured that when all the nonsense settled down, I could handle it on my own. But right now, I just needed to be numb. After a long-winded fifteen minutes in his office, he sent me home empty handed and uneasy. The following day I received a message on my answering machine from his nurse...

"Hello Jimmy, the doctor called in a prescription for you. Unfortunately, he's too busy to see you today, but he did leave a message. He's advising that you leave the club and to start taking this prescription immediately. Have a nice day!"

The comment about leaving the club went right over my head at first, probably because I was so damn used to hearing it. I knew that cat knew me better than that—I'd told him straight out that I wasn't a club member! I knew he dug the Ice Cream Man From Hell, so what was all the confusion? The doctor prescribed me a mood-altering drug called Paxil for my anxiety. Fuck it! I had no idea what it was all about but I popped those pills in sweet anticipation of dreamland. A month into my new daily diet of meds, I chilled out long enough to catch some zzzs. Those little pills prevented the knot in my gut from flaring up and enabled me to get through my day a little easier. It made my brain a little foggy and my eyes blur, but the trade off was worth it. What the medication *didn't* do was change the fact that I was still in danger and it definitely didn't get rid of my hunch that Anna shouldn't be slinging ice cream without protection! It was time to make some major changes. I was burnt out and needed a break—I just wanted to remember what life was like *not* being the Ice Cream Man From Hell for awhile.

With all these thoughts in mind, we packed up the caravan and we moved down south. Turning fifty didn't make me feel any older; it just changed the way I looked at things. For example, why am I fifty years old and still walking around with those big black shiners like I had back in my early days? I quickly learned that it didn't matter where I lived; the Ice Cream Man From Hell had worldwide recognition now. Hell, people were even boot legging my shit in Japan—there was no place to hide. Fuck me!

So, we moved to the southern most point of nowhere. Only

You're Next

a few breaststrokes away from Cuba, this town wasn't even on the map. Even though I had literally dropped off the face of the earth, I still couldn't shake the feeling that I was being scrutinized. After months of living there, the locals calmed down and knew where I stood. The reports went back to the clubhouse stating that I was just a hard working fuck head with a few screws loose. I was a squirrel too busy looking for my next nut to cause any harm. Don't let me give you the wrong impression, they backed down but this ain't no fraternity and I didn't make any new friends. I was given the nod of approval and even though I was still leery…at least my house and vehicles weren't being shot at and I wouldn't have to lose any more sleep over it. Now that things were straight between me and the local fellas, and my script was full, I decided to take some much-needed down time. I spent the next year pounding nails and playing with my chainsaw. Even though *Anna's Ice Cream* had been a hit for over seventeen years, we never re-opened the business after the move. Anna needed a break from the bullshit too. Life in the singlewide felt good, but little did I know it was nothing more than the calm before the storm.

    I had an inkling in my balls to hit the road again because Jimmy needs to get his kicks just as much as the Ice Cream Man From Hell. The south was nice and all but I missed looking at people with a full set of teeth in their head! Before I hit the fluoride reservoirs of the Northeast, I decided to take a detour through Maryland. I pulled into Mel's place well after midnight and was welcomed with open arms. We sat around her dimly lit dinner table and got caught up in conversation for hours. Once you hit Baltimore, the lingo picks up speed and the hours are no longer made up of minutes and seconds. I felt at home again. Mel was lamenting about a car she needed to pick up in Astoria, Queens. She was nervous about driving into the city and it was causing her to procrastinate.

The Full Circle

"Great! Just the kind of kicks I need right now! Let's head out first thing in the morning. I'm down with driving into the city. I know Astoria like the back of my hand, well not exactly, but don't you worry, I'll get us where we need to be. Yes, yes, yes, I'll get you there and back—no problem. Hey, I'll even give you some driving lessons!"

We headed out at dawn and had completed our mission. We visited some friends and we were on our way the next day. Mel was screaming bloody murder from the passenger's seat while I gave the car in tow some flying lessons. Once we hit the Jersey side, I headed straight for Homestead so we could ditch the extra luggage and bang around the ole neighborhood before heading back to Maryland. It was late September 2003 when we stopped at the local filling station. It was at that very moment my life began to take a downward spiral. From the moment Duke's daughter told me that my brother, my best friend, my mastermind and my confidant was diagnosed with cancer—everything fell apart.

I have no time! I have no time! I could be next! What the fuck was I doing sun bathing down south? I became obsessed with thoughts of death, my wristwatch was ticking. I have no time! I have no time! I was suddenly bowled over with a dose of energy I hadn't felt since before I started shoving those little pills down my throat. Not knowing when Duke's clock was going to run out, I decided I'd rest when I was dead. I wasn't going to let anything stand in between me and my mission, and the only culprit I could see were those Fuck Me Meds. I've been educated in self-medication long before needing anti-anxiety drugs, and by no means was it slowing down my alcohol consumption. So why was I on this shit anyway? I had gotten by my entire life without it, and now wasn't the time to be taking a mental vacation. Shit, I had no idea where the last year of my life had gone.

I was totally unprepared for the chain of events that would

follow my decision to stop taking my medication. I was an addict and didn't even know it. My mood swings were atrocious and I couldn't stand to be in my own skin. I became a fucking ticking time bomb—again! My ears were ringing, my dick was limp, and I was drenched in sweat. The pulsing in my fingertips infuriated me! The electric jolts throughout my body caused me to cringe and twitch. The jolts would drive me out of bed in a fit of rage! I no longer feared my enemies; the only thing I feared was myself. All I wanted to do was jump in my truck, drive up the coast in the middle of the night, and hang with Duke. It was the only distraction from my physical pain. I was acting like a maniac. Anything and everything set me off!

Every time I'd see Duke, it was obvious he was getting worse. Was it the fact that my best friend was literally decaying right in front of my eyes that was fucking with my head? All I knew was that I was slowly and unbearably going insane. Were my worse fears coming true? Had I caught it? I had no concept of reality—I was living in a blackout. I'd wake up in my truck outside of Duke's house in Jersey confused. I couldn't remember leaving home or the thousand miles in between. I didn't know what else to do but turn to the man that prescribed me the poison. The signs of physical addiction were evident. I had no idea that this was part of the package. I wanted answers. I wanted to know what my doctor had done to me! So I gave him a call…

"Leave the fucking motorcycle club? What fucking motorcycle club? You know me better than that! What the fuck is going on? I'd rather die than feel like this. What is going on inside my body, inside my head? Doc, what the fuck is going on?" I was completely irrational, I was detoxing, and I was scared.

Shortly after I had hung up the phone (by ripping it out of the wall and throwing it out the window), the other line rang, it was the police. The doctor had put a restraining order against me. Now I was really on my own. My head was cracked wide open

The Full Circle

and my demons slowly started chiseling away at my skull. This all couldn't have come at a worse time. After all it was *their* favorite time of year—*December*.

I was roaring up the coast again to see Duke when my cell phone rang. Like a blade pointed at my heart, I panicked every time that damn thing would ring. I never knew when I was going to receive the phone call about Duke and the reality was it could be any second. I picked it up. On the other end was the voice of a producer from the *Discovery Channel*. They were filming a spin-off of Monster Garage. A crew was touring the country looking for radical vehicles and their owners for a television show and a book to be released in 2004. They'd be at my doorstep in two weeks if I was interested.

Yes! Yes! Yes! This would be the first big break for the Ice Cream Man From Hell's Pro Street Ice SCREAM truck! With this kind of exposure, I'd be able to book the truck for nationwide tours. "I'll be ready and waiting!" I hung up the phone. I couldn't believe it, a moment of clarity, I was back in the saddle—this was huge! The *Discovery Channel* had successfully targeted the biker market and finally…I was in. Anna! Do you understand now why we built this truck?

For a moment, I felt like myself again because my sense of humor was back in my step. I pulled into a truck stop to take a piss and grab a cup of mud. I'd be in Jersey by the time the sun came up, and I couldn't wait to tell Duke the news. I walked into the john and started unzipping my fly, "Hey, is this where all the pricks hang out?"

Through all the years of sleeping in ditches, living on peanut butter and jelly sandwiches, and walking around with a bloody lip. For every mile, every notch on my belt, and every urine stinking hell hole I've pissed in—the urinal cakes had never smelled so sweet! Success! I had to laugh out loud. However, the stranger pissing next to me didn't think I was so funny…

You're Next

"Hey, what are ya some kind of faggot wearing two different color sneakers?"

"No man, I'm just neutral!" I looked down. A red Chuck on my left and a black Chuck...**Wham!**

I got up off the filthy tile floor. I stood up and wiped the moldy moisture off my face and looked in the mirror. I guess I should've just pissed on my rear tire like a fucking dog, because that's what I usually do..."Now that was a good one!" Not only did I have a big black shiner but my cock was still hanging out. Apparently, I wasn't done pissing when the guy clocked me because my jeans were soaked! I'm unsure if that prick knew who I was, but it didn't matter, it would be a funny story to share with Duke.

The day of the *Discovery Channel* shoot came, and I was up for over twenty-four hours in preparation for their arrival with the help of a bunch of my friends—no rest for the wicked. I had every piece of flash I owned spread out on the lawn. A lifetime of collecting for this very moment...life-size monster statues, vehicles, smoke and mirrors, I worked feverishly to set the stage. Luckily, my latest shiner had cleared up but my anger level was through the roof. I was still on the rollercoaster of withdrawal. Even Anna was starting to avoid me. At the drop of a hat, I was screaming at people and flaring my arms. I had notions of choking everyone around me, even myself. I was climbing the walls to get those electrical jolts and pulsating headaches to go away. This glorious moment I was experiencing was turning into a test of my inner strength...I was suffering for my sanity.

We were halfway through the photo shoot and ready to change locations. Anna handed me the phone and I flew off the handle. I had no time for phone calls right now, who the fuck was on the other end?

It was Ray's wife. Ray Zag, a life long friend and a major asset to the Ice Cream Man From Hell circus had dropped dead

The Full Circle

that morning of a heart attack. We were one of the first to be notified. As soon as Anna handed me the phone she walked around and kindly asked everyone to back up, knowing that my actions would be completely unpredictable once I hung up the phone. One of the producers immediately piped up...

"Look Jim, we understand if you need to break for the afternoon."

"Fuck that—I have no time! Ray may be dead but I'm not! What is everyone standing around for? Let's go! I'm sure Ray would've wanted me to keep going!"

I climbed into the passenger's seat and Anna drove to the next location. I had no choice but to keep pushing. If I stopped now I'd surely go over the edge or leave town to crucify some nameless face. Violence was my only known cure for that knot in my gut and right now it was on fire! I was having a mental break down.

In five...four...three...two...one...ACTION! The second that camera rolled I immediately turned Jimmy off and the Ice Cream Man From Hell on. Years of being in the licking business had conditioned me for that very moment...

"That's a wrap. Good job everyone. Jimmy, you were great! We made art here people!" When all was said and done, I still had one more picture to take. I stripped down to my faggot ass mismatched sneakers, lit a flare, and shoved it in the crack of my ass. The onlookers started running away and although the photographer was absolutely mortified, he managed to capture the moment before I mutilated myself! The next day I sent the photograph to Duke, just to let him know that although he was dying, I still had the fire in my ass for both of us!

I was at the highest point in my career and the lowest point in my life. The Ice Cream Man From Hell was known worldwide throughout the biker culture. The 1954 Pro Street Ice SCREAM truck had just gotten major exposure and I was getting ready to sign my book deal. But I didn't care about any of it—Duke was dying. I was too blind to see. Meanwhile, I was consuming enough alcohol to cause a slow and excruciating death and it just wasn't working. But I gave it one for the Gipper. Wait, who the hell is the Gipper? It was January, the holidays were over, and I managed to scrape up enough energy to drive a thousand miles north. I needed to seal the deal on my book.

It was my last manic blast up the coast and the last time I'd ever see Duke. It took me over four months to detox from those fuck me meds but the anxiety and depression still lingered long after the drugs were out of my system. The truth is, it wasn't the medication, it wasn't the booze, it was Duke's death that nearly killed me. I had hit rock bottom, but somehow I needed to pull myself up by my Converse and focus on my book.

Duke and me

The Full Circle

I met Angelina Desolate my author, at a quiet park for the first of several interviews. We sat in the grass and popped a cork. I snapped when she hit play on that tiny tape recorder and started asking questions. I felt like every question that she asked was totally out of line. "You mean everything I've worked my entire life to forget, you want me to remember? You mean I got to re-hash the drama of all my family's mental illness, my infidelities, my violent behavior, my bust, my father, my mother, my brother, Skeets, Jeff, the Mafia, the motorcycle clubs, those fucking nuns and now Duke?! FUCK YOU—I ain't talking!" And like a dirty rotten kid, I scrambled to my feet, grabbed the first good size rock and chucked it at her! "This book is about the Ice Cream Man From Hell, not me—FUCK YOU!"

I was so freaked out, who the hell did this chick think she was? Jimmy had nothing to do with the matter at hand. She was writing a book about the Ice Cream Man From Hell. If her mission was digging for *my* personal opinions on life, death, and all the garbage in between, well, that's all she was getting and in my eyes that pretty much summed it up. "Like I said kid, this book is about the Ice Cream Man From Hell—it's not about me."

Talk about being kicked while you're down. Every time I got together with this chick it felt like I was at the shrinks. My dreams became tortured, everyone in my life who had died started paying me visits in my sleep. Talking about the road was depressing—Duke wasn't going to be around next season, or any season ever again for that matter. "Heller? Heller! Heller! I don't want to talk about fucking Heller!" I became uncooperative and my household was tense. After throwing a fit, I'd spend days on end asleep on the couch. I just wanted to quit. The bottle was the only way I could make it through the interviews, it was the only way I could be open. Don't get me wrong, I've always known I'm a scumbag, it just hit home when my empty promises and violent behavior started taking shape in a manuscript.

You're Next

I was forced to take inventory of myself and face the truth, and that's exactly what happened in the process of writing this book. All of my concerns started to resurface and I was left with a burden of guilt that was nearly too hard to bear. I knew myself too well all those years ago, and that's why I wanted to move to Ohio immediately after marrying Anna. I can't blame my actions on anything or anyone, it was my own damn fault I had been unfaithful, and in my heart I truly know how badly I'd hurt Anna. I can't say it enough how fortunate I am that she never threw my ass out on the street.

Anna is a woman of morals and she knows what the true meaning of marriage is. She never ran at the first sign of defeat and I know it wasn't fair of me to have thrown so many curveballs her way. Believe it or not, my beautiful wife was behind the scenes for most of the wild road tales of sexual inhibitions that I've shared with you. We've always had our own private set of rules—I was allowed to look but never to touch! Don't get me wrong, she never liked any of this. Her idea of a good time has never been watching a bunch of gals hanging all over her husband. But she's dealt with it like a trooper, got through it like a champ, and she usually bit her tongue. Why? Because she's my wife, that's why.

Would Anna's life have been easier if I had stuck it out at the engineering company? Damn straight it would've been, but here's the thing…it doesn't matter to Anna. Her burning desire in life has always been to stand by my side, support me, love me, and take care of me. How did a fucking loser like me get blessed with such a precious gift? Why did this stenciled angel fall in love with me? I don't know the answers to those questions, but what I do know is that I'm the biggest motherfucking idiot for playing with fate and potentially screwing it up. She is the most important thing in my life and I'd die without her! My body would've probably been found in a dumpster sometime back in the mid '80s if it wasn't

The Full Circle

for the love of this good woman!

Anna has always respected my space when it comes to my religious beliefs and my feelings about the holidays. Her family had instilled a strong sense of faith in her, but she never pushed the envelope with me even though I've carried on like a child with all my self-centered acts. Like flat blacking her Christmas trees and smashing her Santa Clause with a hammer. This is how I repaid her kindness and loving understanding. Believe it or not, despite all of my bullshit, she's always kept her faith.

I was not intentionally doing these things to torture her. It was me who was tortured. Even after twenty-five years of marriage, I still have a lot to learn from her. I've always known that the charted course of success requires faith, but I'd been fist fighting it all the way because of my horrific experiences. Anna, I'm sorry for all I've put you through over the years. And oh yeah, I'm sorry

your feet were always cold. It was me who was taking your slippers over the years, not the doggies. Anna...I love you more than life itself.

    After reminiscing about all my years of hatred towards nuns and faggots like Father Fitzjames, I realized that the Catholic religion had cock blocked me from my faith. I'd created a world of hate based upon my childhood experiences and didn't even realize it. Several Christian motorcyclists had approached me to discuss the quest for faith and I've always blown them off. "What? Just because I'm the Ice Cream Man From HELL, everyone assumes that I need to be saved?" During the climax of the violence and my notoriety in the industry, it must've been apparent to others that I needed something bad.

    Back in 2000 at Laconia Bike Week in New Hampshire, right before giving into the meds, this guy Mark approached me. He was a good-looking cat who appeared to be so physically untouched by the evils. Even though he was only slightly younger than me, if you put us next to each other you'd think I was his Pappy. Mark never laid his beliefs on me...I've always made sure of it because I'd keep my distance even though I've always liked him. You see, he was clean and sober unlike myself, and he belonged to a Christian motorcycle club. I was taken back that year when he asked me to share in a simple prayer with him. I was cornered, and as usual a little confused, so I decided I'd have to sidetrack him and bust his chops about his chrome dome — you know what I mean. He'd make Mr. Clean jealous! I did my dance in an attempt to entertain him, but he was persistent and I gave in, "If it'll make us better friends Mark and if it'll get you to shut the fuck up, why not?" I made it clear to him that I didn't want to be involved in any of that voodoo shit like pedaling pamphlets, baptizing shoes, or pancake breakfasts...just a simple prayer. In a split second it was over and I'd gotten through it.

    "Hey, Jimmy, God just shined his light on you. Not too

bad, huh?"

"Yeah Mark, not too bad." I wasn't really sure what had just happened, actually I was pretty sure nothing had just happened. Mark assured me that he'd see me later and with his big grin and a hearty handshake, he melted into the crowd and I went back to my sidewalk act.

Later that evening among the swarms of faces and camera flashes, I saw Mark out of the corner of my eye. With that peaceful smile, he handed me one of my own business cards with something typed across the top.

"It's the *Prayer of Jabez* we said together this morning Jim...short and sweet, use it when you need it!"

"Hey man! How the hell am I supposed to give out this business card now, people might get the wrong impression—I'm trying to work over here!" I stuffed the card in my top pocket and smiled.

Months later, somewhere on the road, I was lying on the floor of my trailer missing the hell out of Anna. I couldn't stop thinking about what the fuck I was or wasn't doing wrong. My mind wouldn't let my body rest. A few tough guys wanted to talk to me and I was indecisive as to what to do. Do I just lie there and let it pass, or do I charge straight into the fire? My hatred started guiding my thoughts to make a move, but I forced myself to stand still in an attempt to rationally think it through. I fumbled around in my vest pocket for a phone number and found the business card that Mark had given to me. I had forgotten all about it. I grabbed my flashlight and read the *Prayer of Jabez* over and over again...

Oh, that You would bless me indeed,
and enlarge my territory,
that Your hand would be with me,
and that You would keep me from evil.
That I shall cause no pain.

You're Next

I woke up with the card on my chest and was startled—it was daylight! I had gotten an entire night's sleep and I was still in one piece. I was ready to pack up and go home. After shaking off the webs, I hit the street for the word. The word was me. I'd managed to dodge a serious conflict by being in the last place anyone would ever suspect...asleep in my trailer saying my prayers. Usually, when my instincts tell me something's not right, the last place you'll find me is in my trailer. It's too obvious, instead I spend my time bobbing and weaving a confusing circle of tracks. I was stone cold stunned. That little prayer had kept me out of harms way!

I kept that prayer close to my heart for years, and I still carry it around today. I believe it's what began to open the door to prepare me for Duke's message. As confused as I was, I had no choice but to take serious heed to what Duke had whispered in my ear shortly before his death. What he had told me would forever change my life and was very simple—*Shake the Hate*.

When Duke knew he was on his way out—all the rage, the violence, the revenge, that ripened from his fears no longer existed. He came to realize that none of that bullshit mattered. It took the awareness of his death for him to see it for what it truly was—nothing. Now was my chance to break the cycle, Duke had given me the answer and for the first time I believed it.

Shake the hate didn't sound like a bunch of hippie liberal bullshit coming from the mouth of a hardcore bastard like Duke. Yet at the same time, it was the hardest time to accept this information because everything in my life was going south.

My life felt like a cruel joke. God was the puppet master and he was having a good laugh every time he pulled my strings—and believe me, he kept me dancing. Addiction, detoxing, restraining orders, giving and receiving punches, curbing my violence, stepping on my own dick, not wanting to remember my past. Oh yeah, don't let me forget the most recent roll call of deaths...Duke,

The Full Circle

Ray, Indian Larry, Johnny Jett, and my dog Marley! This all happened in such a short time frame. So short that it's fair to say it happened all at once...I could only perceive this unbearable chain of events as a wicked twist of fate for the sole purpose of fucking with my head. It took a lot of guts and soul searching to realize that this was nothing more than perfect timing—I needed to receive Duke's message more than anything else right now! In order to save me from doing any more harm to myself or others—*that I shall cause no pain.*

Looking back, there have been people in my life that have been trying to convey this same message. I just couldn't hear it, or even see it, so I ignored them. What the fuck did they know? They weren't standing in my shoes, they had no idea—but Duke did, and that's why it struck a cord to the depths of my soul. Oh it struck a cord alright, I heard what he said, and I believed him. Great! Now I'm really fucked! I believed it but how in the hell can I achieve it? You tell me, how in the hell is a guy like me, that's lived the life I've lived, that's done the things I've done, live without fear, violence, anger, revenge and hate? This was a question that I had no idea of the answer. Yet I knew I had to find out.

For years I'd crash at Bitty's after an event in my blood stained uniform. I'd sleep soundly in her basement, but only after I scrambled to cover every window. Her place has always been a safe house for me and I'd sleep in her basement for days on end after a motorcycle rally to lick my wounds. She's been a life long friend of mine and Anna's and she's never judged me when I'd crawl into her pad with a busted up face and road worn...and a few weeks worth of dirty laundry dragging behind me. Bitty's got two beautiful girls who love me so much that they call me Uncle Stupid, and she'd always shoo them off to bed when I showed up because she didn't want them to see me that way. She's never discouraged me. She's always been a great support even though she's never actually seen this Ice Cream Man From Hell at work. She's never even been to a motorcycle rally.

For the last fifteen years, the only visual she's had of the road has been the aftermath, the crash, the crawl, the terror, the tears—the pain. So, how could she possibly lend encouraging words? I didn't know that answer, but what I do know is that Bitty's always been a great friend to me and Anna and she's always been an important part of my mastermind. I consider her my spiritual adviser. She can always see things for what they really are and she has a gift of shining the light through the liquid darkness of lies. She's been trying to give me this message all along. I just wasn't ready…not until I had heard it loud and clear from Duke.

In spite of the serious danger Bitty Baby knew I was facing, she always found the strength to repeat those same encouraging words…"Jimmy, just keep doing what you're doing because it works!" She did the only thing she could, she gave me what I needed, encouragement and support to just keep on keeping on. When she realized I was finally ready to receive her message, she shoved that Love not Hate thing so far down my throat that I choked…

"Jim, hate is only a manifestation of fear."

"Fuck you, I'm not afraid of nothing."

"That's not what I'm saying, Jimmy."

That's when she handed me a cassette tape. She told me to listen to it and then maybe I'd have a better understanding of her message. *A Return to Love* helped me see what I was missing from my life. After listening to it and accepting it, I could move on with my positive thoughts.

After she explained it again, I finally got it…it made sense, I had my answer. I could feel it, hear it, smell it, touch it…I was ready now—so I could see it! So I did a spin around and threw on my cape, I jumped to the ground and said…Good God Almighty—I am the *Hardest Working Man in Ice Cream* and even though I walk the line, my message has been the same from the

The Full Circle

very beginning—Party in Peace.

Bitty Baby always reminded me of that, she knew it was part of my success. Through all the years of laughs we've shared while breaking bread, Bitty knew I had a talent. It was obvious to her that the people who surrounded the Ice Cream Man From Hell, did these wild things of their own free will. My special gift, as she calls it, is how I touch people's lives. I make them feel good about themselves and just let them do what the fuck they want to do—and believe me, as you now know...they do!

It's so easy to lose sight of all the positive things that are going on around you and become consumed by negative thoughts. I know everyone can relate to that. You know when things are going great, I mean really great. You feel like you finally got everything figured out, life is running smooth then—**Bam!** A 2 x 4 smacks ya in the back of the noggin! Just when you thought you got a break and were able to bask in the glory of the day then—**Bam!** Some guy clocks ya in the eye for telling a joke and wearing two different color shoes.

When I decided to take a pro-active approach about my violent behavior, (fuck you Fran, I'm still not going to no head shrinker), I decided to play a little game with myself called, *How Long Can Jimmy Go Without Getting a Black Eye?* Just like a recovering alcoholic, I started crossing off the days on my calendar. Man, I was furious because in order not to receive a black eye, you can't give one. I was going through withdraw again, that's right, withdrawal from violence. Believe it or not, violence is just as addicting as any other poison, but just like any other addiction, if you put your mind to it and look towards a higher power—you will prevail!

I've come to find out there's a balance in life. I've taken great risks in being the Ice Cream Man From Hell and for that, I've had to deal with great hardships. When it's so bad that you just can't seem to make it through another day, you've got to use one of life's greatest resources—faith.

Now, I'm not here to get all religious on you, and I'm sure as hell not here to preach. Take it or leave it because you've probably observed by now, I ain't no fucking saint! I don't care who your higher power is, other people have been fighting those wars since the beginning of time. All I'm saying is, if a reformed Catholic like me can walk back into a church after all these years of spitting on nuns, anything is possible.

One afternoon, I was driving home in a fit of self-rage. I was annoyed and desperate, my day hadn't gone as planned, nor was I on schedule. I noticed a sign on the side of the road that read, "Fresh Fried Fish." So I pulled over to grab some southern goodness to share with Anna. A striking black gentleman in a suit was standing beside the road wiping the dust off his shoes as I approached the fish stand. After I paid for the fish, the gentleman approached me with an invite to stop by his home anytime. I had a chip on my shoulder, so I copped an attitude with him—I thought he was getting cute with me. The gentlemen calmly smiled and thumbed at the building behind the fish stand. It was a church. I thanked him for his kind gesture and now that I felt like a complete jerk, I jumped back into my truck. I couldn't shake the prominent image of this man from my mind all weekend. My hunches told me that I should go to his home that Sunday for service. The pastor's simple act of kindness opened my heart to a newfound family. Who would've ever guessed that fish would feed my soul for years to come?

I awoke a force that had been asleep inside my soul by approaching it with love, not hate. But get this, I still hate nuns, but that's okay because they got nothing to do with it. Love not Hate man, ya dig? Without faith in some higher power and without faith in yourself, it's impossible to obtain your ultimate desires. You must believe in the tits you cannot touch, the thongs you cannot smell and especially the things you cannot see. Our thoughts and dreams are intangible at the time that we conceive them, and in order to turn them into reality, we must have faith. Each and every one of us has the power to live out our desires, if we chose to have the courage. With almost all of my friends gone and the world on my plate, even I can stand in front of you, and say—I truly believe in miracles!

"John Lennon said it from the start...Love, Love...that's what this world needs so much more of ...Love, Love."
— *Gerry Gabinelli*

Chapter 12

By Any Means Necessary

I've never been comfortable with the idea of writing this book, even though for several years a dear friend of mine has been trying to encourage me to write the damn thing. She claimed that my stories were too unbelievably true *not* to. It's just my crazy life and I've sold a few popsicles along the way, but who the hell would want to read about that. I make people laugh and feel good — so what? Then it came to me. If I'm going to do this, then I've got to do it right. Which means — I've got to come clean. So wipe that wiseass smirk off your face and listen up!

There's no question that I've proven that you can achieve your goals large or small, no matter what hand life deals you! Working and never knowing for what, is the biggest question we're all faced with. Whether it's material possessions, love, money, or power, we all want something. Understand that your desires and goals don't have to be solely for the purpose of financial gain — That's bullshit. *You may be rich right now and not even know it.* I mean just think about it, my trike has seen more *ass* than a Port Authority toilet. Can you put a dollar amount on that? Life can be whatever you chose it to be, once you make a decision about what you want and stick to it. Fuck what the world thinks! This is about *your* life, right here and right now. We all have desires, but how do we make them happen? By never accepting the word no, and by never giving up — That's how!

I ain't no super hero but I can tell you this, with every

punch in the face that I've taken, I've gotten right back up, well...maybe not *right* back up, but I'm a persistent little prick that refuses to give up! Listen up folks, Lady Luck doesn't exist, and if she did...I know she wouldn't be half as wild as some of the biker chicks I know. Use *your* talents to make them wanna scream— Forget luck! Stand up for what you want. I don't care if that goal is as small as getting out of bed in the morning or winning first place in the "all male buns" review—Just do it! Never be ashamed if the day ever comes when the world's got you so punched out that it might just take everything you've got to pull yourself up— Just do it!

We're all good starters but most are poor finishers, because we allow ourselves to be defeated by the world's negative views. Things have become too easy in this life, we have too many choices. As a whole, our society has become a group of unconscious mice working from nine to five for a piece of cheese. It's up to you to find the drive, the burning desire, what makes you tick, what makes you feel good, and feed that desire in order to succeed. You'll know when you got it because it'll keep you awake at night!

There's nothing easy about this way of thinking. You might even find yourself in a spitting match the whole way through. The world might even try to beat you down at every corner. You got to be prepared to fight like a brave warrior and refuse to accept defeat. Have you ever tried to apply for a permit anywhere in the USA? Bureaucracy, it's like a brick wall, so get out your jackhammer!

When I was sentenced to jail, I made it my burning desire to serve out my time without fucking it up. I refused to get caught up in the vicious cycle of re-sentencing and living out the rest of my days labeled as a loser. All the odds were against me and the statistics will tell you my chances were slim to none. I made sure my life didn't go down the tubes. I broke the cycle because I wanted to, and I was the only one who could make that happen. Do you

You're Next

think the State of New Jersey put forth any effort to ensure that I didn't rot in the human meat market or become state raised? Fuck No! If anything, all they did was tax me at every curb and discourage me every step along the way.

I refused to leave my fate in the hands of someone else, my family was too important. Changing professions, staying in my garage, keeping my head clean, I wanted it bad enough to fight the good fight against my demons—and I won! How bad do *you* want it? No matter how many times you may be kicked around or hear those oh so familiar words. (You're out of your mind. That's impossible. You can't do that. It's never been done before. What makes you think you can do it?) Fuck all that, you got to keep marching on, and just remember...the world doesn't deny dying to anyone!

There've been times when I've wanted to do just that, especially after Duke's death. Life is tough...and sometimes the crazy thoughts in your head can overpower what you truly believe in and know in your heart. That's why you got to be persistent and determined in order to control your own destiny and never let it control you.

I tried to get my brother Heller to adapt to my, "Fuck You Theory." Maybe he would've been better off if he'd accepted *my* theory instead of those whore nurses who force-fed him all those fucking pills. By doing things *my* way...I've trained my mind not to become a product of my environment. It's all I know and it's what keeps me going. I've refused to let any doctor, priest, judge, lawyer, nun, or newspaper determine my fate. Practicing autosuggestion...repeating positive thoughts over and over again and feeding your own mind will eventually lead you to believe that you *can* achieve anything. "It's only a bad trip...I'll be just fine. It's only a bad trip...I'll be just fine."

Educating your mind and controlling your thoughts is key. You have the power to feed your subconscious whatever it needs to win. Stop allowing your precious hat rack to be fed with negative information and worthless opinion! There's no reason for any of us to be a victim. Destroy those negative thoughts that creep into your mind. Your brain receives all information equally, so why not feed it more positive thoughts? We've been conditioned to become a product of our environment through the power of autosuggestion. That's right...other peoples fucked up opinions. It doesn't have to be that way because we all have free will!

Sometimes our loved ones can cripple our drive to succeed. They don't realize that by boldly stating their opinions they can sometimes hinder our drive for success. Although their thrash of the wooden spoon may be based on love and concern for our well-being, their personal fears often turn their reactions into negative opinion. Opinions can be very dangerous things, if you let others persuade your decision making, you will forever doubt yourself and never act on your own hunches.

So stop asking other people what they think! Most people can't decide what they want for motherfucking breakfast, so why the hell are you asking them? Make up your own blessed mind and keep your desires close to you, and *never* allow other people to sabotage your thoughts. Surrounding yourself with good people that you can trust, and a few naked chicks to keep up the moral, will help you to succeed. It'll give you the positive support and encouragement we *all* need now and again.

One of the ways I've been able to achieve success is by surrounding myself with positive thinking people to share my ideas with. Creating a mastermind and surrounding yourself with positive thinking people for the purpose of brainstorming and making the creative imagination come alive will open new doors and set you closer to your goals. Create a mastermind because it's their input that'll help you. In order to do this, you've got to get rid of indecision. This can only be done by being honest with yourself and facing your fears that are causing self-doubt. Taking a good

You're Next

hard look at yourself is one of the most difficult things to do...You'll have no choice but to be honest with yourself. Take what you've learned and use it in a positive way. Your subconscious mind will accept any information that you feed it, negative or positive. It returns to you what you ask of it. *When you take the initiative to do this, you will witness your own miracle!*

In order to be a leader, you must be a decision maker. Once you've set a goal and your decision is made—you've got to stick with it, and fight for it, tooth and nail! That's why self-doubt must leave your mind, heart, body, and soul—right or wrong, you call the shots. Adjustments can be made along the way if needed, just stick with your gut instincts, but never be a greedy little piglet!

Beware not to let opinions be misconstrued with knowledge. They're two entirely different things. When I decided to go forward with this Ice Cream Man From Hell gig, people told me I was crazy. They were right—I am crazy, crazy enough to determine my future. When I had the wild idea that I wanted an ice cream slinging motorcycle, everyone got a few good laughs at my expense. Rather than feeling stupid, and trust me, I'm not going to lie, I did feel stupid in my ice cream get up. Rather than knuckle under to the majority's opinion, I said—FUCK YOU!

The specialized knowledge of Mr. Mott, that old Italian man who'd been in the business way too long, enabled me to turn my wild idea into a reality and I ended up with a freezer on the back of my trike. It was a hit and I knew I was right—Despite popular opinion! Did I give up even though it took eating bologna and cheese sandwiches for seven years till I completed my 1954 Pro Street Ice SCREAM Truck? Hell No! Reaching out to the right people along the way who had the specialized knowledge I needed, such as...Dave Cronk, Ratfink, and Mr. Mott helped me to achieve my goals. It was their knowledge that helped empower me to complete my projects and succeed. We all ate a lot of bologna and made a lot of personal sacrifices to get where we are. If you're sitting around eating government cheese and playing the self-pity game—that's your own damn fault. You've got to take calculated risks in life to get ahead. Do you hear me? I said calculated! Think before you act. Procrastination in life is a slow and agonizing death—worse than the booze!

Start now to eliminate those negative thoughts you have lingering in your mind and start focusing on only the positive and what you truly want in life. You can expect to experience thousands of setbacks before reaching *your* ultimate goals. There's always a trade-off. It just depends on how badly you want it. Peddling a charitable cause like The Home for Wayward Women wasn't just something that happened, you got to take your goals seriously you know. Most people don't succeed because they fall just short of their goal by allowing themselves to become consumed by negativity.

You've got to realize that negative forces, crooked politicians, and fat Italian mothers are always going to try to sneak in and attempt to override your thoughts. So, face the challenges that you're up against and just keep marching forward with full faith and trust. Meet the negative vibes on the playing field of your mind and mash the hell out of them! You've got to have the courage, determination, and persistence to push through all the distraction and trickery along your path to the prize.

Never let money be your excuse…this *is* fucking America, the land of the free! We have every resource at our fingertips to be filthy stinking rich, if we so desire. Ideas attract riches. What are you willing to bring to the bargaining table of life to enjoy your desired riches?

It was my father who taught me the true meaning of, "by any means necessary." Hey, I may be somewhat illiterate and that's the truth, but my father made damn sure that I graduated high school "by any means necessary" so that I could have a shot at the All American Dream. My parents may have struggled but they

You're Next

were no slouches, and I learned a very important life lesson from the wise mouth of my mommy. It's something that I'd like to share with you because we all weren't blessed with an Italian mommy…

> *You've been born in the most fruitful and blessed country in the world. Never show how tired you are. Your quest is to succeed! Sit and a rest, but only for a moment, then get up and a continue. Remember, life's a challenge, the smart and the swift don't always win the race—the person who believes in their dreams will always be a winner!*

It's because of those words that I decided not to leave this earth a poor man. These methods to achieve success that I've shared with you are timeless, and they've been proven over and over again. They've been used by four-foot cotton haired strong arms and successful men who've harnessed greatness such as, Attila the Hun, Pappy, Abraham Lincoln, Pee Wee Davidson, Alexander Graham Bell, J. J. Steel, Andrew Carnegie, Fred Flintstone, Henry Ford and Dave Cronk. Each and every one of these people has applied these success formulas in their own lives. Not of course, for the same reasons or in the same way, but their end results have all been nothing short of success!

In the name of peace, I've been able to give back to the universe by being the Ice Cream Man from Hell—God works in mysterious ways. I'm sure not everyone would agree that my vulgar acts, brutal honesty, and sheer stupidity have liberated the spirits of others…that's okay with me because I got a job to do just like everyone else. Knowing this is how I've been able to openly approach people and have fun with them. More importantly it's allowed others to love themselves in the presence of the Ice Cream Man From Hell. I'm not a braggart, but to prove my point, I'll share this next story with you.

I've had the pleasure of putting a three hundred pound girl on the back of my trike and make her feel so confident and secure about herself, that by the time I looked back, she was topless in front of thousands of people! How many fat chicks have you made feel good enough about themselves to do that? All I can hope is that she keeps up that same spirit when she goes home and looks at herself in the mirror and smiles—that's my mission.

Because my mission has always been the same, and my message has always been positive, seventeen years after the Ice Cream Man From Hell was born I can still come home to where it all began. That's right, before I started pushing popsicles in Cobbleskill, I was breaking into the scene at the Dawn Patrols Annual Run in Bradley Gardens. It's nice after all of these years to be able to drop the nonsense of this gig and go have a hotdog and beer with the boys who warmly welcome me as Jimmy.

I make people feel good and I create good memories, that's what I do—I am the Ice Cream Man From Hell and that's what has served as my means to touch thousands of people's lives in a positive way... *I spread good will motherfucker!*

It's been my burning desire that has kept the Ice Cream Man From Hell on the streets even in the face of danger. I'd never wish the hardships I've experienced on anyone. Who knows, maybe I am a little jerky and a complete fool for marching forward as the Ice Cream Man From Hell? Yes, yes, yes, it's made me a very rich man in many ways. I'm not talking about the green shit, come down south sometime and I'll give you the grand tour of my double wide. I'm talking about the energy, the love, the experience, and the vibe I get from everyone of you that I've had the privilege to touch...that's the kind of rich I'm talking about!

It's made all my hardships nothing more than temporary defeats in my quest for success. My wish has always been to spread my message to my brothers and sisters across the world to Party in Peace. It's up to each and every one of us to do right by one another and the universe! While you're at it, don't forget that laughter is a sure fire indicator that you're on the right track. So don't forget to do a lot of it...and enjoy your road to success!

You're Next

Chapter 13

You're Next

In conclusion to all this confusion you've just experienced, courtesy of the Ice Cream Man From Hell, I'd like to leave you with my closing thoughts to ensure that you got the message! I can guarantee you that no other motivational speaker has delivered his message in quite the same fashion...but here it goes!

We've been reprimanded since our childhood for saying the words *FUCK YOU* because it's dirty and crude. This isn't necessarily true. It doesn't have to be used as a negative. It can be used as your affirmation. I'm here to tell you that it's due to my conscious decision making and my ability to say...*FUCK YOU*, that I've been successful in this game we call life. I've been able to bypass the mindless behavior of indecision because of my, "*FUCK YOU THEORY.*"

Think about it, when you say *FUCK YOU*— it's your final answer. There's no question in your mind as to where you stand, nor is there any confusion for whoever is on the receiving end. When your response is *FUCK YOU*, it leaves no room for persuasion or the opinions of others. When most people are mulling over a situation or are second-guessing their decision, their response too often tends to be..."I don't know? I guess? Maybe? I'm not sure? Whatever!"

All of these are examples of indecisive thinking that will usually leave you open to the persuasion of others. Somewhere in the back of your mind, you really *do* know what you want, but you fear the possibility of offending others by challenging their opinions. Whenever your response is…*FUCK ME…FUCK HIM…FUCK HER…FUCK THAT…FUCK YOU*…and the horse you rode in on! There's *no* question in anyone's mind, including your own, as to where you stand! Hey, you know what you want more than anyone else does—so go get it! Once you start saying it over and over again you'll unleash the power of autosuggestion. You'll no longer be subjected to doing things you don't wanna do. Instead you'll be able to start living your own life—on your own terms!

When you know you're right, stick to your guns. My, *"FUCK YOU THEORY"* doesn't always need to be verbalized. It's actually more effective when followed through with action. If you decide to live by the *"FUCK YOU THEORY,"* then you have to acknowledge that there are other people who live by it too. Part of being an independent thinker is being a good listener. An independent thinker and a leader knows there's a chance that they may've overlooked something, and that's why the mastermind is so important. Listen, be open minded, take in what you need, and leave the rest.

My, *"FUCK YOU THEORY"* is not for everyone but it works for me. Please *do* try this at home, and remember there's no time like the present. You're the only one holding yourself back, march forward in full faith toward your desired goals. If I can dust myself off after being beaten in the garbage can by a nun, keep marching forward black eye after black eye, wooden spoon after wooden spoon, if I can surmount all of this in order to succeed. Let me ensure you that— **YOU'RE NEXT!!!!**

The Ice Cream Man From Hell is available for motivational speaking, fireside chats, and for appearance at your next event.

For more information contact us at

www.icmfh.com

Angelina Desolate is a freelance journalist and tattoo artist. Her work has been featured in several motorcycle publications in the United States and Europe.

Angelina Desolate would like to thank the following people.

Jimmy and Anna—it's people like you in this world that preserve freedom, and we should all be grateful for that. Thank you for believing in me and encouraging my creativity. It was a true honor to write this book.

Bitty and Nicole—who have put forth so much effort, their devotion is the reason why this book is in print and the Ice Cream Man From Hell's story has reached the masses!

I dedicate these pages to my husband Johnny for unconditionally loving a luna-chick.

I'd like to thank the following people for their contribution, time, and attention towards this project.

Special Thanks
Nancy Bocchino
Fran Chelli, LMSW
Old Man Gary
Ken Glynn
Joe Landry
Howie & Sandy Paley
John D. Randazzo, ESQ. a/k/a bikrlaw
Brandon R. Smith
Johnny Socks
John VasKorlis

Photography and Artwork Credits
Cover Design: Mike Barnard a/k/a Psycho Mikey
Back Cover Photograph: Pulsating Paula
Interior Photo Finishing: John VasKorlis
Typeset Design: William G. Carrington

Interior Artwork
Mike Barnard (p. 208, VI, VII, VIII, IX, XII)
Shoemaker Mike (p.V)
Ed Roth (p.194)

Interior Photographs
Melissa Burley (p. 161) Angelina Desolate (p. 130, 153, 167, 169, 171, 172, 174, 191, 195, 222, 266) Dan Howell (p. 164) Mark Langello (p. 264) Roger Lohrer (p. 138, 198) Nasty Nish (p. 247) Pulsating Paula (p. 123, 244) Johnny Socks (p. 177) Billy Tinney (p.124) Anna Trotta (p. 81) John VasKorlis (p. 7, 136, 141, 144, 150, 151, 166, 182, 184, 185, 190, 202, 215).

Bibliography

Life Application Study Bible: King James Version. Wheaton: Tyndale House, 2004.

Burnham, Sophy. A Book of Angels: Reflections on Angels Past and Present and True Stories of How They Touch Our Lives. New York: Ballantine, 1992.

Hill, Napoleon. Think and Grow Rich. New York: Random House, 1960.

Peale, Norman V. Power of Positive Thinking. New York: Ballantine, 1982.

Roberts, Wess. Leadership Secrets of Attila the Hun. New York: Warner, 1990.

Wilkinson, Bruce. The Prayer of Jabez: Breaking through to a Blessed Life. Sisters: Multnomah, 2000.

Williamson, Marianne. A Return to Love: Reflections on the Principles of a Course in Miracles. New York: HarperCollins, 1992.

Additional educational resources that have contributed to my success...

Bike Mags
Car Mags
Mad Magazine
National Geographic
Want Ad Classified
United States Road Atlas

Ride Till Ya Rot!

www.cobbsociety.com

★ ☆ ★

Give the gift of the Ice Cream Man From Hell's Biography!

☐ Yes! I want _____ copies of <u>**YOU'RE NEXT**</u> for 19.95 each. Include $3.99 shipping and handling for one book, and $1.99 for each additional book. Overseas orders must be paid in US funds via money order only.

Make your money order payable to:

ICMFH
P.O. Box 277
Bunnell, FL 32110

Please charge my: ☐ Visa   ☐ MasterCard
Card # _____
Exp. Date _____
Signature _____
Print Name _____
Address _____
City/State/Zip _____
Phone _____
Email _____
Shipping Address   ☐ Same   ☐ Other

Name _____
Address _____

To Order by Phone Call Toll Free (866) 731-2622
Internet Orders: store@icmfh.com
Information: www.icmfh.com

★ ☆ ★

Give the gift of the Ice Cream Man From Hell's Biography!

☐ Yes! I want _____ copies of **<u>YOU'RE NEXT</u>** for 19.95 each. Include $3.99 shipping and handling for one book, and $1.99 for each additional book. Overseas orders must be paid in US funds via money order only.

Make your money order payable to:

ICMFH
P.O. Box 277
Bunnell, FL 32110

Please charge my: ☐ Visa ☐ MasterCard
Card # _____
Exp. Date _____
Signature _____
Print Name _____
Address _____
City/State/Zip _____
Phone _____
Email _____
Shipping Address ☐ Same   ☐ Other

Name _____
Address _____

To Order by Phone Call Toll Free (866) 731-2622
Internet Orders: store@icmfh.com
Information: www.icmfh.com